Primal Energetics

Emotional Intelligence in Action

A work of art in progress

Elisa Lodge 'Wowza'

Booksurge, LLC (An Amazon.com Company)

1SBN:1-4196-1629-3
Printed in the United States of America
Limited First Edition

Cover design by Susana McGuire
Cameron/Baxter Photo
www.theinnstitute.com
mcguirecommunication@yahoo.com
Layout of book by Robert Moore

Elisalodge@comcast.net
www.primalenergetics. com
831-659-4616

A hero ventures forth from the world of common day into a region of supernatural wonder. Fabulous forces are there encountered and a decisive victory is won. The hero comes back from this mysterious adventure with the power to bestow aliveness on his fellow man.

-Joseph Campbell
Hero of a Thousand faces

Contents

A new world is being seeded for a forthcoming grander and far more glorious race than we have previously known.

-Madame Blavatsky

Dedication

We have to learn anew to reclaim the rich physiological, biological potentials natural to all children. In this way, the instinctual wisdom inherent in our own body can guide us.

-Helen Keller

I dedicate this manual to my beloved sons

Ryan and Zachary

Acknowledgments

A loving tribute to James Wanless my dearest friend who gave me the inspiration to synthesize my work on energetic embodiment to the written page. I am especially grateful to Teresa Moore and her husband Robert Moore for creating the layout and offering me so much encouragement. Many thanks to Jane Morba, James Wanless, Andrew Bailey and Hinton Harrison for their expressive photos. Deep appreciation to Heike Be, Michelle Marcell, Susana McGuire and Karin Hildebrand for contributing to the job of editing.

An entire legion of teachers have inspired the growth and manifestation of my work. Hundreds of their quotes accompany this document. A special thanks to my first singing teacher, Mr. Beasly, of the Metropolitan Opera, for awakening my awareness to the healing power of sound. To Lavane Maow for guiding me to feel the soul of emotion as music. To Oscar Ichazo of Arica Institute for teaching me the difference between the ego and the essence, and to actor Rod Steiger who took the time to guide me into the depths of authentic acting. To the late Lee Strasberg who acknowledged and encouraged my hidden talents to be seen, felt and heard.

Writers aren't exactly people. They are a whole lot of people trying to be one person.

-F. Scott Fitzgerald

In memory of Ida Rolf for attuning me to the power of gravity and Judith Aston for embodiment of fluidity in daily actions. To David and Susan Schiffman for all their many years of unconditional loving support. To Connection Magazine for providing space for monthly articles on *Emotional Fitness*. To Victor Sinn for supporting an on-going group of ten years that helped evolve my work. And to Nancy Lunney at Esalen Institute for offering me the opportunity to facilitate such a wide variety of workshops.

To the many teachers who have influenced my work: Chungliang Al Huang, Jonathan Goldman, Fritjof Capra, Jean Houston, Don Campbell, Chloe Goodchild, Paul Rebillot, Gay & Kathlyn Hendricks, Emilie Conrad, Stanislav Grof, Anna Halprin, Gabrielle Roth, Angeles Arrien, Peg Jordan, Chariotte Selver, David Darling, Rhiannon, Jill Purce, Ruth Zaporah, Starhawk, Lynclair Dennis, Elisabet Sahtouris, Rupert Sheldrake, Larry Dossey, Gangaji, Deepak Chopra, Mathew Fox, Brian Swimme and Tom Kenyon.

Blessings and love to my many friends for all their feedback and continual support:. Nancy Knapp, Beverly Toney Walter, Flo Lesur, Delia Horwitz, Pennell Rock, Christen Brown, Julie King, Robert Bolander, Jeff Hutner, Benj Langdon, Stessa Thompson, Leslie Shill, David Dilworth, Bear Olson, Miki Lee, Jane Sullivan, Rahasya, Rick Cannon and so many more. Thank you..

Forward

Primal Energetics is a work of genius. It reflects an integration of our 'cross-over age' where cultures, concepts and disciplines are interwoven into new technologies for living. As my friend and mentor, Elisa lives her message. At 70, she embodies her talk. She is a feeling, vital person committed to the full living out of her authentic self. Her life illustrates the essence of transformation. Like the lotus growing in the mud, Elisa has used emotional dysfunction as the growing edge of her own transfiguration. Her story, not unlike many of ours, exemplifies how to weave the traumatic threads of life into a tapestry of magic that goes beyond the limitations of prevailing personal myths.

With forty years experience teaching in the human potential movement, Elisa's greatest challenge was to revitalize the authentic, primal power of emotional energy that has often been buried in the process of social conditioning. A new paradigm of fitness has been created that rekindles a fluid body language that supports the expressive feeling capacities we were given at birth. Embodying the rhythmical pulsations of emotional energy with breath, sound and movement sets the body's healing wisdom in motion. Regaining this intrinsic knowledge is the secret of sustaining ageless vitality throughout our lives. This is work that needs to be recognized - it does make a difference.

There is nothing more difficult to take in hand, more perilous to conduct, or more uncertain in its success than to take the lead in the introduction of a new order of things.

-16th century Mystic

For those looking to relieve stress, achieve health and well-being, and for anyone wanting an efficient means of transforming emotional blocks, here is the way. Athletes incorporating the primal power of emotional energy into their training program will take a quantum leap in expanding instinctive agility, speed, endurance and stamina. For people who are shy and insecure about expressing themselves; here is a way to uninhibited spontaneous response. Singers, dancers, musicians and actors will discover innovative ways to bring rigorous technique vibrantly alive with authentic, emotive intensity. For people in sales, here is the way of reading people's body language and a powerful means of bringing vital, authentic feelings into communication. For the business world, *Primal Energetics* brings 'emotional intelligence' into creative decision making.

And for all of us who have become enmeshed in the mental domain with no feeling or meaning, I can think of no greater gift to modern civilization than freeing ourselves from habits and patterns that deaden us. Exercising more artful ways to express my inborn passionate power by embodying my feelings rather than talk about them, I have become more energized, healthy, flexible, powerful, compassionate, creative and successful—more me!

-James Wanless, Ph. D.
Strategic Intuition for the 21st Century

Show me your original nature before your mother and father conceived you.

-Zen Koan

Born Brilliant

Introduction

Our innate capacities for the energetic involvement of emotional expression are nothing less than miraculous! We were born with a driving intent to express the beauty and power of our originality.

–John Parker Ph.D.

Just as flowers know when to open, birds know where to migrate, and silkworms know how to transform into butterflies, every cell in our body is encoded with billions of years of instinctive knowledge to navigate us safely into an unknown world. Being interconnected to the wholeness of life, we are a vital aspect of nature's primal vitality. The natural ecology of our being is as expressive as the elements, resourceful as the minerals, changeable as the seasons, self-renewing as thé plants, graceful as the animals, and free spirited as the windy air.

And that's not all. As young children, the primal power of emotional intelligence motivated us into the adventure of continually growing and changing in new and exciting ways. Gifted with fluid grace of motion, electrifying vocal brilliance and authentic facial animation, we could communicate our deepest feelings and desires without the need of words. With an inventive imagination, dazzling creativity, and ecstatic passion fueled with inspired play, we moved through the day with full involvement.

A baby's cells are not really new. The atoms in them have been circulating for billions of years. But the baby is made new by an invisible intelligence that has come together to shape a unique life-form. Aging is a mask for the loss of this intelligence.

-Deepak Chopra
Ageless Body, Timeless Mind

Researchers now affirm that every child, with the exception of brain damage, scores in the creative genius category. Thousands of adults have been tested and only 2% scored at the genius level. Where is our creative genius hiding? How can we free the expression of emotional intelligence in a safe and appropriate way? For the most part, the culture has not recognized or valued our vast expressive capacities as the storehouse of creative genius.

Primal Energetics **reclaims what has been lost – the fluid flexibility, emotional authenticity and creative genius, which are stored in the expressive language of our feeling nature. Breathing, sounding and moving with full spectrum emotional energy is the secret of growing more healthy, ageless, vital and wise.**

As children, emotions are all we have to offer. This energy that motivated us from one activity to another, was our inner truth. If emotions were not valued, it was easy to believe we were not valued. In order to be accepted and win favor with others, our muscular system went to work and shaped our body into static postures, monotone speech habits, and predictable movement patterns to disguise our inner world of feeling. Just as a muscle withers away when unused, the capacity to feel and express what we feel grows dim. If the expression of emotional energy is continually thwarted, this primal power will find stronger ways to get our attention – often surfacing as aggression, rebellion, abuse, addiction, chronic stress and senseless violence. All the anti-depressant drugs and worldly distractions cannot cure the pain and trauma that occurs when losing contact with the soul of our emotional life. The challenge is not to deny or transcend our emotions, it's about discovering how to truly feel and express this primal power in healthy, creative ways.

Feelings make us real and, despite all attempts to stifle them, they will not sit idly by when our intrinsic values are being trampled upon.

-Cooper & Sawaf
Executive EQ

Primal Energetics **is an 'emotional fitness' process that exercises this primal power the way musicians, actors, dancers, singers and children do all the time passionately with soul.**

Awakening to your authentic self is developing intimate awareness and embodiment of the original Source of energy that created you.

-Baird Spalding

Overview

Three parts compose this breakthrough process. After the overview, which lays out the map of *Primal Energetics,* I share my story of healing and transformation. The second part introduces the *Five Catalysts,* which ignite a fluid body language that supports the authenticity of emotional energy to flow. The third part exercises the physiology of *Eight Primal Energies*, which integrates all emotions into the full-bodied expression of natural ecstasy – the celebration of our radiant wholeness.

My Story: From Woe to Wow

People often ask me, "At age 70, how do you sustain your amazing energy and still have the physical flexibility of a child?" *Primal Energetics* is the secret of my ageless vitality. Like a lotus growing out of the mud, the trauma of physical/emotional abuse, a disfiguring skin disease, cross eyes, and crippling inhibition were my greatest teachers. Physically expressing my pain in dramatic expression with breath, sound and movement, opened up a whole new world of alternative, healing possibilities that radically transformed my health, vitality and very life into renewal.

I have been teaching expressive arts therapies, movement/dance education, sound healing and innovative bodywork practices for decades. My mission is to help us all reclaim the expressive beauty and power of emotional intelligence – before conditioning and traumatic occurrences adversely shaped our lives. Regaining the youthful physiology that unleashes vital aliveness opens the way to heal and transform anything that ails.

As the philosopher and anthropologist, Ashley Montague, has revealed in his book, *Growing Young,* "We are designed to grow in an unending state of development so conspicuously exhibited by the child. A youthfulness of spirit offers us continued flexibility, curiosity, playfulness, imagination, creativity, openness and resiliency to grow and change in new and different ways. In this way, we will not become the ossified adults prescribed by society."

Five Catalysts

Living in a world undergoing radical change a more fluid, adaptable, emotionally fit body language is required to move us feelingly into a new and different future. The *Five Catalysts* uncover a quantum physiology of consciousness that supports emotional energy to flow. Together, in unified harmony, the *Five Catalysts* have the power to shift us from rigid conformity to fluid adaptability, from mental analysis to creative synthesis, from domination and aggression to heart-felt interaction with others and the planet. Here is a brief introduction of the *Five Catalysts.*

The quantum self is a more fluid self, changing and evolving at every moment into a larger self. It ebbs and flows, but is always in some sense being itself.

-Danah Zohar
The Quantum Self

Catalyst 1. Sacred Actor: Artist of Being

Many of us had to put away imaginative play and act out prescribed roles in order to conform and be accepted. Entering into the magical realm of the *Sacred Actor,* which represents the creative genius of your multidimensional self, total freedom of expression comes back into play. The first step is enacting your habitual social role – the familiar stance, vocal pattern and walking style as your greatest creation. Conscious embodiment of the public persona means you are no longer lost in the part. Embodiment of the Soul of Emotion supports the primal power of your authentic self to take center stage. With heightened awareness and acceptance of the multifacets of your identity, the ego and the essence join forces and 'interplay' in harmony.

Find out who you are, and do it on purpose!

-Dolly Parton

Catalyst 2. Fluidity of Being: Quantum Body in Motion

The second Catalyst honors your body as a unified field of energy interconnected with all that is. Exercising a fluid body language in ever-changing motion transforms protective/defensive boundaries of muscular density into spontaneous, flexible adaptability. Coming into union with the uplifting support of gravity while sitting, standing and walking the waves of unpredictable change can be met with instinctive prowess and natural grace.

In the endless avowal of that selfhood which is divine, we use our translucent bodies in a new language that expresses the glory of our being.

-Ruth St. Dennis
Divine Dancer

Catalyst 3. Breath Olympics: Champion of Life Force

The third Catalyst dissolves shallow breathing habits by activating oxygenated aerobic power to freely flow through your body. All degenerative disease and the debilitating affects of aging are caused by oxygen starvation. As the prime mover of all action, Ecstatically breathing with emotional energy is most effective in cleansing and recharge your body of toxins, fatigue and stress. From lovemaking to sports, being a champion of life force revitalizes the stamina and endurance to go that extra mile and effortlessly reach ecstatic states of bliss any time you wish.

Catalyst 4. Mother Hum: Inner Voice of Feeling

All of life is composed of vibration and it's all humming! Like a dolphin's sonar language, this fourth Catalyst brings you into 'sympathetic resonance' with an ultrasonic genius that can vibrate vital energy into the atoms of your cells and positively affect your health and vitality. Humming with different emotional energies can diminish pain, synchronize brain waves, improve motor skills, dissolve debilitating moods and calm your mind by bringing your awareness into the present moment. In an era requiring rapid pace thinking, humming while reading and working at a computer can generate more intuitive resources and strengthen retention of information.

To nurture our spiritual roots into growth, we must embrace the pre-verbal language of original creation – a language that precedes the intellect and resounds the sacred in all things.

-Matthew Fox
Original Blessing

Catalyst 5. Song Talk: The First and Future Language

The fifth Catalyst attunes you to the ecstatic sound current that flows through all of creation. Making up original languages with a diversity of melodic rhythms offers unlimited permission to delve into the primal depths and expanses of feeling without mental deliberation. As a future language, *Song Talk* is an effective means to develop more telepathic and empathetic understanding in our communication with others. When fluid, feeling tones are interwoven into your known language, trust is strengthened to select the melody, set the tempo and change your tune any time you wish.

Primal Yoga: **Groundwork for the *Eight Primal Energies***

Originally, the system of Yoga reflected the flow of nature's elements and the fluid flexibility of its creatures. With the advent of formalized postures, the feeling heart of expression was exchanged for precise expertise. With exploding violence, addiction and rapid pollution threatening the planet, perceiving the body as a living ecosystem that is interconnected to the vast energetic resources of nature is essential for our very survival.

Of the 100 trillion cells inside each one of us, only 10% are actually human. The rest belong to bacteria, fungi, and other microbes.

Josie Glausiusz
The Body is a Planet

In preparation for embodiment of the *Eight Primal Energies*, 'original postures' are created that unleash the instinctive dexterity of your creature nature. Activating more fluid creativity in any static posture generates more feeling resources that can help you thrive in any urban jungle

Audibly breathing and sounding while wiggling, undulating, writhing, rolling, slithering, creeping and crawling on different sized balls prepares your body to express, without reserve, the dynamics of emotional energy. Recent discoveries have uncovered that stunted mental development and a rigid body language often result when primal movements have been inhibited in childhood. Exploring the different movement possibilities of the mutational process, from fish to early human awakens fluid adaptability and heightens awareness of personal and collective sustainability.

Eight Primal Energies

Even with all our smarts, we are a culture that is still struggling with poor self-esteem, exploding violence, massive addiction and chronic stress. Screaming at sports events, watching violent movies, yelling at people we love, pounding pillows over traumatic events or taking addictive substances are not adequately doing the job of channeling the buildup of emotional energy.

Different from therapy, and closer to how an actor heightens feelings to create a role, exercising emotional energy with breath, sound and movement is highly therapeutic. The secret is recognizing and heightening the sensations of emotional energy pulsing through your body. Heightened sensory acuity of emotion offers more creative options to express your feelings in communication with others.

Without awareness of our relationship to Soul, no one can ever become as fully human as we're intended to become.

-Paula Reves

The most definitive aspect of this process is making a clear distinction between emotions that are produced by repetitive thinking patterns and the energy of emotion that is the primal force of inner guidance. There is often enormous confusion between these two states of consciousness. From this holistic perspective, all emotions have equal value. More specifically – when labels and value judgments are removed – emotions are *feeeelings* of sensation, pulsing vibrations of rhythmical energy that compose the molecular structure of our body and the larger body of the world.

Only one percent of our feeling sensations reach our awareness. No wonder we become insecure in knowing what to do and how to move forward in our lives.

In essence, emotions are music that moves us into harmonious action. In the new physics, the universe in an enormous stringed orchestra, our body is a musical instrument that resonates in tune or out of tune with the musical continuum vibrating throughout creation. Healthy living entails building trust in spontaneously moving with the inner voice of feeling

This 'emotional fitness' process exercises the soul of eight emotions with breath, sound and movement. By soul I mean the originating intelligence contained in emotional energy. The eight emotions are: Peace, Love, Chaos, Fear, Anger, Vulnerability, Laughter and Ecstasy.

Our deepest emotions are essential guides, and that our species owns much of its existence to their power.-

-Daniel Goleman
Emotional Intelligence

The Soul of Peace is interwoven throughout all the primal energies. With embodiment of peaceful energy, you possess the magical power to shift in and out of any emotion as effortlessly as a musician plays different kinds of music. This breakthrough program culminates with aerobic embodiment of 'natural ecstasy' that rejoins *all* emotions into radiant wholeness. Healing breakthroughs of relatedness and synergy occur when all emotions, including the most volatile, can be expressed with pure pleasure.

Moving through any mundane activity breathing with the ecstatic rhythms of oceanic fluidity, explosive fire, peaceful repose and wind swept passion is the secret of continuously releasing toxic buildup and rejuvenating our very lives with ageless vitality. As body, heart, mind and soul interplay as one, anything becomes possible!

Emotional intelligence is so valuable because it makes our fragmented selves feel whole again.

-Jeanne Segal
-Raising EQ

You don't have to be angry or sad to participate in this process. Developing emotional fluency – the ability to express any emotion and dissolve it at will– is an immediate way of actualizing personal power. Being emotionally independent offers a wealth of creative options in how to heal and transform what ails. Like a pendulum, we have the ability to swing back and forth between restricting our emotional life or letting it guide us through an increasingly chaotic world. The choice is ours. What follows is a short description of the *Eight Primal Energies*. The exercises are called *Activations*.

Our mission is not to bring the calming presence of peace to where it is not, but to reveal peace where it is hidden from sight.

-James Twyman
Emissary of Light

1. Diamond Mind: Radiant Peace

The first primal energizer attunes you to the Soul of Peace as the underlying substance of your essential self. The practice of embodying tranquil breathing patterns, spacious humming vibrations and contemplative movements inspires the realization that you are no longer trying to *act* peaceful – peace is who you are at the core of your being. With embodied knowledge of this serene power, you can clearly feel when it's time to slow down, relax and release the stresses of the day. Visualizing your mind as a multifaceted diamond opens up a peripheral vision to see the 'big picture' – a whole-sighted awareness that can apprehend a peaceful state of mind in any stressful situation.

2. Heartbeat: Loving Compassion

The second primal energizer illuminates awareness that we are all connected to the same heart, the One Heart of the universe. Separated from the original source of this all-encompassing love creates enormous heartache. Merging your individualized social role with the Soul of Love can quickly heal the split between thinking and feeling. When all emotions are honored with equal value, even your unlovable parts can be embraced with unconditional acceptance. Bonding with the essence of loving compassion creates unshakable rapport with others and the planet.

Consciously entering a chaotic state is an opportunity to restructure our physical bodies into a more flexible arrangement, more suitable to the unknown. Constructive use of chaos frees us of old structures.

-Richard H. Lee
Editor of China Healthways

3. Shake out the Crazies: Order in Chaos

The third primal energizer unleashes a little madness to prevent the big madness! Breathing and sounding while shaking out deadening layers of conformity and emotional buildup unleashes unbridled creativity to improvise your life with uninhibited brilliance. As a mover and shaker of emotional expression, trust is gained to unleash lightning-quick impulses without rational deliberation. Freedom of response supports the creative art of risk-taking as a practical means of living in a world that is becoming increasingly chaotic.

4. Guardian Angel: Fear Alert

The fourth primal energizer exercises your 'startle reflexes,' which are designed to shock all your systems awake in an instant. Embodying the Soul of Fear as the life preserving, primal power offers undaunted fearlessness in moving into an unknown future. When daily exercising the energetic pulsations of the fear response, endless frightening thoughts generated by the intellect relax their hold on your mind. Research is discovering that brain cells continue to grow when short doses of rapid percussive stimulation are directed into the bones, muscles, and cells of the body. Attuned to the source of inner protection, there is renewed excitement to live life to the fullest.

As we accelerate into the next century, sharp eyes and quick reflexes are needed to navigate ourselves into an unknown world.

-Barry Minkin
Future in Sight

5. Rain: Healing Vulnerability

This fifth primal energizer exercises your 'crying muscles' whether you're sad or not. Like rain moistening the parched ground, breathing, sounding and moving with the sporadic rhythms of vulnerable energy loosens up and strengthens the entire midsection of your body. As your ribs, organs and diaphragm become more mailable, a balance of hormones are released that help dissolve the buildup of pain, loss and disappointment. From this healing, transformative perspective, vulnerability is our strength.

6. Volcanic Power: Pure Anger

To be warm and loving is important, but it is equally important to be fierce when necessary, and come out kicking ass!

-Clarissa Pinkola Estes

In what part of your soul have you stored the pleasure of being big and bold with your body, voice and gestures? The sixth primal energizer coaches you how to fully express the intensity of pure anger in creative, life affirming ways. Rather than dumping the buildup of this energy on outside influences, expressing the Soul of Anger as thunderous, volcanic power gives you unbeatable strength and decisive know-how to meet challenging conflicts with courageous confidence.

7. Hilarity: Authentic Laughter

The seventh primal energizer coaches you to laugh with the truth of your moment-to-moment feelings. This means you don't have to be happy to laugh or have something to laugh about. If you're miserable, laughing in a miserable way instantly loosens up unproductive moods. Exercising the percussive rhythms of laughter makes it easier to laugh through all insufferable dramas, unrealistic idealism and stupid mistakes that are a part of being human. The endorphin of pure joy is fully liberated when skipping with rhythmical laughter.

8. Celebration: Natural Ecstasy

Reclaiming the lost passion of our body is not merely sexual in nature, but the radiant fire that animates our entire being in pure joy.

-Wowza

Ecstatic energy dances in every molecule of your body. Conscious embodiment of natural ecstasy eroticizes your nerve fibers, warms your flesh, arouses your arteries and pumps blood into your heart with undivided passion! The focus of this last primal energizer is to weave all emotional energies into the rapturous harmony of ecstatic expression – now this is something to celebrate! Moving through the day breathing with passionate aliveness supercharges your personal magnetism and jump-starts your charisma.

Embodiment of the physiology of natural ecstasy is experiencing at a molecular level that all of life is making love to God.

Questions and Answers

Your inner truth will set you free. But first, it will piss you off.

-Gloria Steinem

When exploring new ways of being, many of the traditional beliefs we've absorbed interfere with our need to grow and change. As an analogy, imagine how disconcerting it must have been to discover that the world was round rather than flat. How many questions and disagreements arose when attempting to refute this undeniable discovery? Below are some questions and concerns people have when starting this process.

I was taught that primal instincts are barbaric and not to be trusted. An assumption exists that our instincts have not evolved, and should not to be trusted. Believing this instinctual way of knowing is barbaric, savage, and uncivilized, the body becomes a prison, with muscles forming into armored guards in an attempt to block the dreaded enemy from coming out. Whatever we disown will surface in a maladaptive manner.

When impulses of sensation are perceived as an original language that awakens and alerts you to the present moment, gut-level feelings become your greatest ally. If we can't trust our 'insides,' who or what can we trust?

I have a tendency to explode in anger. Why would I want to exercise this volatile emotion? If the energy of anger has been labeled as a negative emotion, once again, your body goes to work to physically inhibit its expression. Angry tirades are often unleashed to release the buildup of tension. I want to add, with so much emphasis placed on development of the mental mind rather than support of the feeling heart, our American culture is the most violent society in the history of recorded civilization. The weapons of war budget are bigger than all the war budgets in the world put together. In fact, the promotion of violence is a multi-billion dollar business. Studies suggest that between 10 million children witness some form of domestic violence annually. The average American child witnesses 12,000 murders and more than 150,000 other acts of violence on TV just by watching a minimum of 3.5 hours a week.

Daring goes hand and hand with losing fear of exposing your emotional authenticity. The expression of big and bold energy gives you the needed courage to act decisively.

-Moni Yakim
Creating Character

Violence sells because it reflects the most deeply repressed aspect of our psyche. Programmed to be obedient and never question authority, this same authority can quickly control our mind. With the mass extermination of indigenous peoples along with the rain forests that keep the air breathing, it is imperative for our survival to enjoin with an original intelligence that is guiding us into a quantum reality of 'unbroken wholeness.'

Channeling explosive emotions into ecstatic expression is a magical way to quickly move through the toughest internal obstacles. To identify, accept and express strong emotions in artful, creative ways, is to feel life in all its fullness.

What's so smart about emotions? Contrary to conventional beliefs, the thinking brain grew out of the neurological seat of emotional energy. Candace Pert, author of *Molecules of Emotion* has written, "The molecules of emotion run every system in our body, and this communication system is a demonstration of the body/mind's intelligence, an intelligence wise enough to seek wellness."

A new report on violence in America has found that over the last 30 years, big city violent crime increased by 40 percent, and firearms possession has increased over 120 percent.

-Ray Suarez

More specifically, the DNA molecule pulsates as a giant hologram hooked up with the nervous system of the planet in which past, present and future information exist concurrently. Your DNA strands, if stretched out end to end, are over 125 billion miles long! This inborn biotechnology contains over a hundred trillion times more information than the most advanced computers. As Dr. Deepak Chopra indicates in his book, *Perfect Health,* "The cells memory of perfection contained in the DNA cannot be lost. It is only covered over by erroneous beliefs that obstruct this intelligence from being acted upon."

Are you asking me to act out emotions in a phony way? As young kids, we were masters of spontaneous emotional expression and we were anything but phony. Before we could say, "I love you" our arms instantly reached out to hug and be hugged. When forced to eat something distasteful, our voice and gestures signaled a clear intent that everyone could understand. Social roles are developed to project how we wish to be seen. The habit of excessively smiling to convey happiness, looking stern to appear smart, or projecting a dominating demeanor to control others, forces our body to remain in static patterns that rarely deviate from the role. When identified with these masked facades, peace becomes inertia, fear becomes mania, laughter becomes sarcasm, sorrow becomes self-pity, and

Marvel at the ingenuity in which divinity hides itself in order to find itself.

-Alan Watts
The Book

anger becomes manipulation. As our materialistic lifestyles are becoming irreconcilable with our mission to become fully human, and our educational systems still train children to conform in uniformity, reclaiming emotional intelligence is the very preparation we need to meet the future with an open, loving heart.

Walling oneself off from our expressive vitality happens at great cost. This is where really brilliant ideas are located, where 99% of our potential creative genius lies.

-George Land

How can I stimulate emotions of laughter and ecstasy if I've been chronically depressed for years? Most of our culture joins you in this respect. Lots of talk and more pills are the mainstream prescription in dealing with depression. Most of us do not live in our body we live in our heads. Spending precious time in the ivory tower of the mind adults think about 50,000 thoughts a day - or about one million thoughts in three months. Half of these thoughts are negative! The debilitating habit of reliving life's distressing experiences or fretting about what will happen in the future would make anyone depressed. The false veneer, surface politeness, and lack of genuine feeling that is characteristic of 'terminal adulthood' has served its usefulness.

Primal Energetics is a non-drug intervention that prescribes ingesting massive amounts of emotive breath, sound and movement to regenerate natural vitality and intuitive awareness. As depressive patterns are perceived and amplified, revitalizing inspiration is awakened that triggers rejuvenation on all levels.

Generating excitement is a better medicine for depression, hopelessness and loneliness than anything that comes out of a bottle.

-Stella Resnick, Ph.D.
Pleasure Zone

Six Benefits

Fit, Creative Living

In a culture that is becoming increasingly more mechanized, most exercise regimens reflect a solid model of body mechanics that prescribe ironclad, repetitious exercises that attempt to buff up the body with 'abs of steel.' Going through the motions with a blank face, clenched teeth and a deadly serious attitude have served its usefulness. Research is proving that most mentally driven exercise drives over half of the people who start these fitness programs, drop out and return to sedentary lifestyles.

At last, you don't have to stop what you're doing to become fit! Sitting, standing and walking while breathing and humming with ecstatic energy tones and strengthens your body from the inside out.

Generating full-bodied passionate power can help you accomplish all your tasks with effortless ease. For instance, breathing with the energy of anger builds volcanic power and inner strength. Humming with vulnerable energy acts as a gentle rain that moistens all your cells and clears loss and disappointment. Walking with the percussive energy of fear firms your startle reflexes that protect you from danger. Dancing with the energy of ecstasy generates the potent fire of pure aliveness. Stimulating more wave motions to flow through your spine generates enormous circulatory power that keeps all your systems juicy and alive.

Feet die of boredom for lack of walking in interesting places, and the heart doesn't enjoy being treated as a pump.

-Thomas Moore

Exercising emotional muscles not just physical muscles invigorate all the systems of the body and strengthen a presence of mind.

Radiant Health

Dr. Bernie Seigel is quoted saying, "Repression of emotion is the number one health hazard." Without a synergistic flow of emotive chemistry, our system becomes increasingly more toxic. Circulation dries up, skin sags, bones become brittle and disease builds with alarming intensity. Addictive compulsions, such as the urge to drive at reckless speeds, consume alcohol and hard drugs, are often a substitute for chemical deprivation.

The energizing power of ecstatic breathing can purge us from lethargy and fill our body with renewed health, excitement and passion.

-Frank Natale
Trance Dance

The body is a profound miracle of molecular energy that contains an apothecary of chemical frequencies designed to sustain our health and vitality throughout life. The brain is capable of producing any biochemical response when strong intention and energy is connected with this process. For instance, tear ducts are designed to cleanse toxic buildup, while the quick responses of fear mobilizes the energy to kick and run to protect our life. A gush of excitement unleashes a hormone (ACTH) that dissolves depression. Feelings of love produce a chemical called oxytocin that increases the heart's pumping action. Generating ecstatic energy with breath, sound and movement releases required opiates that promote a 'natural high' without the use of drugs.

Stimulating full spectrum emotional energy as a daily fitness regime releases a balance of chemical ingredients that can effectively ward off psychosomatic symptoms of disease.

One exciting discovery is the knowledge that the trillions of cells in our body completely transform themselves every seven years. You may wonder with this built-in power, why the body wears out at all. Before a cell dies, its memory is passed onto the next cell being born. It is the massive buildup of past trauma, negative beliefs and repressed layers of emotional energy that prevent the cells from fully rejuvenating themselves. Exercising the rhythmical, sensations of emotional energy with healing intent is highly effective in stimulating the trillions of cells to grow more healthy and vital with each passing year.

The more emotional charge you can generate, the more life you can contain and the more pleasure you can experience.

-Julie Henderson
The Lover Within

Intuitive Awareness

Born brilliant, we all possess the incredible gift of intuitive insight. It is still rare in most schools around the country that intuitive know-how is developed as a valuable talent of direct cognition and wise insight. Instead, we are taught how to retain massive amounts of secondhand knowledge, which is quickly forgotten.

Amazing sources of oracular wisdom and prophetic insight are released when learning how to intuit the Soul of Emotion's unique rhythmical signals as a language of emotional intelligence.

Honoring emotions as high-powered intuitive advisors can offer instant motivation to activate your hopes, dreams and desires into manifestation. What hidden gifts and talents do you possess that is waiting to be expressed? At the end of each chapter, you are invited to stand before a mirror and energize a specific desire with emotional energy. Intuitive responsiveness is intensified when physically enacting a desired accomplishment in present time. As the master genius, Walt Disney, once said, "By intuiting your dreams and energizing them with your intention, they will manifest in wondrous ways. Always remember that the whole thing was started by a mouse!"

Intuition is charged energy, an emotion that puts us in motion. So feel it and do it now!

-James Wanless
Intuition@work

A Youthfulness of Spirit

What contributes to the debilitating process of aging? The habit of 'sameness!' Living life in repetitive behavior patterns forces us to breathe, sit, stand, walk and talk with little variation in the matter. To make my point clear, I'm reminded of an amusing story of two caterpillars inching their way along the ground. Suddenly a brightly colored butterfly glides by. "Humph!" said one of the caterpillars, "You'll never get me up in one of those things!"

In a flash of insight, take wing as a butterfly soaring freely into a new world of unfolding mystery.

-Dorian Brown

Without surprising doses of novelty pulsing through the nervous system, our body sags down into deadening decline. By not growing we become old. Opening to 'newness' means moving through the different stages of life as a surprising adventure – a challenge in spontaneously changing and growing in more enlightened ways.

There is an exquisite butterfly forming out of your caterpillar state that dazzles mental comprehension. Can you feel it? Being at the threshold of a new mutation, a youthfulness of spirit is coming alive in your heart.

The spirit, being eternal, is forever young. As I embrace and honor age 70 with a flexible spine, limber joints and energy to burn, I propose that the outworn need to 'act our age' needs revamping. I wish to emphasize that ageless vitality is not about trying to act young, which means sustaining a mask of pretense that can never let down the image. Sustaining any emotional attitude for very long is exhausting!

All ages need to be perceived with equal value because each age contains fertile seeds of new, creative beginnings. If I identified only with my chronological age, which reflects the conditioning of stereotyped behavior, I would consider myself too old to create a pioneering body of work and feel too inhibited and inertia-ridden to birth it into the world. Here is a quote is from an Indian Elder that beautifully expresses the ageless spirit. "It doesn't interest me how old you are, I want to know if you will risk looking like a fool for the adventure of being alive. I want to know if you can dance with wildness and let the juicy feeling of ecstasy fill you to the tips of your fingers and toes – without cautioning me to be more realistic or to remember the limitations of being human."

The dead hand of tradition, and the power of our own expectations will no longer force us to do exactly what everyone else our age is doing.

-Ken Dychwald
The Age Wave

Play of Genius

More than silliness, childish frivolity, or indulging in exhibitionist behavior, reawakening the 'play instinct' is the secret out of which creative genius springs. Play is the original fitness of the universe. It may even be said that the nature of existence is celebratory play – ecstatic rejoicing of the unlimited creative potential we all share in common. Brian Swimme, author of *The Universe is a Green Dragon* expresses it beautifully, "The adventurous play of all life forms burst into the sublime diversity of the past five hundred million years. All of this profusion of being and beauty is the outcome of creative play, of risk, of surprise!"

Keep away from structures that do not cry, the philosophy that does not laugh, and the greatness that does not bow before children.

-Kahil Gibran

Most children are trained with rewards and punishment to follow outer authorities demands to grow up as soon as possible. This usually means stop that 'silly playing' and start acting like a serious adult. Hyperactive tendencies in children just may be a desperate attempt to break out of rigid molds of conditioning that deaden the life force of their playful spirit. Children are master players of creative ingenuity. It is time we modeled their rich biological resources in order to reclaim emotional intelligence as the very preparation we need to meet an unknown future.

How can we live life in the spirit of celebration? Exercising the 'play of genius' as the ultimate fit activity keeps our baby-wise brilliance and elder-wild passion singing and dancing throughout life.

Perceiving our lives as 'living art' in progress all the many actions of the day can be explored with more artful creativity. Any repetitive drama, and even the most negative habits of mind can be dramatized with masterful enactment. When life and art are enjoined in creative interaction, there is unlimited freedom to breathe like the wind, kick up a storm, punch through the rut, leap with courage, speak with heart, laugh without reason, hug with love and unleash our natural gifts and talents with grace, boldness and daring. The world itself becomes a magical playground in which everyone encountered is a potential playmate that helps us unveil and celebrate the wholeness of our being.

Charles Garfield, in his book, *Peak Performers-The New Heroes of American Business,* discovered that successful leaders possess strong patterns of childlike behavior. Having the magical knack of turning work into play, wonderful things start happening. These outstanding people spontaneously perform with clear energy, are at home in their bodies, are highly imaginative, have unbridled enthusiasm, a flourishing creativity, intuitive know-how, and can express honest, heart-felt feelings with others. These healthy, vital qualities are the bottom line of *Primal Energetics.*

By ctivating your native instincts will make your work and your life richer, more rewarding and fulfilling.

-Robert J. Kriegel

Our mission is to become fire.
Passionate, wild hearts dancing.
And the time is NOW!

-Elliot Sobbel
Wild Hearts Dancing

My Story

From Woe to Wow

Sharing your story of primary wounding and how you transformed your pain, adversity and despair with unwavering courage is what can inspire others to do the same.

-Cheyenne Saying

One of my favorite pastimes as a child was gazing at clouds changing into whatever my imagination could conjure. Several years ago, when feeling frustrated about how to bring my work out into the world, I gazed into the sky and noticed that a large cumulus cloud had taken the shape of a movie screen. Before long, a dark figure loomed in its center. In my inner ear, I heard a voice echoing a greeting, "Blessings and praises dear child, I am the cosmic casting director. Rejoice! The part you have come to play in this lifetime is awaiting your full embodiment. You have sprung from a long lineage of 'primal energizers' that are here to rejuvenate the passionate soul of humanity. During this challenging time, you are opening new frontiers of expression to heal people's separation from the source of their original, feeling nature."

Draw your chair up close to the edge of the precipice and I'll tell you a story.

-F. Scott Fitzgerald

I blurted out, "I'm totally confused how to accomplish this enormous task." With a wave of his hand he said, "My child, being a pioneer is not always easy. I encourage you to write your story of emotional wounding and the unique healing discoveries you've made." I moaned, "My writing skills are totally underdeveloped. Besides, how can energetic expression be articulated on the written page?" With a loving smile he said, "This practice will help you balance the mental and creative hemispheres of your brain. Being 'whole brained' will make it easier for you to communicate to your fellow humans how to thrive with emotional authenticity in a radically changing world.

Trauma and Transformation

My parents, each in their own way, taught me well how to withhold the expression of my feeling nature. Any outburst of spontaneous emotion would infuriate my father. His favorite device for keeping me quiet was reaching for the dreaded razor strap. When he made use of this devise, I would rigidify every muscle in my body to prevent myself from crying out. I believed if I could withstand any amount of pain, he would appreciate my bravery and be kinder to me. What kept my love alive for my father was watching his sullen mood shift when a Viennese waltz was playing on the radio. Standing motionless, as if transfixed in a dream, he would spring into motion and whirl around the living room in ecstatic surrender. Oh, how I wished to be swept up in his arms and be whirled into dancing oblivion! When the music ended, it was such a shock to see his beautiful dancing spirit return to his sullen state of mind.

It is not the years themselves that age us. It is the way we have learned to live them. Giving up a little of our true selves at each step, limberness diminishes with reduced movement, and the feelings, playfulness also diminish with reduced expression.

-Gay Luce

Living in the midst of emotive hand grenades going off between my mother and father, a scaly, oozing rash appeared on my forearms. It itched like crazy. When the rash spread up my arms and made its way up to my neck, I begged my mother to let me wear long sleeved blouses to school. This request was denied because she believed fresh air and sun would heal it. When the rash came to rest on the cheeks of my face, I was mortified with shame. I can still hear the kids yelling as I walked to school, "It's leper girl!" Turning to their friends, they would whisper, "Don't get close to her, you'll catch it!" On hearing those words, my very soul contracted to avoid the pain.

Six months after the arrival of the skin disease, my left eye pulled into the corner of its socket. The doctor said I was cross-eyed. The remedy was to wear thick, corrective glasses. I really didn't mind wearing them because they offered me a protective mask from the daily onslaught of ridicule. What bothered me the most was the terrifying chill I would experience when a teacher would ask me a question. Feeling dizzy with confusion my mind would draw a blank. When the teacher told my parents I had dysfunctional learning abilities, all my father could say was: "You stupid kid, how can you be so dumb?"

You are never what they believe you to be. You are even more than you think that you see. There's a much greater truth. When you look you will find the key is right there in your heart and your mind.

-Gina Otto
Cassandra's Angel

My playground was my imagination. I loved to create wondrous movies in my mind that often started by visualizing myself sitting in the center of a magnificent web of many-colored strands that hovered in the sky. From this lofty place, I had a bird's eye view of any areas of the world in which my services were needed. My favorite role was portraying a female Robin Hood who guided hungry, frightened and abandoned children into a magical kingdom that provided them with delicious food and tender loving care. I came away from my inner adventures knowing, no matter how stupid or ugly I was believed to be, powerful forces lived inside my heart that nobody could beat out of me.

The day of my eleventh birthday, my mother bought a floor-length mirror and hung it on my bedroom wall. Mirrors were my enemy. I could not stand to look at the ugly rash that covered my body. On this day, I had an impulse to cover my face with an old Halloween mask. With my face covered up, I noticed my body, perhaps for the first time in my life. I was shocked to see how my shoulders rounded around my chest and how my chin tilted down into my neck. My chest looked like a dark hollow cave hiding my heart. I winced when noticing how tightly my elbows were pulled into my waistline.

I deal with this disease by looking at it as one of the best teachers I've ever had. I treat it with respect. I try to love it. I talk to it. I'll say: "Do not worry, I do not hate you."

-young person with Aids

Seeing my body in this way, I doubled over in anguish. Wishing i could disappear forever, every muscle in my body tightened up into a deadly grip. Nothing was going to make me breathe. Suddenly a burst of energy burst through my resistance and forced me to gasp for air. Even when overtaken with dizziness, I feasted on this air as the most delicious food I had ever tasted. It was my first real experience of taking a deep breath and what it felt like to experience energy running through every part of my body. Once again, I tightened my body and did everything I could to keep from breathing. As massive gushes of fresh air pushed open my lungs, I opened my mouth and gorged myself on all the heavenly air. When I finally returned to my normal state, my body. was tingling all over with pulsing sensations. What is this breath that insists that I live?

Ugly Dancer

The next day, when I was alone in the house, I was compelled to experience more of this intoxicating experience. While standing at the mirror, I doubled over and held my breath for as long as I could. When the dramatic moment came, my arms flung open and I gasped for air. With my head spinning in a light-headed trance, an exciting idea entered my mind. If I can't be a beautiful dancer as my father says, I'll be the greatest ugly dancer in the world – now that's something I could really be good at!

There are three kinds of dancers: those for whom dancing is physical exercise, those who dance to express emotion, and those who hand over their bodies to the inspiration of the 'soul.'

-Isadora Duncan

With no paralyzing inhibitions getting in the way, I twisted and contorted my spine into every shape imaginable. All my inhibiting sensibilities went running for cover when breathing with the ferocity of a wild windstorm! What enormous pleasure it was to let loose and roar with all my might! After spending weeks exploring this strange activity, I looked at myself in the mirror. Why, I could barely recognize myself. My sunken chest had come out of its dark cave, and my rounded shoulders appeared more open. My face had a lovely glow that awakened something in my heart.

One afternoon, while exploring dancing with new and different moves, my father walked into the room. I stood frozen like a hunted animal about to be shot. With disgust in his face, he shouted, "What are you doing – acting nuts?" I blurted out that I was dancing. All he could say was, "You, dance? You don't even have legs to stand on!" Oh, how I wanted to scream, "I'm an ugly dancer and I do have what it takes!" Instead, I stumbled out of the room and ran to an old cemetery, which was my private play area.

As I crawled into a corner of a big stone slab, an enormous pressure was building behind my eyes. Displaying tears was my dreaded enemy. I believed any show of tears would make me appear weak in my father's eyes. On this day, no amount of tightening could contain this overwhelming force. In spite of my best efforts, a river of tears gushed from my eyes. After this outpouring of tears, I felt newborn, like a white sheet blowing in the wind to dry. Who knows, maybe my tears are simply like falling rain washing out all the pain and loneliness that depresses my heart.

The child is a maker of stories, draws and paints without hesitation, hums and dances its moods, until it is plugged in and the artist is driven underground.

-Frederick Franck

Mother of the World

That night in bed, another wellspring of tears were building up behind my eyes. Fearing my tears that would never stop, I distracted myself by gazing at a picture hanging on the wall. It was a beautiful woman with a golden halo framing her head. She was sitting on top of a mountain and from her hips flowed a winding waterfall. A little child played at her side.

Once, when I asked my mother about the woman, she told me the picture was called, *Mother of the World*. In my distress, I imagined this beautiful woman reaching out to hold me in her arms. As I felt her arms enfolded me in a sweet embrace, she hummed a lullaby that melted my heart. In my inner ear, I heard her whisper, "Dear child, you are loved." The *Mother of the World* loves you and will always love you."

Suffer the little children to come unto me, and forbid them not, for of such is the kingdom of God.

-Mark 10:14

From that day on, I visualized this loving being as my inner companion I called *Humma*. Her humming tones of tender feeling would get me up in the morning, go to school with me, console me when I felt lonely or abused. In my imaginative world, I visualized *Humma* not only easing my pain, but also easing the pain of all children that had ever been abused. On two occasions, the warning intensity of her humming voice saved me from serious harm. Even living in a battlefield of abusive treatment, the realization of a compassionate presence living inside my heart gave me renewed hope in life.

Feeling emotionally split between two worlds was my greatest struggle. Tapping into such freedom of expression in my inner life and acting so inhibited with others was most confusing to my young mind. All this outrageous energy I was experiencing was obviously wrong to express in public, and yet expressing it was the only time I felt what it was like to be fully alive. Perhaps my shy behavior was a means I used to protect the preciousness of my inner life.

A nightingale is a creature who sits in darkness and sings to cheer its own solitude with sweet sounds.

-Unknown

Once I forgot myself and spoke up to my mother with my full voice. She immediately interrupted, saying, "It's unladylike to sound like that! Sound nice and people will like you." I wanted to shout, "No they won't! Being so shy, they don't even know I exist!" Unable to integrate these two radically different states, I continued to spend my time living in an inner world of my own making. Turning my bedroom mirror into a movie camera I visualized myself as the star of the drama who could make the audience cry. The 'Little Match Girl' was one of my favorite parts to play. The scene would start by gazing into a window and witnessing a family sitting down before a delicious Christmas dinner. Starving with hunger, I burn the last match to keep myself from freezing to death. Looking once more at the loving family, I whisper, "I am such a pitiable creature. May I die in the arms of God and end this misery."

When words cease, the voice of the Great Mother is heard. She hums tender lullabies in your heart and makes your soul dance with limitless joy.

-Chaynne Saying

As I expressed these words, I blurted out, "I'm too young to die! Whatever it takes, I will live! This outburst of expression helped me realize I was 'acting' the role of a pitiable creature rather than being a pitiable person. With this growing awareness, I would turn the entire day into a movie of my own design. Imagining a hidden camera following me through all my daily scenes turned mundane activities, like getting out of bed, brushing my teeth or walking down the hall into living Technicolor.

As the weeks went by, I began to view my parents as supporting actors in my movie. Catching my father bellow at my mother at the top of his lungs, he became a warlord battling the inner dragons in his disturbed mind. One day, I spontaneously imitated his heavy gait and bombastic vocal tone. During this embodiment, I was overtaken with sadness. I recalled the story he told me of the abject poverty he endured as a child in Vienna. At seventeen, when released from prison for stealing food to feed his brothers and sisters, he decided to run away from home. Somehow, he managed to hide on a ship sailing to America. He was soon caught and the authorities were going to take him back to Vienna. There was no way he would let this happen. As the ship landed, he jumped overboard and swam to the Brooklyn Bridge. That night he slept under the bridge with his only possession, a nickel in his pocket.

The subtle and powerful vibrations that can be produced by the human voice serve as an ideal resonating force for stimulating, purifying and balancing the energies that generate wholeness.

-James D'Angelo
Healing with the Voice

Somehow, through enormous hardship, he eventually made his way to Hollywood, California. And in 1918, he got one of the first movie contracts to dance in films. Dancing was the great love of his life. When he told his mother about his new dancing career, she wrote back that she would disown him if he continued his foolish interest in dancing. She had spent good money for his trade as a tool and dye maker, and it was up to him to provide for his brothers and sisters. Forsaking the love of his life, he buried himself in a world of machines that made him roaring mad. How tragic. A voice whispered inside my heart, "Give up what you love and make your life a living hell." Gaining deepened understanding of my father's pain helped me achieve some distance from his bombastic behavior.

When I focused on my mother as a supporting actress in my movie, I got in touch with how much I resented her need to keep me in a protective cocoon that was slowly smothering me to death. With a broader perception, I saw her as an actress playing the part of a beautiful scullery maid tending to the insatiable needs of a raging bull. When imitating my mother's darting eyes, high-pitched voice and nervous gestures, a deep pain stirred in my chest. I recalled the enormous sorrow she felt when losing her ten year old son a year before I was born. My father had taught him well how to act 'like a man,' which meant to deny any show of feelings. Refusing to complain about the severe pain he was feeling, his appendix ruptured while playing baseball. He died in the ambulance.

It's as though we were all amnesiacs, having forgotten our truer identities; seeing, like the underside of a weaving, only a fraction of what's before us, unconscious to the ground of our own being, the unguarded river of life.

-Thomas R. Condon

With a growing understanding why my mother did everything in her power to insulate me from harm, more creative options opened up when relating to her. For instance, I remember my mother forcing me to wear a sweater when leaving the house. On this occasion, I spontaneously acted out her frantic tone while wailing, "Oh how terrible! If I don't wear a warm sweater, I'll obviously freeze to death on this hot, summer day." In that moment, an odd thing happened. My mother stopped in her tracks, sat down and became very quiet. She took a deep breath and said, "Is this how I appear?" I said, "Yes mother." Lowering her head she shook her head in disbelief.

The growing awareness of my acting prowess made it harder and harder to hide what I was genuinely feeling inside. I recall an incident when my father yelled at my mother for putting his socks in the wrong drawer. When she did not respond, he threw a rubber boot at her face. As she yelped in pain, I shouted with thundering intensity, "Stop it! Stop it! Stop it!" As my voice faltered, I whispered, "Please Daddy, we love you. Stop hurting us" As his eyes widened in disbelief at my outburst, I feared he was going to reach for the razor strap. Instead, he stood motionless for a few moments and walked away.

Their armor is imprinted with its causative emotion. We see not an angry man, but a frozen symbol of rage; not a sorrowing woman, but an emblem of despair.

-Trudi Schoop
Won't You Join the Dance?

A few weeks after this incident, something had clearly changed in my father's attitude. At dinner he announced he would lose his long earned seniority at work, but he had decided to leave the factory forever. The house was sold and we moved to Florida. Taking this unconventional deed seemed to lighten my father's spirit. He still lost his temper and paid me little attention, but he never hit my mother or me again.

Healing Power

An event, which tapped me strong flows of emotion happened when the minister of our church proclaimed in a big booming voice: "Don't feed the body's passions! The body is the site of temptation. You must protect yourself against the dark forces of animal lust intent on destroying you!" Having experienced so much ridicule and emotional persecution in my young life, those torturous words made my stomach churn in agony. It took everything I had to keep from jumping up and shouting, "How dare you say such awful things about the body? What do you think the body feels like when it hears such frightening things? I'll tell you what it feels, it feels miserable!"

For if a man should dream of heaven and waking, find within his hand a flower as a token that he had really been there, what then, what then?

-Thomas Wolfe

With no physical outlet for my frustration, I scratched the ugly rash on my arms without letup. This was my first recognition that there was some connection between pent-up emotions and the scaly skin covering my body. What finally quieted me down was envisioning *Humma* humming a sweet lullaby to the devil himself. In that instant, he transformed into a miserable, red-faced baby fraught with pain. Rocking him in her arms, the Mother hummed, "You are loved wounded one, the Mother loves you." Tears came to my eyes as the concept of 'original sin' melted into unconditional love.

Unsure of our own value, insecure about our own worth, we can become gullable in accepting the rules and structures of patriarchal authority.

-Starhawk

That night, my skin was itching so bad that I dug into my flesh until blood spurted out all over the sheets. Utterly exasperated, I screamed, "I hate you, skin!" Instantly, I felt a sharp pain stab my heart. Inside my inner ear, I heard a voice shouting, "I am not horrible! I am a mighty power trapped inside you. Let me out!" I had no idea what this meant. With my arms itching like crazy, I groaned and moaned out the pain. while writhing my body with the ugliest motions imaginable. In the midst of this experience, I felt my skin was 'itching' to be touched. Humming with compassion I stroked my poor little arms. In a few minutes the itching magically diminished. My skin appeared grateful for my tender loving gesture. Before I knew it, the rash that I had endured for so long, was becoming paler. By the end of the month, my skin appeared baby soft and clear.

I saw you once, Medusa; we were alone. I looked you straight in the cold eye. I was not punished, was not turned to stone. How to believe the legends I am told?

-May Sarton

Shapeshifting

After an operation, which corrected my crossed eyes, I went to the mirror and witnessed my naked face without heavy, corrective glasses. It was also a momentous moment when I noticed soft curves filling out my skinny body. Delighted, I took a walk up to the ridge overlooking the ocean. Breathing in the sea air, I pulled my hair loose from its tie. As I approached the top of the hill, I spread open arms to embrace sea and sky. Taking a deep breath, I flew down the hill with utter joy. As I ran through the waves, a man with a camera walked up to me and said, "I have just captured a picture of pure radiance!" I had no idea what he was talking about.

A few weeks later, the picture of me flying down the hill appeared on the cover of a popular holiday magazine. The caption read, *Radiant Beauty under the Sun.* I was stunned to see myself portrayed in this way. That same week, while walking through a shopping mall, another photographer took a picture of me sitting on Santa's lap. This photo appeared on the front page of the Miami Herald. The next afternoon a woman called and said she was from the Chamber of Commerce who would like to sponsor me in the upcoming Florida Gladiola pageant. Me, in a beauty contest? Were they kidding? Two hours later, I opened the door, and sure enough, it was the woman from the Chamber of Commerce. I just stood there, unable to say a word. She picked up my discomfort and whispered in a cheery voice, "We love your fresh, winning smile and natural presence. We'd be honored to represent you in the upcoming Gladiola beauty pageant." She paused for a moment and said, "Oh, by the way, do you have an evening gown?" I stammered, "No, I don't." She laughed. "Oh, that's all right. We'll get you one!"

When you stop to relax long-standing patterns of action that have become automatic and deeply ingrained, you experience deep somatic upwelling of sensations and feelings-powerful currents of response which are not verbal.

-Stanley Keleman
Embodying Experience

Two hours later, the doorbell rang again. Sure enough, there she was holding up the most beautiful red dress I had ever seen. With a merry twinkle in her eye, she said, "This is for you!" My only response was "I must be dreaming!" When I closed the door, I sat with the red dress in my lap and burst into tears.

Love on the Runway

My first love affair was with an audience of strangers. Stepping onto the stage for the first time and feeling loving acceptance from the audience, I was free to come alive as never before. Walking down the runway I didn't just pivot, I whirled with uninhibited abandon. When taking my final walk down the runway, I caught a glimpse of my father. I didn't expect to see him because earlier he made some excuse about not feeling well. In that timeless moment, my body stiffened up with embarrassment. The urge to hide myself was profound. But as I slowly walked by him, I saw tears rolling down his cheeks. I couldn't believe it. After all those years of lack of recognition for my being, my father appeared visibly moved by my presence.

You saw the Snow Queen riding in her crystal sleigh, not as evil but as refreshing goodness.

-Diane Wakoski

I received the shock of a lifetime when announced the winner. Walking across the stage with hundreds of people cheering sent massive chills through my spine. When handed the microphone, genuine gratitude filled my heart and I spoke with enormous pleasure. After I got off the stage, a man approached my mother and wanted to know how I learned to conduct myself such spontaneous elegance. If he only knew until this minute, I stumbled over my words and moved with awkward steps. When being driven home, I mused how remarkable it was that there was some force inside that could create massive change in an instant. How remarkable.

As I arrived home with my crown and bouquet of roses in my arms, I found my father turning everything upside down on his desk while shouting, "The most valuable stamp in my collection is gone. I told you never to get near my stamps! Where did you put it?" I stammered, "Daddy, I never touched your stamp collection." Glaring, he yelled, "Don't lie to me! What did it do, walk out of the house by itself?"

Live to shine, love living the song. Live to love. Sing and shine on!

-Nick Page
Sing and Shine On

The extreme contrast between intense elation and painful inflation, once again, left me in a state of confusion. Soon, I heard my mother crying out, "I found it! I found it! You put your new stamp in your old notebook. Here it is." I knew my poor mother had raced around the house in a fitful state looking for this precious item. She would do anything to keep the peace for my father's benefit. In that moment, a belief formed in my young mind. With all my joyous good fortune, I was flooded with the heartbreaking news that longing for contact and closeness with my father was unacceptable. No matter what I did, I would never be the 'precious item' in his eyes. My mind went crazy with thoughts about never being enough. I kept analyzing and deliberating what could be the matter with me. I tried so hard to figure out in my head what I needed to do to be loveable. Will anyone love me just as I am? If I only knew at the time how limiting thoughts can influence the shape of one's life. These beliefs certainly shaped my future relationships with men.

The male shadow has to do with the suppression of traits which are perceived as belonging to women and inappropriate to men. Most men hide their tender feelings in the Shadow.

-Marcia Starck & Gytnne

Queen of Queens

Here I was at age fifteen, a representative of Florida's Gladiola industry, traveling throughout the state and appearing on TV. My mother became my official chaperone. This was by far the most thrilling experience of her life. During this year of exciting activity, her whole life opened up. She started practicing Yoga and became enormously interested in health food. The food blender traveled with us far and wide.

First-class flights on airlines, limousines whisking us from one engagement to another was heaven on earth. After winning the beauty contest, '*Queen of Queens*' of

Palm Beach, I had the honor of dining with Prince Obilinsky and the Duke and Duchess of Windsor at the famous Whitehall Hotel. At the event, everything went well until the finger bowl appeared at the end of the meal. Totally unaware of its true purpose, I drank it! The Duke of Windsor, without blinking an eye, drank from his bowl. As I recall this event, I honor him for this gracious act and acceptance of my original innocence.

Become a maverick who can step outside the boundaries of consensus thought, always risking ridicule.

-David Jay BrownStern
The Dark Goddess

Riding on a wave of success, I became the *Florida Citrus Queen* and traveled 100,000 miles throughout the United States and Europe as their official spokesperson. One particular day, I appeared on the *Today Show* in the morning, the *Arthur Godfrey* Show at noon, and flew to Los Angeles for the *Steve Allen Show* that night. When I returned from this trip, Governor Collins honored me as Florida's favorite Goodwill Ambassador. At nineteen, I won the most coveted title of all—*Miss Florida.*

For an entire year, I was flooded with support and good wishes that I would become the first Miss Florida to win the title of Miss America. Even though many people were singing my praises, my inner self was clearly informing me that something was radically amiss. Awakened by my acting classes at the University of Miami's Ring Theater, I had an overwhelming urge to drop what I was doing and become an actress. From this new perspective, beauty contests began to look like a glitzy charade that could no longer hold my interest. I was also becoming painfully aware of my difficulty in being a normal teenager.

All of life is full of successes. Enjoying the success happening in the moment is the greatest success.

-Janet Dunn

Alone by myself or on a stage in front of strangers showering me with acceptance, it was easy for me to be my free-spirited self. In the presence of my peers, my shy self ruled the day. Not knowing how to relate with kids my own age, I got the reputation of being stuck up and conceited. This hurt me as much as being called 'leper girl' as a child. The people who sponsored me in the contests were happy that I didn't run around like other girls. This meant I could be trusted to represent their products. How could I get out of all this? I would soon find out.

There She Is . . . Almost!

There I was on stage with Bert Parks with all of America watching. The magic that had swept me with rapture, the energy that had lifted me to cloud nine was clearly gone. In its place was a polished, seasoned professional, smiling and pivoting to perfection. With so many friends in the audience rooting for me, I tried my best to pull it off, but my heart was no longer in it. As I heard my name called as one of the five finalists, I was stricken with a numb sensation that threw me into a panic. What remained were two questions that each of us had to answer. This final interview would determine the winner. As my name was called, I pinched my hands to ignite that old magic. Nothing seemed to work. All I could do was wait to receive the question that would change my beauty queen life forever. It was, "What would you do if a burglar entered your house at night?" Ordinarily, I would have answered like a queen, politely saying, "Why, I would remain poised and self-assured under any adversity." But instead, I froze in abject silence as my mind coursed about in a dizzying frenzy. Coming from I don't know where, I whispered, "My father taught me jujitsu, and what I would do is *EHEHKKKK KKKKK! POWWWWW!"*

As a blood-curdling wail exploded through my lips, I kicked my leg to high heaven, which sent my crinoline skirts flying! Bert stood mummified in disbelief. And all I could think was, "Oh, my poor mother!" Leaving that stage was beyond a nightmare. As I ducked behind the curtains, people turned their backs to avoid looking at me. My friends just shook their heads, their eyes filled with sadness. Blasting out that karate kick had blown all the circuits out of my self-image. For certain, this uninhibited act marked the end of my beauty queen career.

Humans by nature are surprising creatures!

-Tom Kenyon
Brain State

It was years later that I had a good laugh over this strange incident. The Palm Beach Post reported the crossfire of women's rights advocates protesting the Miss America Pageant. Host Bert Parks had been torched in effigy and the crowd had stormed the exhibition hall yelling accusations that the contest was lily-white, racist and pro-military. The article went on to support the growing self-defense practices for women. In the center of the page was a picture of me in a white gown kicking up a storm. The caption read, "If Miss Florida of 1957 had been in the contest today, she would have won!"

With the many scholarships I was awarded in the contest, my desire was to study acting in New York, City. When I told my mother that I was leaving home, she was sure I wouldn't survive without her help. To extricate myself from her clutches, I agreed to continue my studies at Columbia University. During this time, a friend arranged an interview with Lee Strasberg of Actor's Studio, one of the most respected acting teachers in the world. When entering his kindly presence, I was trembling with nervous excitement. Lee gave me a great gift that day when he shared that the modern beauty queen represents the ancient Goddess archetype that was worshiped for thousands of years.

When the goddess queen danced until her skirts flew wide around her, humankind opened its heart with joyous delight.

-Unknown

He encouraged me to become aware of the body language and unique energy that I had accessed in playing the role of a modern goddess. And even more important, Lee encouraged me to find parts that reflected the ugly duckling role that had ruled my young life. My task in this process was to unify my fragile vulnerability and the regal confidence as important aspects of an actors craft. What was often judged as an inferior quality, became a valuable ingredient that could used in the creation of character roles.

Movie Star

After being accepted into Lee's classes, I was shocked that the most successful actors were still struggling to connect with their authentic feelings. One of them was Marilyn Monroe. Becoming a movie star, she had captivated the world with her sexuality and ultra glamour. Below the surface, massive insecurity ruled her inner life. Lee suggested that we work on a scene together. I was beside myself with excitement. The first time we got together to practice, she was in tears. Several teenage boys had climbed up to her apartment on the seventh floor and tried to break through the window. She confided that her greatest struggle was not getting devoured by crowds of people.

As women released themselves from the feminine mystique of domesticity, the beauty myth took over to carry on its work of social control.

-Naomi Wolf

One evening, I went to the theater with her and experienced what she went through out in public. When we left through the back door of the theatre, I pushed people away from grabbing her body. Each time our rehearsals ended, I was compelled to imitate Marilyn's soft, whisper-like voice and the undulating rhythms of her body. In the midst of this enactment, I could see that she very cleverly hid her fears by slowing down her vocal tempo and gestures. I feel in this way, she achieved that famous combination of fragility and heightened sexuality.

The practice of playing different roles was clearly revealing the characteristic role I play in life. Like Marilyn, we both learned to hide our feelings by creating social roles that projected an image of what we thought would please others. She projected a sexy role to please men, and I projected a pretty all-American girl image that was hiding an unlovable child within. Unfortunately, all the fame, fortune and champagne could not quiet the growing volcano of repressed emotions that lay hidden behind her sexy facade.

Following her tragedy, two more actresses that I knew took their lives. Each of them had been physically abused as children and learned to shut off their emotions in order to survive. It appeared as if the primal power of emotive expression was the enemy, something to hide and disguise with a mask of pretense. As I walked through the streets of New York after a broken love affair, I felt like a butterfly trapped in a cocoon. What would it take to free the butterfly inside – not just on stage, but in real life?

To me the Goddess is a combination of all of the emotional energies, the heavenly and the earthy merging together

-Shakti Gawain

The role I caught myself playing with the men I loved shocked me the most. Feeling unlovable made me depreciate my being and do whatever it took to sustain a man's love. Just as war veterans may experience a flashback when an alarm clock sounds or a fire truck passes, my panic trigger was a nasty look or a loud, angry voice. Trembling with fear before a man was feeling in love! How was it possible to feel so secure on stage, and so subservient in a love relationship?

My mother's relationship to my father flashed in my mind. Why, I'm duplicating her anxious gestures and high voice of quiet desperation. In that moment, I remembered my acting teacher's advice in accepting adverse physical gestures as a blessing that could be used in the name of art. When enacting these qualities of behavior as an actor would, they released their hold on me. Without this awareness behavioral attitudes became an addictive habit that keeps us from growing and changing in new and different ways.

The latest incarnation of Oedipus, the continued romance of Beauty and the Beast, stand this afternoon on the corner of forty second street and Fifth Avenue, waiting for the light to change.

-Joseph Campbell

Time Bomb

One night, I had a nightmare of seeing a time bomb ticking away in hundreds of people's bellies. I wanted to cry out and warn them, but the words caught in my throat. In the next scene, armies of men, women and children began fighting each other while, one by one, the bombs inside their bellies exploded in pain. I decided to create a one-woman show called, *Time Bomb*. My desire was to illustrate the enormous expression of emotional energy that is held inside us all, and how important it is to have healthy, creative ways to unleash it.

The piece starts with a woman who spent her life projecting a pleasant image as a means of protecting her heart from pain. One day she discovers she's pregnant with an explosive bomb ticking away in her belly. She shakes off this shocking realization by becoming preoccupied with busywork. Statements were broadcasted into the theater: "Smile! Be happy! Shake off your troubles! Think about something nice! Stop being morbid!" With her belly racked with pain, she turned to the audience and proudly declared, "I will not fall prey to my negative emotions! Never, never, never will I allow a moment of frustration, pain or irritation, and God forbid, anger, to be seen!" As the ticking of the time bomb grew louder and louder, she whines, "I'm such a nice person, why am I being treated in this way?" Caught in this horror, her lovely mask twisted and contorted into a monstrous shape. Unable to hold up the facade any longer, she doubled over in agony.

My greatest desire was only to live in accord with the prompting which came from my true self. Why was that so difficult?

-Hermann Hesse

The audience gasped in disbelief as I unleashed my ugly dancing into chaotic dismemberment! Slumping to the floor, I slipped under a sheet and retreated in silence. After a few moments, a mournful soul song poured from my lips. Like the phoenix rising from the ashes, I emerged from under the sheet as the *Mother of the World* wearing a beautiful rainbow robe. Slowly, I made my way to the edge of the stage and opened my arms, whispering, "The *Mother of the World* loves you, will always love you. Honor your heart-felt feelings; the sadness, grief and joy."

Humming with arms outstretched in loving embrace the audience spontaneously hummed with me. Together, from muteness to outcry, we wailed out a torrent of pain, anger and sorrow. As our voices blended into *Om*, the universal sound of unity. I whispered, "Reach out and hold a neighbor's hand. Being members of one great family, lets us look into each other's eyes unafraid."

Unexpressed emotional energy stays in the body like a small ticking time-bombs. They are illnesses building in incubation.

-Christiane Northrup

Upon leaving the theater, I glanced at the headlines of a newspaper that announced a nuclear bomb testing program. To me the atomic bomb represented all the repressed emotions that have been trapped in the mental mind. How many wars will it take, and how many young men need to die before we all shout, "Stop! War is an insane way to handle conflict." Whatever can bring us all into unified connected with the world as one body is paramount. Out of this union with all that is, more healthy ways will emerge to express the driving force of this primal power.

Hollywood

In the mid 1960s, I went to Hollywood and was typecast to play 'pretty girl' parts on TV and films. After playing a series of these roles, my desire was to expand my talent by playing character parts that would unleash my expressive freedom. I worked hard to convince my agent to send me up for character parts, but he laughed at the idea. How exasperating, even as an actress I'm playing out a social role that is hiding my real gifts and talents inside. To release this frustration, an ecstatic dance of emotive sound expression unleashed my anger as thunderous lightening streaking across the sky. The tears that rolled down my cheeks became a gentle rain that was washing out my hurt. My

Nothing under heaven can arrest the progress of the human soul on its pilgrimage from darkness to light, from the unreal to the real, and from death to immortality.

-Jacquelyn Small

The child draws and paints without hesitation, hums and dances its moods– until this 'artist of being' is driven underground.

-Frederick Franck

very breath became the wind that ignited an outrageous wild woman who was made of blood and guts, seaweed and stardust. She moved with animal magnetism and had no trouble speaking her mind.

The next day, I added a foreign accent to this primal woman and paid a visit to my agent. When I walked in, he had no idea who I was. That afternoon he sent me up to play a British sergeant in the television show, *Hogan's Heroes*. I got the role and became a semi-regular on the show. For the next five years, I got character parts in shows such as *Ben Casey, Dr. Kildare, Get Smart* and *Mission Impossible*. I even got to play a sexy part in a movie with Jerry Lewis and had fun being one of the girls in a movie with Elvis Presley.

Presence of Zen

In the late sixties, the 'human potential' movement was popping up all over Los Angeles. I attended every consciousness-raising program I could find. My time was spent studying Yoga and Tai Chi, creative dance and sound healing. I also became fascinated with eastern spiritual practices that honored the divine presence of God in everything.

Recall the satisfaction of playing well and the pleasure of being a successful performer. This leads to a stimulating sense of exciting anticipation.

-Laurence E Morehouse
Maximum Performance

One memorable experience was studying Zen meditation with a Roshi from Japan. When I walked through the door, I entered a temple of peaceful, simple beauty that was filled with the aroma of incense. Watching the steam circling from the iron pot and listening to the wind chimes outside the window, an inner smile spread through my body.

A big part of the training was answering paradoxical riddles named Koans. These riddles are to be answered with spontaneous engagement. One afternoon, while cursing my own stupidity for failing to answer my koan, my lower back went into spasm. In a split second, I breathed and wiggled with wild chaos. Trembling from head to toe, I was shocked to notice the pain in my back had loosened its hold. After this radical experience, I went to sit with the Roshi in Zazan. He gave me this koan, "What is the meaning of the bird singing outside the window?" Instantly, I started chirping like a bird. His eyes widened as he quickly asked, "What is the meaning of love?" Without a moment's hesitation, I reached down and profusely kissed his folded hands. Now he was beaming from ear to ear. He threw open his arms and kissed me, first on one cheek and then the other! Looking directly in my eyes, he shot out another koan. I was so flustered by his loving demonstration that I mumbled some intellectual gobbledygook, after which he hastily rang the bell and Zazan was over.

When was the last time you drank a glass of water and really drank it?

-Roshi Susaki

Raised to appear passive and quiet most of my life, sitting meditation had served its usefulness I moved on to explore Hatha Yoga, which blended physical training and spiritual awareness. After two years of study, I was invited to teach Yoga at Atlantic University in Boca Raton, Florida. My biggest struggle was sustaining a controlled breathing style in the postures. I was drawn to explore the creativity and freedom of instinctual movement that existed in any repeated posture. Experiencing movement at a cellular level, led me to express the primal creature that the posture represented. Released from the confines of structure, my stretching capacity expanded ten fold.

One afternoon, while observing people go through the postures with little inspiration, I coached them to audibly breathe while activating their 'bushy tail.' With titillating laughter, I witnessed participants stretch way beyond their normal capacity. Unknown to me, the director of the department was observing the class through the window. He called me into his office and said, "Why were you laughing in Yoga?" Not knowing what to say, he warned me to stick to the proper program. Being conditioned to sustain proper postures that resist change, a desire was forming to stretch beyond the traditional doctrines of eastern or western spirituality into the sacred nature of the body's wisdom. The passionate power of my being directed me to create a *Primal Yoga* process that offered people more permission to express their feelings and create original postures that could meet the body's instinctive needs in the moment.

The primal power existing in animals and all of nature, is a viable energy to embody,

-Jonas Rernard

Body Wisdom

A traumatic experience occurred in which I crunched the vertebra in my neck in a car accident. The pain in my neck drove me to explore a whole new world of alternative healing practices. My husband was open to exploring the body's potential as much as I was. One afternoon, we attended a demonstration of a new form of bodywork called *Structural Integration*, also called *Rolfing* after its creator, Ida Rolf. This strong willed woman had discovered a means of manipulating connective tissue to create a more flexible body in balance with gravity. After witnessing her transform a man's rigid body into malleable flexibility, I was inspired to learn how to do this amazing feat.

Only human beings have come to a point where they no longer know why they exist. They have forgotten the secret knowledge of their bodies, their senses, their dreams.

-Lame Deer

During the training, Ida eventually found out that my husband was a sensitive artist and commissioned him to design the anatomical drawings for her new book. We spent two years flying back and forth between her home in New York and Esalen Institute in Big Sur, California where she conducted most of her trainings. My husband became a *Rolfer* and I went on to study with Judith Aston, a brilliant teacher who was expanding Ida's work into a system of movement education. Judith's work demonstrates how to experience greater ease and fluidity of motion in all the other varied activates in daily life.

In the next few years, I mirrored hundreds of people's habitual movement styles; the way they breathed and talked, and how they 'stood' in the world. Being trained as an actor, I was drawn to help people enact their own conditioned tendencies as their most brilliant creation. This engaging process confirmed my notion that we are all actors on the stage of life who have forgotten we are acting. As a person's character was perceived as the mask they used to survive, more of the hidden aspects of their essential being spontaneously came bubbling up to the surface.

A man named Buck comes to mind who was the epitome of the 'he-man.' He complained of enormous stress in his shoulders and lower back. Towards the end of the session, his body relaxed and become more fluid. As he was about to leave, he immediately tightened up and returned to his super-controlled image. When I brought this to his attention, he commented that even though he felt better, he couldn't go around acting like a loose noodle. As long as he believed this, it was impossible for him to make any real changes in his behavior.

In another session, I coached Buck to gaze into a mirror while tensing and relaxing the muscles that shaped his self-image. As the tensions began melting away, a memory returned of being called a weakling by his father. In order to win his dad's approval, he turned his body into rock-hard stone. He also confessed that his wife complained of not knowing how he felt. And no wonder. The role he created prevented any vulnerable feelings from being seen. Learning to breathe and move with greater fluidity opened him to the realization that being fluid meant he could be strong and flexible, vulnerable and decisive – fully himself.

About the only difference between stumbling blocks and stepping stones is the way you use them.

-Bernard Meltaze

I recall a woman named Terry who found it difficult to make friends. Being raised in a high status environment, she cultivated a hyper-straight body language that was often intimidating to others. When I enacted her 'social role' and asked if I appeared approachable, she immediately said, "Of course not!" When coaching her to enact her own posture, vocal style and movement patterns as an actor would, a quiet miracle happened. All the protective veneer had softened. Amplifying her own 'character' traits as an actor would uncovered more of her authentic essence.

Kids at Risk

My interest in coaching people to embody their social role with conscious awareness, opened the way to teach a theater program for 'kids at risk.' I called the program the *Sacred Actor.* This 'artist of being' represents the creative brilliance of our multidimensional self. It was becoming clear that there is allot of confusion in recognizing the difference between the ego and the essence. When identified with conditioned tendencies of the social role as our real self, real change is difficult. My focus was revealing the enormous healing and healthy vitality that is unleashed when actualizing our 'shapeshifting' skills.

We become trapped in postures that are out of balance with gravity. Occupying a rigid structure leads to chronic stress and ill health.

-Ida Rolf

When I first entered the class, the kids were jumping around and talking with loud, abrasive voices. I knew they would resist being quieted down, so I joined them by making even louder noises with enormous pleasure! Shocked by my behavior, the room became quiet. When inviting each kid to say their name, I mirrored their vocal tone and body language with respect. I shared that reflecting other people's behavioral patterns with respect, is a great spiritual practice that keeps me from getting stuck in any role.

To make this point clear, I had each kid say their name again while the class mirrored their specific vocal style, emotive quality and posture back to them. With no value judgments attached to this experience, enormous enjoyment was unleashed. At the end of the process, this group of frenzied young people became unified into a field of good-will.

A spiritual science which will keep the physical body a perfect temple for the soul and higher harmonies of life, is a crying need.

-Genevieve Brady
The Human Form Divine

The next acting task was to free the creative power of breathing as the prime mover of action. I guided them into remembering what it was like to play with a toy airplane while flying it around the room. They laughed when realizing it was the audible breath that brought the whole experience unforgettably alive. When the breath is the prime mover their movements became instantly fluid and dynamically flexible. When I directed them to return to their familiar social role, they instantly returned to their static posture and shallow breathing habits. It was a real eye opener to experience the difference between inspired aliveness and habits of mind that rigidify the body.

Once they could demonstrate how to coordinate their breath with fluid motion, I devised a scene in which they identified themselves as 'primal athletes' in training to become 'champions of life force.' With ceremonial power, they entered Mount Olympus where the aerobic games would be played. Placing a half mask on their face, each one had one minute to breathe with unpredictable, kaleidoscopic power. The group mirrored each unique aerobic contribution. In this way unlimited creative resources were being exercised that went way beyond anything they had ever experienced.

The next task of the *Sacred Actor* was to empower their vocal expression by identifying with the primal forces of nature; a thunder storm, a volcano erupting, a forest fire or huge waves crashing against the rocks. When unleashing emotive sound supported with fluid movement, these 'rebels without a cause' burst alive with full, uninhibited aliveness. The last task was to enact a scene in which they were the future leaders of a new tomorrow. Each one had an opportunity to share their newfound mission statement before the group. Getting to know their essential worth through direct experience, many vowed to help their brothers and sisters free up their creativity to better survive in a fragmented world.

Synergy is the result of teaming up with the opposites. Synergy takes place when the whole is worth more than the sum of the parts.

-AnnMcGee-Cooper

On returning home, my marriage began to unravel at the seams and was soon over. In the midst of my sorrow, all my unlovable issues came to the surface. On this occasion, the wild woman living in my soul persuaded me that it was better to love and feel hurt than not to love and feel nothing. Honoring this truth helped me remember how much my husband had enriched my life. His genius gave me an artist's sensibility that helped me discern shapes and infinite spectrums of color. He opened my eyes to the intrinsic power of nature as my true nature, and refined my ability to perceive beauty in the dreariest surroundings.

There need be no one confining role in your life than there is a single role for an actor. Just as Marlon Brando can become a punch-drunk dock worker in one film and a Mexican bandit in a second, change is always possible!

-Warren Robertson
Free to Act

We are One Body

Back to Esalen, everybody was talking about a teaching master from South America who was presenting a three-month training in New York City called Arica. His name was Oscar Ichazo, who had spent most of his life mastering the different spiritual traditions around the world. The Arica Training was a synthesis of his vast spiritual experience. He created a technology of conscious enlightenment that became known as even more powerful than any mind-altering drug. His major message is that all of humanity is composed of one body and dualistic notions that divide people and countries from each other cannot continue if we are to survive as a species.

At this point in my life, I was starved for ritual and yearning for the sacred. For five years I was a trainer for Arica Institute, working with a team of people teaching 'forty-day' trainings around the country. Typically, seven or eight trainers would lease a big house in a major city. We then rotated all our jobs — from working in the office, cooking meals to baby-sitting and teaching in the training programs.

The urge to see the body spiritualized, to metamorphose into something else, is in our hollow bones.

-Steven Larsen
The Mythic Imagination

Being an only child and raised in isolation, it was a revelation to live in a community of peers who were exploring their spiritual potential in practical ways. The Arica Training was most influential in helping me to perceive my ego, the social role that never feels enough and thereby craves outside acceptance. The vast array of spiritual disciplines was slowly uncovering the unifying power of my divine essence. One memorable practice, which was conducted with over a thousand people, was called *Trespaso.* It was an 'eye gazing' meditation, which brought me into sympathetic union with others as an extension of a vast identity that had no end. .All these many holistic practices were giving me renewed hope that we can wake up from mass hypnosis when realizing that we are 'one body' at an energetic level.

We walk through ourselves, meeting robbers, ghosts and giants, but always meeting ourselves.

-Stephen Dedalus
Ulysses

World of Therapy

As life would have it, I fell in love with and married one of the most established group leaders at Esalen Institute. For over ten years, we co-led workshops teaching people the principles of Gestalt therapy, Psychosynthesis and Bioenergetics. People in all sorts of transitions, whether burned out CEO's or housewives leaving thirty-year marriages, found their way to our workshops. Bright, healthy and educated, they were now seeking to heal the past that money, status or expensive toys could no longer satisfy.

We provided a safe haven in which they could share their struggles and gain greater acceptance and personal freedom to discover their essential self. I witnessed magical transformations occurring when people could divulge deeply buried secrets or painful trauma without judgment. As we gathered together to go our separate ways, people would invariably groan about re-entering the 'real' world. This usually meant forsaking genuine feelings, the integrity of intention and live in the colorless abstraction of a conditioned facade.

The awareness that because every individual is intimately connected with the entire cosmos by the operation of objective laws within their own bodies, there is no separateness except as a mental hallucination. When we understand this, we are completely at peace with our past.

-Oscar Ichazo

Many people dealt with this problem by creating whole lifestyles of 'recovery' in order to give themselves legitimate license to unleash expression of their emotional life. In oder to accomplish this massive task, precious life energy is spent dredging up old traumas and worst-case scenarios to keep the fires hot for ongoing therapy sessions. It was becoming more and more obvious that continual focusing on past trauma kept encouraging more of the same in the present.

Going deeper than talk therapy, I desired to uncover the original energetic potential we possessed before social conditioning shaped our essence into contrived roles of behavior. Who am I before wounding of my soul occurred? It made sense to uncover and strengthen our original physiology and its innate emotive powers of expression with more artful creativity. *Expressive Arts Therapy* most closely reflected this desire.

Channeling past trauma, guilt, shame and insecurities through the creative use of breath, sound, movement, mask drama, music and drawing offered people the possibility of perceiving their very lives as 'living art in progress.' Through this awareness, the *drama* of life is transformed into the *play* of creative discovery.

A human being is part of a whole, called by us the universe. The delusion that thoughts and feelings are something separate from the rest, is a kind of optical delusion.

-Albert Einstein

Healing What Ails

We always teach what we need the most. After my second marriage dissolved, I felt humbled to the core. I decided to cancel all my teaching activities and get lost in the wilderness of Big Sur. One afternoon I climbed up on a high ledge to meditate on how to heal my aching heart. As the sun warmed my face, an ancient lullaby hummed in my inner ear. It was the *Mother of the World*, my beloved companion who had nurtured me as a child. Her inner voice of feeling hummed, "There is a little one in you who still believes she is unlovable and unworthy of a man's love." I moaned, "But I've done all kinds of therapy around this issue." The Mother interrupted, "This little one is not an issue that needs fixing. Being pure love, she needs to be loved just as she is."

When hearing these words, a vivid memory of my father's abusive nature came into awareness. In that instant, I let go of all control and sounded out all the violent tones that I had ever heard from my father. Deeply shaken from this outpouring of emotion, I felt the hidden pain that a man feels when losing contact with his nurturing, feminine soul. When sounding out all the passive, submissive tones that had shaped my life with men, a luminous being appeared I instantly recognized as the *Father of the World.* Looking deep into my very soul he whispered, "I love you." On hearing those words, the ugly duckling child in me contracted in pain. This divine being exclaimed, "Oh child, you are beautiful just as you are! Here are your dancing shoes. Dance the dance only you can dance."

In the next moment, I witnessed the *Father of the World* merging inside my own father's broken heart. It was as if all the unresolved pain of his miscarried life vanished into thin air. With exuberant, waltzing music playing in the balmy winds, I felt him pick me up in his arms and whirl me into oblivion! When I came out of this altered state, the masculine and feminine soul living in my heart was dancing in love.

As I stood up to walk home, two dark, piercing eyes that were burrowed in the bark of the redwood caught my attention. In my inner ear I heard, "I see you! You are part of me and I am part of you. We are one!" I whispered back, "Yes, this is true! I feel your presence as part of my very own nature."

As I opened my eyes, everywhere I looked; ancient faces peered out at me from trees, wildflowers, rocks and clouds. Seeing fields of wild lupine and orange poppies smiling up at me, I smiled back at them. As the gusty winds blew through my hair and intoxicating smells of sage exploded my senses, I heard all of nature whisper, "Your body is made of dust and stars, seed and stone. You shine in the lightening, you roar in the thunder and move as flowing waves!"

In a delirious instant, I kicked off my shoes, pulled my old shirt down to my waist and ran bare-breasted into the wind. Leaping and dancing through fields of Lupin and over the grassy hills I embraced the sky, ocean, and wildflowers as my brothers and sisters. Yes! Nature is my extended family! As my breath was spent, I threw my arms around my shoulders and honored myself as nature's work of art in progress.

Humanity needs to listen , until such a time as the voice of the Souls heard throughout the universe as the only voice of compassion and reason that has ever existed. When this occurs, all of humanity will be truly free and the voice of the Soul will sing until the end of time.

-Fred Wolf, Ph.D.
The Spiritual Universe

Penetrate the character of your masked identity in order to reveal the truth of your essential being.

-Jerzy Grotowski
Towards a Poor Theatre

Earth Altars

Every day, I feverishly ventured through the wilderness, forging for nature's abundant treasures—green moss, gray lichen, gnarled bones, twisted roots and dried leaves. Laying them out on the ground, an intuitive force moved through my hands and formed these precious gifts into Earth Altars. Each one I conceived honored the wild face of nature's blessing. One of the first Earth Altars I made was from cow patties and bones. I exclaimed, "Blessings to our common humanness. I honor your wisdom of composting and recycling matter into vital gardens of beauty." In moments, I heard a reply: "Blessings to you! Thank you for your recognition!"

Another Earth Altar was made from rotting pumpkins. Its

"I am an earth child," she said proudly, "And this planet is my home."

-Lillian Smith

decomposing face looked like it had manifested from some alien species. I asked if it had a message for me, it replied: "I am the farthest part of yourself. Be not afraid to live large. You are as vast as the universe itself." I was stunned into the realization that nature never rejects me; it only illuminates my uniqueness and connectedness to all of life.

With growing excitement, I was drawn to bring nature's gifts home and create primal masks to help me embody the elemental powers of my true nature. The glue gun became my greatest tool. Hot glue was the trick that held the lichen, leaves, stones, shells and dried flowers in place. When I placed a primal mask on my face, I entered into the soul of a radically different state of consciousness. With renewed inspiration in my shapeshifting powers, there was instant permission to follow the spirit that lived within the face.

One afternoon I entered the wilderness and forged for green moss, seeds, stones and bones. As I spread out these treasures, a new face of nature came alive in my soul. It was the ancient archetype of Green Man, the lover of Mother Earth, the giver of vegetation and nurturing abundance. Wearing a hand-made cloak covered with green leaves and blossoming flowers, I placed him over my face. In that instant, Green Man awakened harmony between my primal strength and fragile vulnerability.

The Sacred Mask

Being so taken with the power of the masked metaphor, that I created a seminar at Esalen Institute called *The Sacred Mask Experience*. The elemental power of masks to liberate and transform consciousness is a lost treasure I wanted to renew. By concealing the conditioned social face we wear and donning a mask, the genuine emotional facets of our nature can be more affectively revealed. Each mask offers a special kind of permission to 'shapeshift' into a body language, voice and creative imagination. Regaining a vital vocabulary of expression strengthens the ability to shift in and out of any limiting role, attitude or behavior at will.

There is no escape from our interdependence with nature; we are woven into the closest relationship with the Earth,

-Barnard Cambell

A 'two-faced' mask was created that dramatized the conflicting parts of our nature. A woman Kitty comes to mind that desired to free her voice but she was painfully shy. To illustrate this point, one side of her mask represented her inhibited self, and the other side represented her 'soul singer.' Kitty came from a religious background that believed strong emotions were demonic forces that would take over her soul if they were expressed. Naturally, singing out her feelings was virtually impossible. What turned things around was removing the labels attached to emotion, and perceiving them as the living music of her soul. With her two-faced mask in place, she tilted her head and enacted the painfully shy persona that lived in fear of expressing her natural talent. As she slowly rotated the mask to the other side, the soul singer burst free from a lifetime of repression. The entire class was aghast when Kitty belted out tones from the very bowels of the Earth herself. When she finished, I beckoned her to take off the mask and sing with an open

The epidermis of the skin reveals the self as part of the ecosystem.

-Joana Macy

heart. This accomplishment helped her to trust the original sources of her energetic aliveness, rather than be ruled by thoughts thrust on her by others.

In our last ceremony, I gave each participant a 'white mask' that represented the *Holy Child* of original innocence. Before the mirror, I instructed participants to tell their social role not worry; it will never be abandoned. With inclusion of the conditioned self, it will have less need to sabotage what is new and different. Engaging in a pre-verbal whispering language of serene energy while moving with fluid gestures ignited the *Holy Child*, the pure presence of our being into action. Often a rush of tears would pour out from behind the mask. when seeing themselves without their conditioned face. As people's eyes met with no protective/defensive boundaries getting in the way, pre-verbal talk was sung with infinite variations of feeling.

The neutral mask is the instrument of metamorphosis, a way to reach the powers to which it appeals.

-Bari Ralfe

These sonic communications between their soul and another's soul gave us a glimpse into a new world that is the embodiment of unconditional love. When the participants took off the white mask, layers of tension and strain had magically vanished from their faces. People also exclaimed they were breathing with a depth of feeling response they had never experienced before. Many agreed it was as if they had just undergone the ultimate beauty treatment - a fully rejuvenated spirit.

I was so moved by this 'expressive arts' experience, I desired to create a 'happening' in public that merges artful expression into a mundane, daily life experience. With a group of my students, we elected to wear the white mask in a crowded family Laundromat. Our focus was to enter a meditative state and let original innocence be the prime mover of the task. When we entered the Laundromat, a few people expressed shock and several others appeared as if we didn't exist. The children were utterly transfixed. They watched our every move with wide-eyed wonder.

In some way, the deepest meaning of the mask has to do with finding our faces before we were born. This is truly a search for our roots in the deepest sense, a quest into the field of life's vitality.

-Steven & Robin Larsen
The Healing Mask

With deep calm, I don't ever remember folding my towels and sheets with such dedicated meticulous care. Every gesture was felt from beginning to end, with no mental distraction. As we continued with our simple tasks, it seemed that everyone in our midst dropped into being more present and open. Towards the end of this process, we took off our masks while still sustaining this spacious open quality of attention. I couldn't help musing, what would it be like to perceive our very nature as living art.

Identified with the *Sacred Actor*, the body becomes an artistic process rich in creative resources. Opening more multifaceted dimensions of our nature would reveal new roles and new plot lines that could unleash more intuitive awareness in dealing with the complexities of life. When all else fails, what would it be like to tap into this original innocence that can see the most unsolvable problem with fresh eyes.

Monster Mask'

For my next seminar, I wanted to uncover the cultural 'Shadow' – that dark part of our selves we often do not want to acknowledge because we've been trained not to. When the potent power of our instinctive, primal nature is judged as bad, or worse, evil, this alienated energy goes underground and stirs up mayhem in our mind. An angel repressed turns into a demon. If anger is perceived as something bad, this belief engenders a whole series of thinking patterns that can drive the mind crazy with rage.

Looking long enough into the eyes of the most frightening inner monster, can transmute this monster into an awesome treasure.

-Paul Ribblot

A divided mind is in the habit of constantly looking for assumed enemies to unleash its pent up rage. This maddening condition sustains conflict on all levels.

Hall Stone made a profound statement in his book, *Embracing Ourselves*. He wrote, "The disowning of demonic energies contributes to the 'monster pool' of the world. The darkness of our world cannot be solved by love, unless that love is an expression of an aware ego that can encompass these demonic energies." The *Sacred Actor* represents an aware ego that embraces all emotions as the language of God.

Making a Monster mask and performing it before others is an effective means of channeling the disowned side of our social persona into living art. Once the mask is crafted, participants sit for a half-hour in front of a mirror and gaze into the eyes of their mask and breathe with the feelings that emerge. I was the first to perform the Monster for the group. This enactment was dedicated to my father who had abandoned his dancing spirit and was consumed with monstrous rage.

In one hair-raising moment, the Monster burst alive and erupted with seething, hissing, snarling sounds. With flared nostrils, clenched jaws and tightly bound fists, the raging beast leaped about with volcanic fury. Glaring at the participants, it roared with thunderous streaks of lightning: "You call me evil - the devil! Don't you know who I am? I am the BIG BANG! I am volcanic power erupting to grow new land! Yes! I am the potent strength of nature, conceived out of the One Energy of creation!

When the shadow is recognized and integrated,a wholesome, unified sense of self naturally develops.

-Stark and Stern
The Dark Goddess

Without my volition the Monster sprang in the air with arms flailing and shouting, "Wake up! Use the power of anger to become strong and mighty in spirit!" Suddenly, the Monster's body began to twitch and tremble as it slowly crumpled to the ground. With great weariness it looked out to the group and whispered, "There is nothing outside of God." Like a small baby, it curled up and went to sleep.

After my performance, each participant went through the same enactment in their own unique way. As exploding emotional energy was released through the Monster mask, all the distorted features of the mask magically softened and appeared more human. When the mask was removed, people's faces glowed with radiance.

Shortly after this event, I noticed the breakdown of something I wanted to avoid; the pollution of precious oxygen sources and the growing waste dumps of undigested materialism. What was once paradise was now only a faint whisper on polluted winds. I struggled with the knowledge that so many religious beliefs have conditioned us to take dominion over the Earth. When we believe that our true home lies in heaven, we have no trouble filling the air with toxins, infesting the atmosphere with smog or dumping waste into the great waterways. What can one person do to affect this overwhelming problem that is consuming nature?

Theater of the Earth

I'm not sure what created the turning point, but before I knew it, I had drawn together a troupe of conscientious people and created *Theatre of the Earth*. Living in cooperation and reverence with nature was our central theme. As modern shamans, we helped each other root out numbness, apathy, despair, anger and frustration about what is happening to our home.

Time was spent in the forest listening to the Earth's voice in water, wood and stone. Our focus was to embrace nature as our extended body. This Earth is a living being. We are a part of her body. Her pain is our pain, her fate is our fate. This means we do not end with the skin. Our molecules are made from the air, water and soil. Salt remnants of ancient oceans flow through our veins and ashes of expired stars live within our genetic chemistry. The birds, the insects and vegetation are all aspects of our nature. In this open, aware state, we would forage for natural materials to be used in the creation of a mask representing the soul of a perishing creature, a rare plant or an ancient tree about to be cut down.

In our performance art pieces, we invited a creature or element of nature to occupy our body. As the modern poet Gary Snyder expressed, "The shaman speaks for the wild animals, the spirits of plants. By stepping out of his human role to put on a mask, the mind of nature speaks through him."

Being a channel for this elemental power or creature to speak through us, we all marveled how specific healing information, about how to heal the destruction of the environment would spontaneously pour forth without any deliberation.

One of the group pieces I created was about a sky god who attempted to dominate Mother Earth by using up her natural resources and turning them into war material. A former Green Beret who had fought in the Vietnam War agreed to play the part. A woman in the workshop, who felt like she had been trampled on and treated like dirt, played Mother Earth. The Green Beret opened the scene by sitting in a tree and throwing hand grenades onto the ground. Dry ice was used to create a vaporous toxic wind that finally toppled him from his high position. As he landed on the ground, Mother Earth mulched him into compost to feed her depleted soil. As the warrior of war was recycling into dismemberment, Mother Earth emerged and transformed into a sky goddess spreading golden seeds across the world that began germinating the presence of peace. Out of this growing garden of renewal, the warrior emerged as Green Man. This ancient lord of vegetation and lover of Gaia turned his war machinery into preserving the nature of life itself.

Primordial power cannot be given boundaries. It is ineffable and beyond thought. It is known only through becoming it.

-Mandukya Upanishad

Look about you. The environment is burning up in a thousand places. But there is no fire escape other than knowing we are one with nature.

-Jim Nollman

Like the wind itself, the breath of God permeates all of nature. Breathe as the breath of God and transform your life.

-Unknown

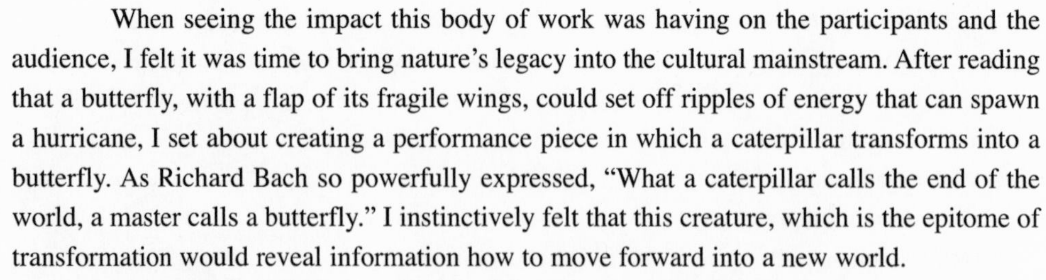

We do not come into this world; we come out of it, as leaves from a tree. Every individual is an expression of the whole realm of nature; a unique action of the total universe.

-Alan Watts

When seeing the impact this body of work was having on the participants and the audience, I felt it was time to bring nature's legacy into the cultural mainstream. After reading that a butterfly, with a flap of its fragile wings, could set off ripples of energy that can spawn a hurricane, I set about creating a performance piece in which a caterpillar transforms into a butterfly. As Richard Bach so powerfully expressed, "What a caterpillar calls the end of the world, a master calls a butterfly." I instinctively felt that this creature, which is the epitome of transformation would reveal information how to move forward into a new world.

I started this performance curled up in a fetal position dreaming what it would be like to take flight into a new domain of expression. I breathed out bolts of chaotic energy for several minutes. Intoxicated with oxygen, I experienced long silken threads regurgitating from my mouth. As these magical threads wrapped themselves around my body, it suddenly occurred to me that I was weaving my own death! With that thought, my muscles imploded into an airtight cocoon. As I struggled to catch my breath a voice whispered in my inner ear, "*Let go and let God.*"

When finally surrendering all my efforts, my physical form melted down into a puddle of gelatinous fluid. With no solid body to call my own, I realized I was still very much alive. In the next instant, instinctive ferocity filled me with strength of purpose. As massive energy pushed up against the walls of my protective cocoon, I exploded into newfound freedom. With gusts of fresh air filling my lungs, I spread out my wings and soared into a new consciousness.

Sitting quietly after this experience, the voice of guidance spoke through me. "A new mutation is stirring in the caterpillar nature of humankind. A future self is coming forth to inspire wholeness in the heart of the world. As an evolutionary catalyst, you are to model for others, a 'fluidity of being' that honors the life force as the prime mover of creation."

When I say the fate of the sea turtle or the tiger is mine, I mean it. All that is in my universe is not merely mine; it is me.

-John Livingston

As I opened my eyes, George Land's book *Breakpoint and Beyond* was lying on the floor. This book focused on awakening business corporations to support personal and collective sustainability. Being the master of change, Mother Nature runs the most productive business in the world. Adapting nature's methods for dynamic creative expression is what *Theatre of the Earth* was doing through performance art.

We move through the wilderness of physical forms that look on us with affectionate looks.

-Baudelaire

In transcending old belief systems of lack and limitation enormous power is available to recreate ourselves and our world. What am becoming? How can I bring about circumstances in which I can be of greater service to the common good of us all? Can I purposefully and knowingly enter in this great natural current of change and inspire more healing, transformative possibilities into actuality? Once more, my insides were urging me to take a leap of faith and move out of my comfortable self-enclosure. There is a world out there that is calling for greater aliveness, and I'm being called to be a bridge.with a world at Breakpoint.

Wild Woman in the Workplace

My friends laughed when I expressed an interest in 'primalizing' the world of business with nature's laws of change. Being a master of extremes, I started this new venture refining my shapeshifting abilities; investing time in learning the corporate language, cutting my hair and purchasing a classy power suit. Within six months, I walked through the door of Sun Microsystems and co-led a seminar with a friend who was well seasoned in the corporate world. The theme was raising self-esteem.

My friend started the workshop by announcing she was the rational left-brain and I was the creative right brain. Together we created a whole brain! We embodied this task with a touch of humor. After lunch, I entered wearing the power suit with a tone that meant business and my cohort glided in bursting with creative ingenuity! A strong bond took place when participants enacted subservient/dominant social roles and contrasted these roles with communicating with authentic feeling. As protective/defensive layers of tense behavior softened, a more supportive and accepting climate appeared in which creative inspiration began to soar.

The last half of the program offered different ways to integrate passion of purpose with the personal power necessary to implement greater creativity on the job. Participants were excited about the program, but without sufficient support from the top down, they were fearful of taking new actions that might risk their job. This realization made me pull back and create a workshop at Esalen Institute called *The Physiology of Leadership — Shapeshifting into the 21st Century.*

In corporations, the idea that working can be fun is still novel.

-Laurence E. Morehouse

This embodiment process fosters a fluid body language and expressive vocabulary of feeling that strengthens an authenticity of being. I started the workshop by announcing that new growth and productivity is not about sitting still and playing it safe. I invited participants to bounce on large Physio Balls while sharing what they feel most passionate about. Within minutes of this activity, their social roles melted and free-spirited energy was on the rise. The heart of the process was personalizing emotions as a team of intuitive advisors that offer high quality management and gut-level know-how. *Pow Wow Brainstorming* sessions turned on the brilliance of the creative right brain when participants learned to think and communicate on their feet - the secret that keeps a team energized and motivated. Catching the wave of impulse by verbalizing intuitive insights with boldness and daring triggered genuine feelings and true enjoyment. As creative innovation danced together with left-brain logic, mutual support for each other's natural genius radically increased.

The emotional task of the leader is PRIMAL. It is the original and the most important act of empowered leadership.

-Daniel Goleman
Primal Leadership

Quantum Physiology

Corporate work opened the way to present a *Quantum Physiology of Consciousness* for a group of physicists who had joined together to share their research on the unified field theory. Contrasting a Newtonian/Cartesian body language with the fluid, energetic principles that reflect the unified field is one way to heal separation at a molecular level. The first thing I did was exchanging their chairs for Physio Balls, which represented the unique blueprint of the DNA. The bodymind being one and the same, the more innovative movements they generated, the more innovative information would be uncovered. So, for an entire week they bobbled on these balls while listening to lectures and brainstorming together in small groups. Frequently, they were reminded to stretch out their spines by relaxing over the ball and letting their heads dangle. Released from the pressure of being upright, the fresh blood flowing into their brain kept their brilliant ideas percolating. Unleashing more fun, playful ways to breathe, sound and move on the ball magically released tension while helping them take in more oxygenated vitality throughout the day.

To change one's life, start immedetly Do it flamboyantly. No exceptions, no excuses.

-William James

I also spent time coaching them to become more physically and emotionally expressive while delivering their brilliant contributions. They practiced drawing out their equations with fluid hand gestures rather than speaking in monotone voices that could barely be heard. This made it easier for people like me to understand new and different concepts more readily.

As our awareness grows, so does the web of life– for we are the universe becoming aware of itself.

-Joanna Rogers Macy

Toward the end of the seminar, one physicist was struggling with a missing element in his equation. I invited him to audibly breathe while drawing out his equation on the ball with his butt. This experiment created a lot of laughter that soon turned to amazement. As he stood up with a dazed look on his face, he rushed to the blackboard and scribbled out the missing number of the equation. Miraculous feats are normal when our particle-like intellect and wave-like essence join together in harmony. Identifying with a quantum perspective shifts difficulties into creative opportunities and problems into solutions of wholeness. I have been test marketing the *Quantum Body in Motion* as far way as Zurich and London, Tokyo and Greece, Taipei and Hong Kong China with great success.

Violence Exploding

The importance of creating a healthy container for the expression of emotive energy came about when I was a presenter at an *Explosion on Violence* conference. A handful of people from around the world had gathered together to share transformative stories how they dealt with violent episodes that occurred in their life. The participants, ranging from a retired military general to a young gang leader, agreed on one thing — people everywhere are struggling to keep violent emotions under control and it's not working.

You have to be taught to hate and fear. You have to be taught from year to year. We are taught to hate a person's race, the color of someone's skin, some one's culture. You get the picture.

-Karol T. Truman

This powerful country of ours has the highest incidence of interpersonal violence among all industrial nations, and violence among youth is increasing with each passing year. Everywhere in today's world, people express anger, often in destructive, inappropriate ways. Gun rampages in public places have become a typical news event. The top stories on our local news are often nothing more than a review of the most sensationally violent acts in our community in the past day. During each year, women were the victims of more than 4.5 million violent crimes, including approximately 500,000 rapes or other sexual assaults. Over one hundred million dollars is being spent each hour on manufacturing death machines. It takes $14,800 to maintain a soldier versus $230 to educate a child. Is it any wonder that 2,000,000 children are doped up with prescribed behavior modification drugs and countless others that have barely enough food to survive.

Just as I had done with 'kids at risk,' I invited participants to release their frustration around the issue of violence by identifying with an active volcano exploding out its fury. Out of this raging inferno, new ground is being created. With audible breath, sound and movement, the whole group burst alive with thunderous energy that made the floor and walls shimmy! Many commented what a pleasure it was to unleash such volatile energy in such a free spirited way. My parting words were: "Teachers, educators and parents – stop 'shushing' children up at the slightest opportunity. The entire wordless sound making is an intuitive language of inner guidance that is an effective means of releasing emotional buildup. When children's emotive expression is valued, they will not need to grow up hurting themselves and others with violent outbursts of rage.

It's not whether you get knocked down. It's whether you get up again.

Vince Lombardi

Emotional Fitness

When I came home from the conference, I walked by a local fitness center and watched a woman walk her dog on a treadmill while reading a magazine. There was something about this scenario that struck my heart. The hard body muscle-mania style of fitness that follows set-in-stone guidelines, strengthens machine-like behavior that deadens our fluid, creative nature. From this observation, I had a strong desire to bring feelings into fitness.

Where do we go from a world of insanity? Somewhere on the other side of despair.

-T.S. Eliot

With a burst of enthusiasm, a book called *Emotional Fitness* began forming in my mind. Exercising the physiology of emotion with coordinated breath, sound and movement would do so much in healing layers of stress and anxiety. Sitting down and writing a book that dealt with the energy of emotion, at first, seemed virtually impossible. I could barely distinguish a proverb from and adverb!

Just as I had finally synthesized most of these ideas to paper, my computer crashed. All my precious work was gone without a trace. The idea of losing this material was more than I could bear. Once again, I was forced to take my own medicine. Standing before the video I went through the emotive workout with a vengeance! When my energy was spent, I meditated on what had happened.

Repetitive forms of fitness support a two-by four- world of narrow choices and limited possibilities.

-Jane Anderson

Suddenly, I heard a voice whispering, "I am the Soul of Peace. Nothing is ever lost. Breathe long and deep. Know I am with you through all adversity." Another voice hummed, "I am the Soul of Love. A dear friend is coming to your aid. Don't lose heart." As I released a long sigh of relief, another voice sang out, "I am the Soul of Ecstasy. Go to the party and dance with passion!" The idea of dancing with passion seemed absolutely ridiculous to my intellect. It ordered me to get on with rewriting what had been lost. Out of nowhere an angry voice shouted, "Don't you dare! Go to the party now!" At the party, I danced non-stop for two hours, which helped to release the tension. When leaving, I shared my unfortunate predicament with a friend.

The next day, she sent a computer expert to check things out. He found the data in a few minutes. In stunned silence, all I could say was, "Wow!" In the light of this intuitive revelation, I came to see that each emotion has a specific job to keep us healthy and safe from harm. The more I embrace emotions with equal value, the more energy and intuitive reliance arise within me.

Supreme excellence – is an openness to surprises that astound even the person who is masterful. It involves surrender to unexpected moves, to new and unexpected responses of the heart – to new illuminations and complete surprises!

-Michael Murphy

Every week I set about exploring a specific emotion while sitting, standing, walking and talking. Delving into his intense study opened the understanding that emotions are music! It is the pulsing rhythmical sensations that sets our body in motion. As living music, each emotion is designed to soothe or arouse us to take the necessary actions to accomplish our life's purpose. This discovery opened up a desire to bring more emotional energy into language. My favorite intuitive game was spontaneously opening up the dictionary and picking a word with my eyes closed. Next, I would resound the word with a vast array of vocal tones. This simple practice helped me to understand that truth exists in the 'tone' of the word. It just takes sensitive ears to hear it.

In every workshop I conducted for the next several years, the word *Wow* was chosen as a focal point to plummet the depths and heights of emotional expression. As participants used the dynamics of emotion to breathe, sound and move through this all-encompassing word, it was truly amazing to watch long-standing inhibitions and insecurities vanish into thin air. Out of this simple practice, a *Wow Languag*e was developed – consisting of a letter and five vowels that make it easy to express what is often inexpressible in any known language.

Thus the Creator, the composer above all composers, desired to weave a universe of enchantment, a magical kingdom, and so he chanted the Word from which would emerge a symphony of endless creation.

-James D'Angelo
Healing with the Voice

While listening to the flourishes of feeling tones and whimsical naturalness that emerges from this kind of pre-verbal dialogue, a *Wow Consciousness* was forming in my mind. Unlike the mantra *OM,* which upholds a controlled straight-lined spirituality, the *Great Wow* opens up a multidirectional expression of energy that is in alignment with the quantum worldview of expanding wholeness. When *Wow* is turned upside down, the word *Mom* is uncovered as the primordial mother of the world. Beyond all our concepts of right and wrong, there is only the Great *Wow* of ever-expanding love.

Church of Wow

In the beginning was the word and the word was *Wow!"* The *Church of Wow* was created to support a meta-spirituality and explore the embodiment of a fluid physiology that lays the foundation for an interrelated global community that embraces total freedom of expression as sacred. The main body of 'wowship' is communing in the *Wow* Language of Wae, Wee, Wah, Woh, Wuh. With an original language all feeling tones can be expressed no self-conscious concerns. 'Call and echo' sermons set the tone for heart-felt dialogue that exists below all our words. Dances of mutual admiration are a simple and powerful means of bringing everyone together to *Wow* each other's inner beauty and unique qualities of being. *Wow* stories are told that are intended to uncover insightful intuitive information that exists in the most exasperating experience.

The Word contains the life principle of creation. The sound within the word is the great master force containing all things. Bring forth the feeling tones within the word and become free.

-Kirpal Singh
Naam

With this intense focus on the Word, the primal name of *Wowza* emerged. I used this chosen name to encode all the power and energy that lay buried in my soul. Consciously downloading all the qualities of a youthful physiology into this name, is a now a magical tool that helps me open the toughest doors with unstudied grace.

When spiritual masters declare, "*I Am That,*" they are true 'sacred actors' who identify with all forms of existence as aspects of God. As Deepak Chopra aptly expressed,

"We are divinity in disguise. And the gods and goddesses in embryo that are contained within us." My hope in seeding a *Wow Consciousness* is witnessing the old adversarial drama that has existed for so long– between the intellect of cognitive thought and the primal powers of emotional energy –interlaying as one and the same.

Out of many growing pains, the book *Emotional Fitness* expanded into *Primal Energetics*. This manual is paving the way for an evolving quantum body that can move through chaos with sensitive feelings guiding the way. It is a fluidity of being that needs to be continuously revitalized in order to adapt to the enormous stresses of modern life. Breathing, voicing and moving with awareness of our interconnection with the world can do so much to reduce psychosomatic symptoms of disease. Performing arts vehicles and video projects are being designed in order to bring this work into the public arena.

Content that I had finally discovered the lost pieces of a giant puzzle, I heard a familiar voice whispering in my ear. It was the cosmic casting director, exclaiming: "Dear child, good job! Every human contact and situation in your life's movie has brought you to this auspicious moment. Regardless of your early wounding, you have continuously moved forward with ever expanding growth and opportunity. This embodied act of power is strengthening your empathy and compassion to be of genuine service to your fellow humans. This is pioneering work. Let nothing stop you."

As these empowering words touched my heart, I blessed my life's journey and all the events that brought me to this wondrous moment. With tears forming in my eyes, my father's essence appeared before me. I thanked him for the important role he played in shaping my unique destiny. If he had supported my natural talents, I probably would have become a professional dancer. But it was the many obstacles he threw in my path that opened me into a whole new world of alternative healing and transformation. Now, I am instrumental in inspiring many people to dance through their life, to creatively express the feelings buried in their bones, and sing the song only they can sing. How magnificent life is – why, I'm falling in love with my own story.

-As we regain the instinctive power that resides in us all, we are no longer incompetent victims determined by circumstances.

-Margo Adair

To laugh is to risk appearing foolish. To weep is to risk appearing sentimental.
To reach out for another is to risk involvement.
To expose feelings is to risk not being loved in return. But risk we must because the greatest risk is to risk nothing at all.

Famous Amos

Shaman healers are people who can shapeshift into different states of mind and body at will. They are mystic performers, purveyors of wisdom, Sacred Actors.

-Brian Bates
The Way of the Actor

Sacred Actor

Artist of Being

I know of artists whose medium is life itself, who express the inexpressible.
Their medium is Being. Whatever their hand touches has increased life
They are artists of being.

-Frederick Frank
Art is the Way

Playful creativity is what every young child lives for. With the blink of an eye, a child can transform into a tinker bell fairy, a shoot em'up cowboy, or a dragon breathing fire without losing the unique essence of being. Following the spontaneous feelings of the 'play instinct' all the aspects of daily life become a surprising adventure. It is rare that children are supported in maintaining this wondrous gift of playful self-expression. When did you stop singing and dancing through the day? When did you stop enacting all the parts of your story? When did you stop turning work into play? When did you stop listening to the feeling sensations of your inner prompting?

This first Catalyst unites you with the creative genius of your multidimensional nature. True freedom of expression is unleashed when your ego and essence can play together in harmony.

Acting is what most of us think we have little talent for, yet we unconsciously do it from morning to night. We can often recognize our friends playing out smart, cool, friendly or strong roles, and not recognize the familiar role we play on a daily basis. As the philosopher Alan Watts expressed, "The most strongly enforced of all known taboos is the taboo against knowing who or what you really are behind the mask of your apparently separate and isolated ego."

Behind the facade of image, each person is an artist in this primal and inescapable sense, an inner artist who carries and shapes a unique world.

-John O' Donohue
Book of Celtic Wisdom

What is your Character?

When I was growing up, developing a strong character was an admirable thing. This often meant that the character you identified with remained steadfast under all circumstances. When I studied acting in earnest, I derived such pleasure when modeling people's posture, vocal style and movement patterns. With continuing practice, I could recognize more clearly, the 'character' that was being portrayed. Most of these people I modeled seemed to have little idea of the role that was being played out in life. What character in this long running movie was I enacting?

Casting for male, female soap opera types-confused neurotic, cute cuddly type and a prima donna.

Ad from Variety Magazine

When I got my first video camera, I asked friends to film me going through mundane activities and when I conversed with others. Boy was I nice! Seeing that pleasant smile and curved right shoulder in shy response filled me with embarrassment. My mental mind kept trying to convince me that this nice part was the real me, and I was acting phony if I tried to change it.

While struggling with this identity crisis, I read in the Upanishads of Hindu mythology that "God is an Actor" who embodies all of humankind and nature simultaneously. I also learned that in many traditional societies, shaman healers were the original actors. Their gift was to transform themselves into elemental forces of nature; a creature or divine deity in order to gain information about healing illness and sustaining the primal power of the community. By embodying change in themselves, they facilitated change in others. I mused what it would be like to identify myself as a *Sacred Actor* playing me! Enacting this familiar role with unconditional acceptance helped me see that it was a survival tactic of a frightened child believing she was unworthy of love.

Identification with the character structure of our 'social role' is our greatest addiction because the mental mind, which runs this role, is the container for all other addictive tendencies.

Like any good actor knows, the character of our public persona is easy to reproduce because it rarely deviates from its physical patterning. A fixed character structure acts as a self-limiting filter to protect us from anything believed to disturb the status quo. The essence, on the other hand, is an inclusion of all kinds of varied colors and spontaneous expression of emotion that is furthering the expansion of our consciousness. When temperament becomes a repetitious habit, it's only natural that we become entranced by its familiarity. The fatal illusion is to believe this fabricated role is who we really are.

However a person typecasts himself, it's amazing to see how his body leaps to the fore with its gift for unmistakable characterization. If the image of 'power' is to be projected, the body becomes a solid block, rigid and inflexible.

-Trudi Shoop
Won't you Join the Dance?

Limiting beliefs of mind become imprinted in our physical structure. It takes enormous muscular effort to sustain automatic behavior patterns. For instance, when playful urges are believed to be childish, a body language is created to project a serious person who 'acts' smart. When feeling the burden of too much responsibility, a 'dumb' role can be created slumping the chest and slurring words to avoid pressure. With repeated criticism by caretakers, a child's body can shrink in size or blow up in size. These physical habits are shapes that sustain a victimized personality or a rebellious attitude that can persist throughout one's life.

A false veneer goes hand and hand with emotional attitudes that project repetitive qualities of behavior in order to fit in and be accepted by our peers. The mental mind is conditioned to do everything possible to maintain the social role once it is set in place. For instance, most men are trained from infancy to keep it all together. Enormous effort is used to emulate the cultural 'he-man' with flexed biceps, puffed out chest and taut abs of steel. The rock-hard stability of a muscle dominant structure solidifies into armor to act 'unmoved' under any adversity. Developing dominance over heart-felt feelings makes brilliant soldiers of war - deadly machines who can kill without flinching. John Wayne, the All-American hero of the movies, was the classic he-man who remained stone faced to the bitter end. Do you ever remember him looking the least bit pained when he shot someone dead? His 'character' did not permit any show of feeling.

Engaging in daily movements with more creative artistry can take us beyond naturalistic conformity, into realms of imagination and poetry.

-Patti Lupone

When approaching middle age, the malleability of the body becomes more and more prone to aches and pains when lost playing out a social role with little awareness of doing so. When the public persona is consciously embodied as your most brilliant creation, you are no longer lost in any part. A wealth of juicy, creative possibilities open up, enabling you to spontaneously flow into richly textured, multiple facets of a growing, expanding identity.

The media continues to portray women's bodies with a combination of passiveness and seduction. Both stances suggest that woman is man's sexual adjunct. Stereotype attitudes are fun to play when we can step out of them at will.

Multiple Personalities

How many times have we been warned that shifting into a different personality can lead to mental illness? Mental illness is dissociating from one role in order to play another role with no awareness of doing so. This is understandable when thresholds of trauma and pain become too hard to handle. A 'spiritual emergency' is created in which the soul will do anything to break free of past trauma and pain. As Martin Luther King Jr. expressed in one of his speeches, "Each of us is something of a schizophrenic personality, tragically divided against our true nature."

You are not a personality, even though you wear a personality. Perhaps you wear it so tightly that you have overlooked that if you drop it, you remain whole and full, while it lies lifeless on the floor.

-Gangaji

By unconsciously disassociating from the multidimensional nature of our authentic self, we are all afflicted with varying degrees of mental illness.

While I was teaching an acting course at Antioch University, one of my students was doing a research study on multiple personalities. He discovered that enormous physical changes take place when people act out a different role. For instance, a person can be nearsighted in one role and magically become farsighted when shifting into another role! One personality may even have diabetes while the other role does not. Imagine the enormous healing possibilities and healthy vitality that can arise when actualizing our 'shapeshifting' skills with conscious awareness.

Like any child knows, playing a new role is an extraordinary learning experience that deepens awareness of human nature. Imaginative play practice excites the nervous system, stimulates emotional response, increases blood flow, entrains the muscles in a new way and increases coherence between different areas of the brain. In short, play-acting is an extraordinary healthy activity that needs our full value.

Activations

The actor on the stage of life, like his theatrical counterpart, is an artist whose medium is the exploration of a human being's emotional life.

-Steven Lrsen
The Mythic Imagination

Regularity, stability, and predictability of character in a world undergoing massive change have served its usefulness. Moving through the day as an 'artist of being' can enrich all aspects of your life with living color. Imagine the excitement of creating different vocal qualities and novel physical expressions to reveal hidden domains of feeling. Entertain the idea of delighting the listener when playing out all the characters in your story. Play-acting is the natural expression of your essential nature. Reawaken this gift by recalling the young child you once were. This was a time when anything was possible. As you travel through these early childhood memories, revisit special play times when you could be, have, or do anything your heart desired.

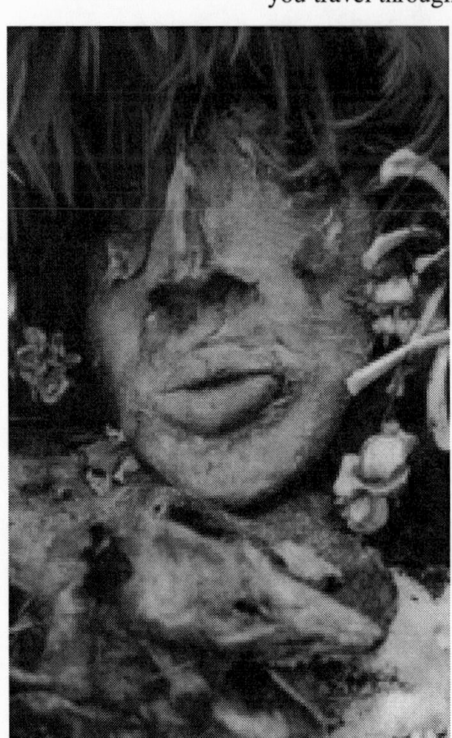

Recall the stories and special roles you loved to enact. What were some of the favorite games you played? Whatever memories come forth, savor and relish the sensory sensations that arise. Notice what parts of your body respond. If nothing comes, make up an experience and visualize yourself play-acting with abandon. Can you recall a time when your playful urges were judged as childish behavior? Do you remember trying to imitate grownups in order to figure out how to 'act like an adult?' What kind of attitudes and physical behaviors did you emulate? How would you describe the adult role you ended up portraying on a daily basis?

Primal Name

Names possess infinite creative power. In many esoteric traditions, the essence of the Word represents the One Energy that flows through all languages. Like the DNA, which is the blueprint of original intelligence, intuitively choosing a *Primal Name* that can be encoded with the *Five Catalysts* and the *Eight Primal Energies,* endows this name with magical 'shapeshifting' powers. Your mental mind will truly appreciate this process because this one word acts as a safe container to unleash unlimited creative expression.

When you realize that you are an actor on the World Stage, you begin to understand that only you can play your part. No one else can take your place. You have something to give to others that no one else can provide.

-Vivian King
Soul Play

Like 'abra ca dabra' in the fairy tales, this encoded name represents the *Sacred Actor* who possesses magical powers to open doors of unlimited creativity.

To start the process, recall the natural energy in nature– the freshness of a spring morning, the passionate warmth of the summer's sun, the lush harvest of autumn and the coldness of a winter's evening. Reflect on the massive waves of oceanic currents, the power of a whale, and a giant redwood tree growing towards the sun. As this natural energy is circulating in your mind, begin reciting the alphabet.

With free-spirited improvisation, play with all the letters in the alphabet while feeling the primal energy of elemental energy flow through you. Go through the alphabet once again and intend three letters to come forward from the depths of your being. Acknowledge these three letters are a gift from your soul that knows perfectly well what sonic frequencies can best serve your true destiny

Write the three letters down on paper. Take each letter and savor it in your mouth. Play with different vowels that eventually become specific syllables. For instance, if your first letter is G, by adding a vowel it becomes Ga, Gee or Go or whatever you choose. Do the same with the next three letters. The vowels are the portals that open up the feeling center of the word. Freely articulate the syllables with your lips, tongue and jaw. Support your tones with lots of free air and keep allowing your throat to remain relaxed.

I can't explain myself, I'm afraid,sir, said Alice, "because I'm not myself, you see."

-Lewis Carroll

Stretching open the vowels with new rhythmic patterns and tonal intensities generates warmth of feeling and resonance in your voice. With continued exploration of your sonic potential, total freedom of expression can be released with exquisite ease.

Mirror of Awareness

There is a Sufi tale about the ego being a marvelous fiction that becomes a novel written by us about ourselves. A polished mirror is needed to see this fictitious character of our creation. The Sufi aspires to become that reflective mirror, the contrasting instrument by which the authenticity of essence can be clearly seen. In other words, the social role is a limited construct, but there is a power within you that can mirror both the ego and the essence of your being.

At first, it may be an intimidating undertaking to act out your social role. In fact, it may be easier to mimic your favorite movie star than embodying the personality that you play in daily life. Great actors like Robin Williams or Jack Nicholson can play the most down and dirty roles imaginable and be fully loved by the audience. Why is this so? Because they love their parts! While studying a part, they exclaim with utter fascination: "Oh, look how she tilts her head and squints her eyes. Let me try that. Oh! I feel so shy. That's great! I can use this vulnerable quality to enrich my role. As St. Bonaventure once expressed, "The mirror presented by the external world is of little value unless the mirror of our soul has been cleaned and polished."

The magic mirror reflected not what was on the surface, but rather that which exists within him in potential, who he can become.

-Jonathan Omer
Man Getting into Step

In the mirror of consciousness, there is no part left out in the cold. Pretense and presence, the observer and the one observed and the creator and creation are all reflected with equal regard as the source of all that you are.

As you gaze at yourself in the mirror, what is your first impression of this person standing in front of you? What is the overall 'image' that is projected - friendly, serious, cool, strong, smart, nice or casual? What role have you been 'typecast' to play in life? How would your closest friend describe your personality? If you were seeing yourself as a character in a movie, how would you describe the role you've been cast in? Notice the posture that shapes your role. What is your standing in the world? For instance, you may lean on one hip and lock your knees. You may collapse or puff up your chest. One shoulder may hang lower than the other. Your feet may be turned inward or outward. Amplifying these tendencies heightens awareness. If embarrassment arises, physically exaggerate it. In other words, play out your moods and attitudes with pleasure!

Not afraid to go beyond normal limits, self penetration reveals the mask covering the essence.

-Jerzy Grotowski
Towards a Poor Theatre

As children, we often modeled the behaviors of people we grew up with. As directors of your life's movie, what role did these people persuade you to enact? Did you audition for this part, or was it thrust on you with rewards and punishments? In our media-rich culture, what favorite hero or movie star did you admire and perhaps imitate? You may have adopted the low-slung model's stance projecting assumed sophistication, or adopted a hyper-straight stance of a smart professional. Whatever qualities are discovered; even ones you don't like embody it with fascination.

Mask of Ego

We have spent most of our lives practicing the repressive conditioning that controls the limit of our current capacity for facial expressivity.

-H. Wesley Balk
The Radiant Performer

Oh, what a sweet mask! Did you make it yourself? As social creatures, most of us have become brilliant at immobilizing the muscles of our face to disguise what we feel. Self-imposed masks can become deeply etched in the muscles of our face. The consistency of this familiar look is one reason why wrinkles and sagging folds appear, even quite early in age. Notice your facial expression. What emotional attitude is projected - aggressive, serious, fragile, smart, or a blank, nondescript look? As a *Sacred Actor*, amplify that pleasant smile, minor frown, or tight upper lip with artful awareness. Notice your eyes. They may be deep-set, bulge out, or reflect a penetrating look. Notice if you tilt your head, which may draw one eye forward and the other eye inward. Focus on your eyebrows. Are they drawn together in worry, disdain or are they raised in a perpetual look of surprise? Once more, amplify these characteristics as an actor would.

Fixed, conditioned behavior makes robots of us all. Consciously enacting any familiar behavior offers the choice whether to continue playing the role or not.

When you look at your posture, amplify tilts, angles, leanings and twists that shape this familiar form. With clearer eyes, your posture may reveal what you are trying to hide from being seen. For instance, you may feel embarrassed about some assumed physical defect. If you were ridiculed for having crooked teeth, a habit may develop of pulling your upper lip over them when you smile. Possessing a large nose in a culture, which prefers smaller noses, you may have developed the unconscious habit of pulling your chin down to make your nose appear smaller. Obsessive smiling, twirling hair with the fingers, fidgeting, toying with rings or a pipe and straightening clothes are nervous habits that spring from self-conscious concerns. Interestingly enough, unconscious habits are the very things that people can't help but notice.

"I'll discuss it with you," she said in a voice that could have been used to defrost her refrigerator.

-Rex Stou

Vocal Style

The social role we are identified with projects an emotional attitude that possesses a specific tone of voice. As you say your name and a few things to describe yourself, pay attention to the tone of your voice. Don't be surprised if you can't hear what you've just said. Say your name a few times more. Are you drawing a blank? One popular tendency to disguise feelings from being expressed is to string the consonants and vowels together into a monotone. While listening to yourself speak, notice if your typical rhythm of tone is speedy or slow. Notice if you tend to speak in the higher or lower registers of your voice.

If we had ears to hear the full range of vibrational frequencies, we might hear ourselves as talking symphonies.

-Tom Kenyon
Brain States

If you're having trouble, record your voice. Pretend you're listening to a stranger. Don't be surprised if you exclaim: "Gee, do I sound like that? I sound so flat and boring." My answer is "No!" This voice that you habitually project reflects your social role, which is a tiny speck of your true vocal power.

Being split off from the flowing continuum of our primal essence, our voice reflects this unnatural split. If your voice sounds like a confident expert, shy student or a cool dude, notice how your posture shapes itself to match the quality of your voice. Bring this familiar quality of voice out into the light of day. Amplify its particular characteristics with respect.

We all have a traditional speech style, a default setting that perpetuates stereotypes. And it denies us options to grow, change, or experiment.
-Sarah Myers McGinty
-Power Talk

If you're a man, how much vulnerable expression do you allow in your speaking voice? If you're a woman, how much potent strength resonates through your tone? Are you comfortable using the high or low part of your range? If not, what specific beliefs limit you from exploring the vast power of your vocal instrument?

Male and female voices are different, yet they aren't different in essence. A voice rich in primal expression can voice both male and female tones and something much more.

When conversing with others, spend a few minutes listening to your predicable tone of voice. Viewing your vocal tendencies without judgment offers more colorful variations of tone that enrich your speaking voice. With increased awareness, more sensitivity increases in hearing and interlaying with other people's tone of voice. This is what 'entrainment' is all about – the mirroring of different vocal styles supports deepened empathetic understanding. Reflecting other people's unique tonal qualities in conversation can radically change the 'character' of your relationships, and expand the dynamic power your vocal range.

A comedian is someone paid to lower his own or other people's status.

-Keith Johnstone
Improv

Status Games

Split off from our soul essence, a strong tendency develops to inflate or depreciate ourselves before others. Living behind a social role makes it difficult to make genuine contact with others as our equal. The fear of 'never being enough' is asking to be dominated, manipulated and downright taken advantage of. Caught in the habit of playing out these dominant/subservient roles with little awareness of doing so, endless power struggles arise that argue who is right and who is wrong. As Daniel Taylor once remarked, "Status games require a counter mask that hides resistant tendencies and lack of confidence."

What follows are scenes that heighten awareness of any status games you are unconsciously playing. Imagine introducing yourself to an authority figure you hold in high respect. Notice if you have the tendency to shrink or hyper-expand your posture. Do you dominate the interaction with your tone or quietly take the low end of the bargain? Now imagine introducing yourself to a young child, housekeeper or employee. What body language is projected under these conditions?

How readily do you absorb blame or project blame on others? The game of 'one upmanship' wipes out any possibility of true intimacy among equals.

If you could listen in, you would hear non-assertive people saying all kinds of negative sentences to themselves.

-Bower & Bower
Asserting yourself

How has your occupation molded your character? Do you fit the cultural stereotype of a doctor, lawyer, expert, parent, teacher, servant or construction worker? If you've settled on a particular viewpoint of the world, do you stubbornly resist hearing any opposing view? Do you get upset when you're not taken seriously? How much time do you spend judging the behavior of others? Can you laugh at your foolish mistakes, or do you immediately want to beat yourself up, or offer a barrage of excuses? You are a victim of circumstance only when losing awareness of your primal essence. When catching yourself engrossed in a status game with someone, invoke the *Sacred Actor.*

Experiential knowledge is the only real knowledge. As a *Sacred Actor*, tune into the body language and tone of voice that sustains a need to victimize or act superior in your interactions with others. When amplifying a status role with artful playfulness, tension is released and more humorous options come to the surface. This artful strategy can also awaken your companion to how he or she participates in status games and have little awareness of doing so.

The important thing is to use the role as trampoline, an instrument with which to study what is hidden behind our everyday mask-the facade-in order to sacrifice it, expose it.

-Jertzy Grotowski
Towards a Poor Theatre

Intentionally raising and lowering your status at will, reveals a third possibility – empathetic resonance for the unique qualities of others.

Walk Primal

Over the years, while mirroring hundreds of different walking styles, I noticed that most people have little idea how they walk. It is even more rare that anyone can reproduce his or her walk with conscious awareness. Recreating your typical walking style opens the door to embody more clearly, the fluid walk of your primal essence.

Take an exploratory walk about the room. At this stage, don't deliberate how to improve your walking style, only heighten awareness of what you discover. For instance, which foot do you use to take your first step? Don't be surprised if you have to stop and

start a few times in order to sense what has become habitual. When moving about, look for areas of tension and amplify them with good humor. Some typical patterns are tightening the neck, squeezing the chest muscles, sucking in belly and contracting the shoulders.

We can walk around our whole life and not be aware of our specific movement style. Developing this awareness is a profound meditation in becoming more present in your body.

More things to notice is your typical speed of rhythm, which body part leads the action, and how much space or lack of space is used in the act of walking. More specifically, do you strike the ground with your heal or do you roll across the ground with your whole foot? Do your toes turn in or out? Notice your overall stride, the extension or contraction of the leg swing in locomotion. Do you push yourself forward by taking long strides to 'get ahead' or take very small steps, as if walking on eggshells? Are the hinges and joints loosely flowing with your movements or held in a rigid manner?

One day you are walking along and you find that nothing and everything have changed. You step forward. You carry on.

-Candida Baker
Women and Horses

Focus on the heart area. Notice if there is a tendency to sink your chest inward, pull it out or draw it up military style. Notice if you feel any movement in your ribs when you breathe. Do you round your shoulders forward, hold them up or pull them back in military fashion? When focusing on your pelvis, does this area move when you walk? Notice if you tuck your tailbone under, or tilt it up. How do you carry your arms? Do they swing with your walk or do they have a tendency to cling to your waistline? Often, one arm will swing in a different angle from the other. When raised in a climate of conflict, the posture and movement is often fraught with counter-pulls in which different parts are moving in different directions at once. Things to notice – your head may jut forward and your chest may pull inward. Your ribcage may rotate one way and your hips may counterbalance in the opposite way.

Being male or female shapes our body language in predictable ways. Here is a simple way of moving beyond restrictive gender roles. Explore walking across the room as the opposite sex. Notice any changes that instantly occur. What feelings and thoughts arise when assuming your other half? Was this easy or difficult? When returning to your regular walk, do you sense it more clearly?

Apparent male and female contradictions contain the parody of paradox.

-Lux Decoda

Sub-Personalities

The primary social role we play hosts a whole array of characters that talk inside our head. These characters are 'disembodied emotions' that think rather than feel. When emotions are mentalized, they are in the habit of relentlessly arguing with us, judging our performance and pushing us beyond endurance. Sub-personalities are capable of creating unbearable noise that like nothing better to do than churning out endless conflict. Being absolutely brilliant at blowing up imaginary fears of doom and gloom, they know just how to throw us into guilt and shame at a moment's notice. When we don't do what they say, they 'should' all over us! Being criticized, ridiculed and made fun of by a bunch of jabbering voices is exhausting.

An actor must be in touch with all of himself and be able to call upon any sub-personality at any time to come and do the work of the character in the play.

-Eric Morris

When critical, incriminating thoughts are played out with full vigor, they can no longer rule your life. You can choose how you wish to think, act and feel.

The point is, don't waste time trying to change what cannot be changed. By diffusing identification with the public persona, you are now free to be a leader of your own destiny. As Gabrielle Roth so eloquently expressed in her book *Urban Shaman*, "The soul plays the self as a consummate stage actor plays a character with detachment and total involvement at the same time." Take pleasure in enacting the head controller – the cruel critic, the relentless pusher, the devious manipulator, the poisonous fanatic, the festering, callous, sly, and ruthless faultfinder that is a mental mind gone crazy. They are all juicy parts to play! In this moment of full awareness, they can no longer run your mind.

Below are a series of statements to get you started. As you express statements of ridicule and judgment, listen to the tone of your voice. For instance, if the tone is harsh and mean, amplify the sound of this quality without words. With increased sonic awareness, the cruelest sounding voice will not intimidate you. No longer fixed and rigid in the meaning of words, the feeling sound below the words will set you free.

How stupid can you be? You idiot!
You act like a total jerk!
Shut up! What do you know anyway?
Forget it. You don't have what it takes!
Lets face it, you're a failure at everything you do!
Who do you think you are?

Private Session

In my private work with clients, I often videotape the session so they have a running documentary of their progress. What follows is a process with a man who was learning to distinguish the difference between his social role and his authentic self. John was the CEO of his own company, which was on the verge of bankruptcy. He had lots of great ideas about how to change things around but had difficulty influencing his employees to explore his new visions. The most characteristic quality of John's posture was thrusting his head forward, which compressed his heart area. His voice projected a stern, hard-edged quality. It was easy to see how his employees were intimidated by the harshness of his style. I first coached John to become more familiar with his emotions by exercising their physiology with breath, sound and movement. Next, I encouraged him to sit in front of the TV and look into the screen. With a video camera in hand, I stood on a stool beside him and pointed the camera onto his face.

Emotional literacy seeks to lead us to consciously coexist with our emotions and reenter that jungle paradise which they guard.

-Claude M. Steiner
The Other Side of Power

John said, "Wow! I never realized how I pull my chin down, which gives me a double chin. Oh God, I remember pulling my chin down as a kid. I thought this gesture would make me look powerful, instead it makes me look deadly serious!"

At that point, I got down from the chair and shot his face from another angle. His eyes squinted in disbelief as he exclaimed "I've never seen myself like this before. I can't believe it; I look just like my father! I see the same look of stern reproach that made me quake in my boots as a kid."

"What ifs" rounded out his daily diet. He was a master at making himself miserable: His misery overflowed onto those around him. He had a black belt in regret.

--Jeamme E. Blum
Woman Heal Thyself

Opening the camera lens to a wide angle, I said, "John, rather than getting caught in judgment, give yourself space to feel your feelings." John gritted his teeth and snarled, "I'm angry!" In seconds he burst out with "I hate you, you son of a bitch! I don't give a damn anymore what you think. You hurt me! I hate you for that!" As I watched John turn his hands into fists, I said, "What do you feel like doing?" John thrust out his fist shouting, "I wish you were dead!" After this outburst, he sat back and became very quiet.

I said, "John, emotions are always changing. Keep noticing what feelings are below the ones you're experiencing."

Tears began to well up in his eyes. With a whisper he said, "My father was so loving and gentle with his horse. Seeing him hug his horse filled me with envy. I wanted to be treated in the same way."

What appeared on the screen was a little boy who still felt resentful for being so harshly ignored. I said, "It's hard not getting the love and recognition you deserve, isn't it?" Covering his hand over his mouth he exclaimed, "Oh God, the way my father treated me is the way I'm treating the people I work with. I can't stand to feel this vulnerable." By now I was focusing the camera on his quivering mouth.

Over time we identified so strongly with the characteristics of our type, we forgot our true nature and 'became' our personality, or false self.

-Helen Palmer
The Enneagram

Then, pointing the camera into his eyes, I said, "John, give yourself space to feel this pain. Give it breathing room to grow and change."

John let out a deep sigh. Watching another layer of John's rigid mask fade from view, I said, "What you've always wanted from your father, give it to yourself now." Without deliberation, he slowly placed his hands on his heart. No words were needed to affirm what was taking place. John tenderly hummed to himself with simple acceptance.

Deeply touched, I said, "You, like many men, have been raised with the belief that showing tender feelings isn't manly. I personally feel it is the essence of manliness."

When I asked John to return to his characteristic social role with its stern look and rigid demeanor, his eyes widened in surprise. His retort was, "No way! Why would I want to go back and do that?" I said, "Because this part of you acted in the belief that this was the only way to keep you from being hurt. This role helped you survive through some tough times, and it needs your respect. In this way, it won't sabotage your emotions from being expressed. Come on John, call on the *Sacred Actor* and play this role as an academy award performance."

Do I contradict myself? Very well then I contradict myself. I am large. I contain multitudes!

-Walt Whitman
Leaves of Grass

On hearing this he laughed out loud. With a renewed twinkle in his eyes, the play of genius came to life with full abandon. John jumped up from his chair and walked around the room with fretful concern. With his head thrust forward, he rounded his shoulders, jutted out his jaw, squinted his eyes and pounded his heals in the floor. As his eyes darted about the room, he mumbled critical assessments to imaginary people in his midst. I jumped up and cheered his brilliant enactment.

Mirroring the Soul

At the end of each chapter, you are invited to create an expressive art ceremony that portrays the social role with deepened acceptance and reveals more and more facets of your multidimensional nature. This sacred practice does not need a stage or an audience to be effective. Perceive your mirror as a holographic movie screen in which all of humankind is sitting in the audience. This all-encompassing audience represents your inner world of sub-personalities.

Enacting your soul means creating a fresh self, an ever-changing, yet enduring self, that can play any role, take any position with full awareness and control.

-Gabrielle Roth
Urban Shaman

A video camera is perhaps the most powerful tool to perceive this developmental process. When you lose heart, you can review the footage and see a record of the different stages of your transformative power. In this way, you're establishing a full color production in which you are the star player of the ongoing play of your life.

I recommend reviewing the video in three ways. You can take one small part of the video and play it over. The first time you see yourself on screen, write down all your critical assessments. On the second screening, mirror everything you see yourself doing. Reflect your unique mannerisms and vocal tone with full involvement. At first it may be a little scary when seeing facets of your social role that you judge as inadequate. On the third viewing, focus on seeing the creative potential that lies hidden underneath the role you project. Be your own cheering team that supports your unique genius to grow and flower.

Why should Robin Williams have all the fun? Why not become the 'peak performance' of the life you have been given. As a *Sacred Actors* on the world's stage, you don't have to cast yourself in the same role for the entire run of the play. You are only stuck in a 'part' if you think you are. As an artist of being, you are the playwright, director and audience all intertwined together.

Ceremony of Acceptance

Being 'whole' there is nothing to get rid of. When all the primary roles that define you are honored and appreciated for the unique gifts and learning they have offered you, they become fragrant herbs in a delightful blend of spices that enrich the uniqueness of your being. Here is an example of some of the roles that define me. May this process support you in acknowledging the many personas that bring out your multifaceted nature.

Uncovering the deepest essence of our identity, offers relief, freedom from the false self that constricts the body.

-Steven Wolinsky
Quantum consciousness

"Hello Dorothy. Dear little ugly duckling, quivering with fear, I hold you in my arms. You are accepted and loved just as you are. I bless and praise the fragility and vulnerability that makes me so sensitive to these same qualities in others."

"Hello Nice Girl. With pleasing smiles, you know how keep the peace and sustain the comfort zone of others. Believing you are unlovable, you act in the only way you know for protection. I honor you as the survivor of a lost youth."

"Hello Beauty Queen. As I announce your name, I lift my head with pride. You are teaching me that we are all kings and queens of greatness. When I tune into your regality, I rise above all adversity into the rich grandeur of success."

"Hello Mama. Your garments are stained with little boy's hands that have played in the dirt too long. Your undaunting patience at keeping the peace has taught me to multitask cooking eggs over easy, hard-boiled and sunny side up, all at the same time! I send you loving praise for pulling off the impossible."

Man only plays when he is in the fullest sense of the word a human being; and he is only fully a human being when he plays.

-Friedrich Schiller

"Hello Sage Woman. As my ageless self, you weather all ages by giving them equal value. And no wonder, your body is made from ancient rocks daily kissed by the elements. You weather all storms with amazing fortitude. Your most precious gift is exuding 'baby wise' wisdom and a well seasoned 'elder wild' nature."

As a *Sacred Actor,* know you can be both rational and irrational, strong and gentle, fun loving and serious, sensual and reserved– all rolled up into one!

Now it's your turn. In front of the mirror, travel down memory lane and pay a visit to the different roles that shape your unique being. See yourself as a little child. Recall how you first heard your name expressed by family and friends. Explore saying it with childlike innocence. Listen to the tonal quality and take time to recreate the body language that represents your younger self. Remember any nicknames your friends used to call you. Sound those names out now. Notice the different feelings that arise. Recall your teenage years. Say your name with the tone and posture of this time of your life. While recreating your teen physiology, say your name a few times more. What is the overall emotive attitude that is being expressed?

The creative person is both more primitive and more cultured, crazier and saner, than the average person. It follows that the creative environment is one that encourages this dichotomy through freedom of expression and movement.

-Frank Barron

Return to your adult role. Consciously recreate the familiar qualities that represent personality. Notice to what degree the child, teen and adult are influencing your present behavior. Perceiving your social role as your greatest creation the public persona no longer has power over you.

I quote Rumi, "What I most want is to spring out of this personality, then to sit apart from that leaping. I've lived too long where I can be reached." Feel what it would be like to stand at the edge of what is the familiar you and what is the unknown you. Who are you becoming? How do you want to make it up? Who is your 'future self' in the making? Whatever you focus upon expands.

For thousands of years spiritual masters have declared, "I Am That." These spiritual masters are sacred actors who identify with all the forms of existence as aspects of God. Honor your newfound power to step out of any familiar persona and become a *Sacred Actor* who can create new roles that serve the common good of humankind. Breathe in "I" and breathe out "AM." While exploring this a few times more, affirm your multidimensional nature with the words, *"I AM ALL THAT I AM. There is nothing I am not"*

Who are you becoming? The a 'future self' is being seeded to interact with a new world in the making. What are the essential qualities of this new being that is being birthed from your soul?

Meditation might be considered theatre. Think of it as a ticket to step outside yourself in order to get some distance on your own little dramas - to become not only an actor on the world's stage but a member of the audience as well. This process helps us understand our personas as the masks that they are.

-Wes Scoop Nisker

Magical Mask

Through concealment of your familiar persona, self-conscious self-absorption dissolves. The creation of a primal mask can help you reveal different facets of your nature that ordinarily do not have permission to seen or heard in daily life. One simple means to get you started is purchasing a 'half mask' that can be purchased in party outlet stores or the internet. Later on, you may enjoy making a mask of your own face with surgical tape and decorating it with meaningful objects from nature. A glue gun makes it easy to attach cutout cardboard to your mask, which adds greater height to mount nature's gifts of feathers, shells, moss, dried flowers, sticks and stones, or anything you choose that has meaning to you.

This mask is a sacred object. Like your magical word, this special object carries a unique spirit that can shift you into new domains of expression. If making a mask seems to complicated, painting your face is another option to explore. As an 'artist of being,' decorate yourself with the face of nature's beauty and power. The nature you are apart of is composed of the same basic elements. As a Native American chant expressed, "The morning mists, the clouds, the gathering waters, and the fire of passion, I am it. The wild rose forever blossoming with primal beauty, I am it."

Being free to act is a great gift. Intent is everything. By saying YES to the play of genius, the Soul of Emotion takes care of the details. Look into your eyes. Breathe deep and drop into your primal essence. Place the primal mask on your face. Who would you be if you didn't know who you were? What new species is waiting to be born in your soul? With impulsive nerve, become irreverent in your reverence. Being poised on the brink of creation, enter the silence. Embrace this silence of mind out of which flows all creative breakthroughs. Listen to your innermost impulses. Allow a new way of expression to come out of the silence. Out of nothing, the wondrous breath arises to lead you into new, undiscovered territory. Don't worry, you won't lose touch with your familiar personality. In fact, with expanded shapeshifting abilities, you can play your social role more perfectly than ever before.

To act means total immersion in becoming the embodiment of another being.

-Marlan Brando

Your flexibility and energy expands when mirroring the essential qualities of different people's body language. Embodying the essential tone and physical characteristics of the mailman, the butcher, the boss, friend and family member, expands your identity and interpersonal effectiveness. In this way, everyone you meet is a potential playmate who has come into your life to reveal hidden aspects of your own identity.

To be authentic, to be real is to say...YES!...to surrender to who you really are in your depths. To be false is to resist your reality in favor of some inherited or conditioned facsimile of the Self. As you face the emotional core of your essence, you face God.

-William Pennel Rock
Performing Inside Out

While going about the day, periodically focus your attention on an object that fascinates you; a bird on a branch or an unusual shape that catches your eye. Describe yourself as the essence of the object. Giving voice as a cumulus cloud or a due drop on a leaf can open up fresh perspectives on any unsolvable issue. Bringing art into life creates an explosion of creative improvisation in which you influence your own future towards victory. Dare to be inventive with your breath, sound and movement.

While watching heavy dramas, amplify the emotions you see portrayed on the screen. Once you enact the emotion, shift into the tone of the opposite emotion. Play practice refines your ability to shift in and out of any emotional state you choose. Cooking dinner playing out an entirely different persona will no doubt bring different ingredients together that will surprise you! Set up a video camera and create your own 'reality theatre' scenes in which any miserable setback and frustrating drama can be transformed into a divine comedy of outrageous possibility.

Being one with the universe, there is nothing or no one that you are not related to. In this context, acting is a profound spiritual practice.

A Fluidity of Being

Quantum Body in Motion

How easy it is to turn the supple and exploratory bodies of infants into machine like bodies with predictable stances and habitual ways of seeing things. How easy it is to give up our experimental authority and lose our fluid vitality.

-Don Johnson

The new discoveries of quantum physics are revealing that the body of the world, of which we are apart, is a unified energy field in fluid motion. There are no straight lines in nature. As the ocean is embedded in a tiny droplet, so we contain the 'ocean of origin' in every cell, muscle, bone and organ in our body. The trillions of cells that compose our molecular system are teeming with liquid biomorphic movements common to all life forms. Our tears, our blood, our sweat still taste of sea salt. Even the curves of our spine's vertebrae reflect the mathematical perfection of a sine wave. Nothing being in a fixed place, everything is swimming in a sea of creative possibility.

With all this new information, how long do we have to relinquish what is most natural in us to be a grown up? What is this insatiable need to freeze our inborn impulses of sensation in order to appear smart? What prevents us from total freedom of expression as our inalienable birthright? One day soon, we will look back to this time, and wonder how we could have held our body in such static postures and limiting movement rigid movement styles that allow so little creative freedom to be expressed.

This second Catalyst introduces a fluid body language that functions according to the laws of the unified field. Exploring the simple dignities of sitting, standing and walking with the uplifting power of gravity offers flexible support and natural grace to ride the waves of unpredictable change.

Becoming universal humans fluid bodies will be essential in this radically new environment. Nature always reinvents old bodies for a new consciousness.

.-Barbara Marx Hubbard

Remaining separate from an expanded consciousness rich in transformative power, the body's juices dry up from lack of novel behavior. Unconsciously sustaining protective/defensive stances that resist change, it isn't surprising that the many diseases plaguing us today are related to circulatory problems. Believing the body is solid and separate, hardening of the arteries, arteriosclerosis, embolism, impaired bowel function and lymphatic drainage reflect the degeneration of fluid flow. Reclaiming a fluidity of being, responsiveness to our feelings and the changing condition of our lives would be a given.

Fish Out of Water

My fascination with fluid movement happened in my teens. One night, I had the most remarkable dream of being a fish swimming through the water. While taking a flying leap into the air, I smelled something absolutely delicious. Nothing was going to stop me from moving towards this intoxicating smell. I was so intent on my task that I grew tiny arms and crawled up on dry land. On awakening, my spine was undulating with a sensuous grace I had never known before.

I later mused that the ability to mutate into a different species is still encoded in my genes. With increasing excitement, I went to the local pool to explore my fluid origins. While aimlessly floating under the water for as long as my breath would last, wiggling waves of sensation pulsed through my tailbone. As I surrendered to my fish-like nature, my body merged with the water as one flowing continuum. When stepping out of the pool, a weightless buoyancy of joyous sensation filled my body. Moving with an incredible lightness of being, I glided effortlessly across the pavement like a fish out of water.

As I entered the kitchen with my newfound fluidity, my mother widened her eyes and spoke to me with a righteous tone, "Young lady, stop acting like a loose woman and straighten up right now!" Instantly, I returned to my 'all-too-solid' flesh. Once again I was struck by the incongruence that existed between my inner and outer world. I quickly realized that moving with more fluidity was perceived as phony, exhibitionist behavior or a sexual signal that would get me into a lot of trouble. All the different exercise forms I explored did nothing to support my fluid discoveries. They all utilized mechanical movement with no feeling flow behind the action.

We are often educated out of rather than into an awareness of the body. The active wriggling of a child's body is urged to "sit still," to restrain its natural impetus towards movement and exploration.

-Jean Houston
The Possible Human

Being fluid and adaptable to change reflects the free-spirited body language we were given at birth. Regardless of age or physical condition, we can reclaim the body's ingenious inventiveness to grow and change with remarkable flexibility.

Tai Chi in Street Clothes

When introduced to the Chinese system of Tai Chi Ch uan, an ancient movement meditation that embodied the natural ebb and flow of nature's elements, I had permission to move with the lightness of the wind, the strength of the mountain, and the fiery energy of a dragon. It was disquieting to me that all this graceful movement dissolved as soon as the class was over. Even the teacher returned to her stiffly held gait. It was time to demystify Tai Chi by exploring its principles in my daily actions.

A wild stallion galloping over the hills, a kitten leaping in the fallen leaves, a bird gliding through the air, and a child leaping for joy, are pure reflections of a fluidity of being.

-Wowza

While studying with Mary Whitehouse, the grand dame of creative movement, I noticed how natural it was to stretch our bodies while chatting together before class. With no self-consciousness, warming up our bodies while talking always injected more high-spirited merriment into our conversations. When talking with friends outside of class, all that playful expression disappeared into the gray zone of colorless behavior. Moving with fluid flexibility simply wasn't a cool thing to do when growing up. The body was more of a decorated or camouflaged vehicle to transport you from one place to the other.

Bushy Tail

Being trained from an early age to "sit still and stop wiggling," I soon grew weary of holding static postures in my study of Yoga. During one of my practice sessions, I spontaneously breathed like a wild creature desperately trying to wiggle free of this imposed containment. While pulsing the edges of the posture, a wiggling dance of pulsation came alive in my tailbone. I imagined these pulsations of energy as the tails of different creatures. With a growing repertoire of 'bushy tails,' I took delight in writhing my torso like a boa constrictor, moving my arms like the tentacles of an octopus and audibly breathing like a hippo!

The tail of a creature tells the universal story of age-old communication with the world at large.

-Brian James

While exploring my creature nature, 'original postures' were created that seemed appropriate to my body's needs in the moment. These postures did not remain silent. With no deliberation from the rational mind, a tonal language of feeling guided me in loosening up tight hinges and joints and pulsed rhythmical energy into my organs. As my trust was strengthened in the free-flowing nature of my body's wisdom, my stretching abilities were increased way beyond what I had ever thought possible. Exploring a broad range of creativity shed more light on the static posturing I assumed on a daily basis – the casual slump, a tilted ribcage, the pelvic rotation and characteristic facial expression. I called my static posturing a 'Habit Yoga. When catching myself stuck in a static posture, I hummed and wiggled my bushy tail with feeling. In an instant my body came fluidly alive with unlimited possibility.

Throughout this manual, wiggling your 'bushy tail' is the magical switch that ignites the dynamics of emotional energy to flow through your spine

Fluid Lifestyle

Being dedicated to the support of a fluid lifestyle, I got rid of my furniture in my living room. Physio Balls are now scattered throughout the space. While working at the computer, sitting on a ball rather than a hard chair helps me to remain energized and relaxed at the same time. It's impossible to slump on a ball - I would fall over! Anytime I'm a little fatigued, I vigorously bounce on the ball while breathing and humming with feeling. Bending over the ball offers my tired brain a vigorous supply of blood that instantly refreshes my spirits.

Though we appear to be solid, we are in fact, liquid bodies, similar in a way to gelatin, which also seems to be solid but is in fact largely water, 'gelled' by the presence of an organic material.

-Daniel Hillel
Out of the Earth

When friends visit, sitting on a ball rather than overstuffed furniture never fails to interject more spontaneous, playful energy into the conversation. Most of my therapeutic sessions are conducted on the ball. As clients shift into more flexible possibilities, existing trauma often shifts into more healthy perspectives. Everyday I give myself a self-massage on a variety of balls. Tennis balls are used to 'clean the bones' of tight muscular attachments that sustain stiffness in joins and hinges. Wiggling and writhing on medium beach balls is a simple, relaxing way to sustain a flexible spine.

Wave Phenomenon

That which fills all of nature I regard as my true body, And that which directs the universe, I also see as my own nature.

-Chang-Tzu

The waves of change are taking root and spreading far and wide. The new physics is asserting that the body is a self-renewing, self-organizing and a self-creating living system in which every part of the organism shares the same blueprint of the future whole. A fluid intelligence is what will ultimately help us thrive in a rapidly changing world. This idea was substantiated when researchers at the University of California at Irvine documented that moving the body while brainstorming releases stress and enhances productivity.

Absorbing information while moving stimulates more creative, right-brained thinking and enlivens the flow of pure creative spontaneity.

Electrical monitors from computer technology are able to chart how energy flows through the body. When projecting a serious mental tone that reflects a rigid body language, the wave motions on the electrical monitors straighten out. When people are in a loving, joyous state, their gestures naturally become more curved. As a result, the screen comes alive with flowing wave motions. When speaking from the mental mind, people are less 'moved' by what is being communicated. Fluid, curving gestures naturally touch the feeling heart of the listener.

The message of God can be felt in the movement of water. The fluids in our cells are the liquid presence of our spiritual birthright. The ocean, our blood are the liquids inside our planet. Amniotic and spinal fluid are all the same.

-Emilie Conrad
Creator of Continuum

NASA has reported that astronauts have greater retention of technical material when doing 'jumping jacks.' 'Moving the body to move the mind' is the motto of the Danish hearing aid company, Oticon. This company developed the world's first digital hearing aid. One major reason they have been so successful is that everyone works at a 'mobile' workstation so that employees 'work in motion.' As its leader, Lars Kolind says, "It's an environment that maximizes walking, talking and acting."

Several of the Waldorf Schools in Marin, California have exchanged hard, inflexible chairs for Physio Balls. At first, teachers feared that introducing the ball will create chaos and they would lose control of the class. After the flurry of excitement, they were amazed that children settled down and were more attentive and more open to comprehend and retain information. And more than that, the children were happier being in school!

Another one of my teachers who is doing so much to further the exploration of fluid movement is Emily Conrad, the creator of Continuum. She first developed her fluid concepts while working with spinal cord injuries. In her class, I witnessed a woman who had been paralyzed for sixteen years grow new quadriceps where there were none. Through the exploration of micro-movements [small cellular undulations] this woman's body reflected the refinement of fluid movement that would make a dancer jealous. Her evolving body of work beautifully demonstrates that the liquidity of our being is the encompassing atmosphere we call love.

Here am I, my body is made of elements that once were stardust, drawn from the far corners of the universe to flesh out, the pattern that is uniquely me, my soul.

-Danah Zohar
The Quantum Self

A new body language is now required that possesses the sensibilities of a universal field of energy. With a fluidity of being, the vast intelligence and passionate power that exists in every cell of our body can more fully been drawn out.

Mystical Scientists

One person making changes in behavior is hard, but a small group dedicated to this one purpose anything becomes possible. While writing this manual, I gathered a group of my clients to explore modeling a fluidity of being in the public arena. We called ourselves 'mystical scientists' conducting research about how a new quantum body language can be implemented in daily life. Our intent was not to be disruptive of anyone's space, only to be mindful and flexible of the changes that were occurring.

Out in public, we blended with the crowd by amplifying the familiar posture of our social role. We also mulled about mirroring the posture and attitudes of people in our midst. Like a butterfly rising out of its chrysalis, we periodically shifted into a fluidity of being. Each time a conscious choice was made to shift, an altered state of awareness occurred that felt so juicy and alive. Shapeshifting in and out of the social role and consciously entering a unifying reality was a genuine revelation for everyone concerned. After a while, we noticed that the people who surrounded us appeared to loosen up and express themselves in more natural ways. If someone was curious what we were up to, 'Logic Statements' were offered. I would often say, "Our group is exploring a fluid body language that releases stress and increases vitality." It was such a pleasure to watch people's eyes widen and become more interested in how to 'walk the talk.'

It seems preposterous to me now, but in the 1960s, we wore panty girdles so that nothing would jiggle and our clothes would glide smoothly over hips.

-Mirka Knaster

Functioning according to the laws of the unified field enhances your ability to pick up feeling sensations of intelligence more quickly. This increased awareness can unleash profound, life-altering results that can turn any intention into reality.

Activations

As a movement analyst, I counted almost 200 moves performed by toddlers in a given day. However, that shrinks to a paltry six or seven performed by adults in western culture.

-Peg Jordan
Instinctual Fitness

In the movie *Abyss*, an unknown species was discovered living in the depths of the ocean. They possessed a 'formless form' held together with a luminous layer of permeable skin. With this adaptable shape, they were able to mirror and play with the physical behavior, facial expression and intelligence of anything they became fascinated with. From a quantum perspective, the body is a formless form that has the same permeability as a cloud taking varied shapes in the sky.

Just as a surfer rides the waves, in invite you to take the opportunity to ride the waveforms of your creative potential that are moving you into a very different future. The *Activations* that follow bring the simple dignities of sitting, standing and walking into the fluid support of gravity. Pioneering more healthy, unified ways of being is setting in motion a more coherent connection with a fluid world dancing in harmony with all this is.

Being educated how not to move, how not to trust the fluid flow of our body. *Dance Stance* unearths static stances into an 'inner dance' of pure aliveness.

The sea is never still because neither are the moon, the sun, or the winds. They move and the ocean resxponds. Never forget there is mystery to be found in the water, winds, and waves.

-Glen Hening

Dance Stance

Taught to stand up straight, stop the wiggling and behave, we try to comply by stiffening our joints, tensing our shoulders, tucking in the belly and pulling in our tailbone. Even the idea of holding such an unnatural posture makes most of us slump down in resistance or contract in defiance. Static posturing is designed to disguise the feeling heart. Being mentally contracted, breathing is curtailed and stress builds with an alarming rate. Regaining a fluid spine not only helps you remain youthful at any age, it is what supports genuine feelings to be communicated with full body delivery. It is an adaptable spine that can authentically reflect the range of emotional energy with fluid dexterity.

One can perceive the body as a virtual-reality suit that we put on to have a certain kind of experience. Yet, over time, we can become entranced that this body suit is reality itself.

-Ric Weinman
Breaking the Illusion-

When static patterns of behavior become repetitive, the connective tissue that holds the structure together becomes tough and unyielding. For instance, while standing, notice areas in your posture that grip, stiffen, tighten, twist, rotate, squeeze and compress your energy. By physically amplifying these patterns, even for a few seconds, there is choice to continue or discontinue the pattern. The mere act of observation - putting attention on your style of standing brings more healthy movement options into play.

Liquid Sphere: Once you have a 'felt-sense' of your typical stance, visualize yourself standing in a watery, womb-like sphere in which you have no trouble breathing. As a liquid medium, imagine your spine is seaweed moving with the currents of the water. This fluid image releases muscle dominant, straight-lined control that sustains rigidity of posture. Encourage this liquid feeling of motion in your spine by creating delicate figure-eight motions that crisscross up and down your spinal column. As this lateral awareness comes more vividly alive, your fluid stance is more like a plant wafting in a soft breeze rather than a solid column that is out of balance with gravity.

Coming into resonance with the field of gravity is a necessary step in igniting a quantum body language.

We are endowed at birth with dancing bodies that are perfectly designed to serve us with ease and enjoyment through a long, active and pain-free lifetime.

-Vance Bonner

Support of Gravity: When we defy gravity's laws of intrinsic balance, the weight of this power tends to pull our structure downward into inertia. When attuned to its power, gravity becomes the very root of lightness, designed to simultaneously uplift and ground our energy at the same time. Standing with the full support of this magnetic current of bipolar harmony is like being 'kissed' by heaven and Earth.

To feel gravity's support, put one hand on your heart and one hand on your belly. Without moving your torso, see if you can see your feet. If you can't, your torso is pulled back of the midline. Play with shifting your torso slightly forward to see your feet. Once you get a glimpse of your toes, slowly bring your head up, and notice how your pelvis, heart and head come into natural alignment. Aligning with gravity integrates and coordinates all disjointed parts into integrative harmony – no part hangs back or moves at odds with the rest.

Flexible Knees: The price we pay for locking knees is chronic back pain and increased stiffness in the joints. There is no sport that works without flexible knee action. Locking the knees places most of the weight back on your heals, forcing the entire body out of the flow of gravity. Becoming flexible is being adaptable to change. To regain this intrinsic flexibility, create a subtle bobbling motion while bouncing an invisible ball with your hand. Sense the coordination between your hands and knee action. Rest your arms at your sides while slowing the bobbing action down to match the inhalation and exhalation of your breath. Sense this subtle sinking and rising action in your knees. Imagine bouncing a ball with locked knees and watch how your body stiffens up. Slowing down and speeding up the pulsations in your knees relaxes and energizes you at the same time.

Embarking into this fluid state of embodiment can be so internalized that no one in your midst would know what you're up to. All they would see is someone radiating authentic dancing aliveness.

Spiral Movement

In all early languages, the word for spiral and spirit are the same. In other words, spiritual energy is spiraling energy. The spiral is the natural, moving form of growth found in the natural world. As a spherical vortex, spiraling through its own center, curving motions combines the inward and outward directions of fluid movement. Creating more mobile diversity in a static posture circulates more energy and releases more intuitive intelligence into your awareness. When your cellular structure reproduces itself during the next seven years, the memory of negative influences that retard the health of cellular growth, are washed clean. This momentous concept is another secret how to sustain ageless vitality.

Chronic solidarity in the body is the source of 'repetitive' strain injuries. A 'fluidity of being' helps shift muscular density into fluid, inner strength.

Spiraling Ankles: The essence of fluid standing is remaining loose and flexible in your ankles. Imagine a clock placed laterally on the floor surrounding your feet. With soft knees and an erect spine, rock your torso around the clock by rotating your ankles. Feel this motion create different pressures through your feet. By gently and slowly rocking side-to-side, the hemispheres of your brain come more into balance. Rocking slightly forward generates more intimacy and rapport in your communication. Rocking slightly back offers more time to deliberate and feel into your condition. Activating spiraling movement in specific parts of the body innovates new neural pathways while generating more energy to flow. For instance, create tiny spiraling motions in your shoulder or in your wrists and notice how light and aerated you feel.

Don't confuse nervous fidgeting with a fluidity of being. Fidgeting, squirming and twitching habits are the body's attempt to deal with a buildup of energy. Being forced to sit on hard chairs with little movement opportunities, children know what to do when school is over – they run to the door screaming their heads off! This action is a safety valve that releases tension due to forced stillness.

What if muscles were treated like they were little oceans, ebbing and flowing, or like fine hair, hanging and waving.

-Patricia Kramer

Emotionally based defiance of gravity leaves tracks of stress and tension in the body,.

-Mary Bond

Enjoy the lightness and agelessness that exists in your body. Play with your potential for moving in a more fluid way.

-Milton Trager

Fluid Sitting

Fluid sitting is not becoming limp and floppy in your chair. It is a dance of balancing motions that are constantly aligning you with gravity's buoyant support. Balancing with subtle light-filled currents of sensation continuously circulates energy through every cell of the body. Take a moment now and notice how your body is forming itself into the chair you're sitting on. Chances are your head is tilted forward or at an angle or your chin is pulled downward into your neck. If you find this is so, it might be disconcerting to know that your head weighs as much as a bowling ball.

Holding your head in any contrived position is what can give you a pain in the neck. Slumping in a chair in a collapsed posture radically curtails breathing. Dropping the head to read creates double chins, tension in the shoulders and intensifies lower back pain. As tension builds in the neck area, eventually the whole body has to turn to look at something. Hyper extending the spine or collapsing the spine reflects two sides of the same coin. Becoming familiar with rigid and fluid ways of sitting, more creative possibilities for change can occur. In other words, you are free to orchestrate a greater variety of expression. that suits your intention.

Amoeba: Our first sensory experience as a fetus in the womb is floating in amniotic fluid. The currents of wave patterns contain us in a weightless world of effortless ease. Recreate this state when sitting in a bath or, better yet, a hot tub. Become an amoeba encapsulated in a luminous bag of skin. As you inhale, notice how effortlessly your arms and hands float to the surface of the water, and as you exhale, notice how they sink towards the bottom.

Turn your hard chair into a pool of flowing, bubbling water.

-Dan Larson

Fluffy Butt: Imagine the seat of your chair is a bubbling spring drawing up vital energy through the core of your being. Locate the big sitting bones, those bony protrusions extending out in the middle of your butt. Perceive them as golden orbs filled with radiant energy. Massage these golden orbs by swiveling around one and then the other with spiraling figure-eight motions. Imagine a clock is drawn on the seat of your chair. Rock around the clock! Zigzag to different times on the clock.

Stooping down in stiff postures is not an inevitable part of aging. It is being shaped by a social role that has developed a stooped, protective stance to life.

While balancing on your sitting bones, notice how your spinal column floats like a buoy on a lake. To test this out, lean back into your chair. You may notice how your tailbone turns under, your back rounds forward and your belly distends. When this posture becomes a habit, your primal power is depressed. With this much pressure placed on your abdomen, potbellies and weighty thighs become the norm. To help counteract this tendency, I recommend using a 'wedge,' anything that lifts your tailbone at a slightly higher angle than your knees.

Loose head: God forbid we should lose our head! When muscular tension is released, your head naturally vibrates with every motion you make. In our headstrong culture, the head is chronically pushed forward, which sustains enormous tension, especially in the eyes. While balancing on your sitting bones imagine a balmy breeze rocking your spinal column. In this fluid sphere of awareness, imagine your eyes are like bubbles in a level. In order to draw a chronically tilted head back on its axis, imagine a face appearing on the back of your head.

Think of rivers and lakes as arteries and blood vessels and rain as the fertilizing downpour of feelings and emotions.

-Ralph Metzner
Green Psychology

Feel where the nose would be in the back of your head, and sniff a beautiful fragrance! Feel where your lips would be and pucker them up to give someone a kiss! Add eyes to the back of your head, and see with renewed insight. Create a subtle wiggle in your tailbone, which brings your torso and head into a fluid dance of deepened support.

There is a vital energy hidden in tense mannerisms. If you fidget with your hands, give them permission to fidget more! When nervous energy is physically intensified in motion, more times than not, this anxious condition relaxes its hold.

Wave movements calm the unconscious as the rocking of the cradle soothes an infant. To lose these primal wave and serpentine movements is to become an alien in one's own body.

-Jalaja Bonheim
The Serpent and the Wave

At this stage of the process, resistance is often felt when opening up defined boundaries believed to protect you from an unknown world. Physical suffering is a great motivator. Moving out of pain may be the first step in looking for alternative ways of being. Letting go of solid, muscular density as a mark of strength can be very intimating.

A shift in consciousness is needed. The question is, where do we end and the rest of the world begins. I thank Tai Chi for giving me a new view of strength that flows from a universal force. I'll never forget a master of this discipline push Mr. America off balance with his little finger. And, I might add, he was eight nine years old. In other words, his strength was as far reaching as the universe.

Walk Primal

Preoccupied with our thoughts, we rarely notice how we move. Whenever you walk with the pure pleasure of your being, you stop comparing yourself with others. The real question is not about, "How good am I performing?" The real question is "How does my movement feel? How can I delight in the perfection of the moment? Take time out to simply focus on the process of your walking style. Let go of the need to control your movements. The whole purpose of expanding awareness is accessing the freedom to explore territory that lies outside your ordinary range of perception. Unless you can recognize how you clench your jaw or tighten your back as you walk, you have no other choice to change your behavior. Refining moment to moment awareness builds a strong bridge that moves you from rigidity to fluidity.

Cultivate the root. The leaves and branches will take care of themselves.

-Confucius

While accomplishing the many activities of daily life, our feet take thousands of steps a day. Walking is interwoven with every aspect of daily living. Invite fluidity into your walk each day. Just as an artist uses a variety of color and a musician uses scales to remain limber, walking in fluid motion support a balanced, flexible, adaptable presence that is motivated by feeling feedback motivated from within our heart.

Nothing is more exciting than knowing that our bodies and our feelings are a clear, open pathway toward our destines.

-Christane Northrup

When beginning this exploration, play with rocking your feet forward and back from your ankles. Even if you think you have flat feet, the bones curve in a wave. To feel the wave motion in your feet more clearly, role through your heal, ball and toe with enhanced articulation. Balancing between the ball and the heel distributes the weight of your body equally over your two feet. The habit of using a big stride curtails this liquid motion.

With your feet supporting your torso and head, 'glide' across the ground with wavy, fluid feet! Experiencing this uplifting, buoyant lightness transforms the ground into an 'aerated cushion' rather than a hard, unyielding surface. A shorter stride supports your pelvis, torso and head to balance over your feet. Walking with the image of roller wheels in your lower legs can help to loosen tight ankles. While gliding across the ground with wavy feet, expand your peripheral vision and notice how accessing this broader vision seems to lift your head into balancing proximity with the horizon. The habit of angling the head forward is a good indication that your thinking mind is in control. Open attention to the landscape helps you remain in the present moment.

Turn walking into an artful adventure. Activating your 'bushy tail' can bring a whole range of dynamic energy into your walk.

Pick three animals that appeal to you. Imagine one of these creature's tails are pulsing with aliveness in your tailbone. Notice how this image instantly affects your walking style. Once you feel the energy of one creature's tail, feel the affects of another crea-

Humanity's survival depends on all of our willingness to comprehend feelingly the fluid, adaptable way nature works.

-Buckminster Fuller

ture's tail. More specifically, imagine what transpires when embodying a rattlesnake's tail and then shifting into the frisky tail of a bunny! This kind of delightful play supports energetic diversity to flow through your spinal column.

Our walk through life is contacting that 'certain something,' a feeling of unity with all things and all persons.

-Janet Person

Being rhythmical creatures, our very spirit comes alive when moving in rhythm with a rhythmical world. For instance, explore speeding up and slowing down your steps while sustaining your link with the support of gravity. A buoyant rhythm creates lighter than air impulses of sensation. By adding sharply defined steps, high-voltage rhythms stimulate your walk with the potency of inner power.

These Activations are designed to help us all to discover the joy of living in our body. A baby is not born awkward. Clumsy motions often mask the pain of not feeling safe and express one's feeling heart in an unknown world.

Mirroring the Soul

There are billions of people in this world and not one is identical in looks and in action. The style of the times, however, is to typecast us into stereotype roles, which literally obliterates the uniqueness of our being. The social role is like a plant that lives in an enclosed container and doesn't get enough water and sunlight. When receiving endless negative feedback that we are somewhat deficient as children, the habit of moving awkwardly with little self-confidence takes its toll. Being separated from the fluid, moving source of life, conflicting forces and emotional upheavals can rule our life.

While standing before the mirror in your familiar way, notice in what ways you are hesitant in really seeing this person that is looking back at you in the mirror. Ironically, the desire to be really seen is what is most longed for, and yet what we most avoid. Being visible also means to be vulnerable and thus, open to rejection. If any of this is true for you, call on the *Sacred Actor.*

Developing the physiology of different creatures enables you to respond in new ways, and expand your physical and emotional world.

-Moni Yakim
Creating a Character

Whatever negative thoughts emerge amplify them as a fun part to play! In this instant, you are no longer victimized my your mental mind. As the star of your drama, you are more capable of being seen by your judging mental mind without being intimidated. Even through visualization, daring to imagine yourself standing before the whole world with fluid openness can cause dramatic changes in energy to occur in your body.

As you pick up ways you have learned to hide who you really are, notice all the still places that have developed in an attempt to keep you safe. Realize that your disapproval of yourself can become a painful belief that is the source of physical aches and pains. Take note where you personal boundaries have become more rigidly defended. Rigid boundaries can be seen as a masked that shields the entire body from the rest of the world. Whatever you discover, bless your growing awareness and acceptance for what is true in this moment.

I want to know if you can walk in grace and power even when it's not a pretty day.

Indian Elder

Experiencing the body as a liquid presence any unpredictable turbulence that arises is simply felt as another wave of feeling in the ocean in which all of life swims together. How would you stand before this mirror is you were to truly claim your inner power? Imagining the interior of your body as an open spacious field filled with vast creative potential in constant motion. Expand peripheral vision and see the space you are in as your extended body. Heightened inner and outer vision allows you to feel roomier and more extended spatially at the same time.

Fundamental change entails embracing newness as a source of revelation. Expressive arts practice before the mirror, can make your play on Earth more fun, exciting and meaningful. It's all about not settling for routine. As a *Sacred Actor*, you are a fish in an ocean recognizing the water you swim in. Gazing into the mirror place your mask on your face and invoke your *Primal Name*. This name represents what is new and different in you. Transcending any concepts you hold of yourself, dance your stance with the intention of encoding this magical name with the fluid flexibility.

In this state of grace, your false identities will fall away, and there will remain an identity more flexible and much more functional than any you now embrace.

-Key Cary
The Starseed Transmissions-

Soften your knees and spiral your ankles while imagining a liquid sphere of light streaming into this chosen name. Draw out waves of tone by extending the vowels in the word with your voice. Using your arms, make the letters as broad and big as possible. Imagine a colored pin attached in succession to various parts of your body, such as the shoulder blade, the elbow, or the nose. Use these body parts as the starting point to draw out the letters of your word. Freely write this name in the space around you with flourishing movements. Imagine the fluid energy of this name setting off a series of wave motions that radiate throughout the entire universe.

The creative intention is a yearning that expresses itself in energy, fluid movement and rhythmical motion. The activity of creation, its expression, is a loving assertion of life.

-Janet Zuckerman

In this performing arts process, you are coming forward to demonstrate the dance of fluid possibility that can send rippling waves of connectedness into the mainstream of humanity.

As the spotlight casts a luminous glow around your body, close your eyes. Imagine you are surrounded by a great sea of water. With relaxed ease, listen to the silence just before a wave breaks. Focus on the sound of a wave breaking and flowing across your body. Open to a source of wonder in which you become this wave of waves that echo its sound across thousands of miles of open ocean. In this timeless moment, open your eyes, witness humanity sitting before you as the sub-personalities of your infinite identity. Layers of stress and long-standing inertia rule their lives.

Just as water dances in the stream, leaves shimmer in the trees and a kitten leaps in the air, regenerating fluid aliveness is awakening the dance of life forever flowing throughout all existence. With your soul voice whisper this statement: "Here in this body are the sacred rivers; here are the sun and the moon, the wind, water and waves of ever changing movement. "

Becoming one with the dance of life is being in rhythm with the world. Slowly begin to sway as rippled clouds floating in the sky. Sense the audience becoming mesmerized by this simple motion. Liquefy your gestures with languid swimming strokes flowing in the air. Embellish your dance with different rhythmic measures, the epitome of bodily freedom. Add drama to you dance by imagining the 'fountain of youth' is streaming up your spine. and gushing luminous light up through the top of your head. With tumultuous waves of life-throbbing energy shimmering around your body, feel your true nature aglow with divine radiance.

Our bodies move more like a river, or a cat, or tall grass in the breeze instead of like pistons and cogged wheels.

-Joseph Heller
Bodywise

In the perfect naturalness of it all, you are no longer dancing, you are the dance. As a master surfer surfing the quantum waves in a fluid sea of joy, wonder, and delight, visualize all of humankind shedding the garments of their mechanized, predicable body language. Witness people everywhere regaining the fluid flexibility to move into the uncharted waters with emotional intelligence guiding their way.

As the dualistic code of degeneration dissolves into the code of regeneration, witness us all joining together to become a global community of souls setting about to purify the sacred waters of life.

Water - blood, lymph, mucous, sweat, tears, inner oceans tugged by the moon, tides within and tides without. Streaming fluids floating our cells, washing and nourishing through endless riverways of gut and vein and capillary. You are that. I am that.

-Roberts and Amidon

Breath Olympics
Champions of Life Force

A wind sweeps my life energies into a harvest, a quantum wave.
I ride this momentum beyond what I can know.
-Carolyn Mary Kleefeld
The Alchemy of Possibility

As children, we were all champions of life force. We feasted on breath, gorging ourselves on this windy air as a steady diet. Aerobic diversity in breathing capacity inspired us to thrive in the joy of discovery as a gift of life itself. What happened to dampen such a wondrous gift? Breathing with the emotional dynamics of a child has had little support in our culture. All these serious breathing exercises we have been told to do rarely inspire us to breathe with full-blooded feeling. Horror movies use audible breathing to scare us out of our wits. Making any sound with our breath is mostly relegated to the bedroom, if we're lucky! How strange, in many circles of our culture, sighing with pleasure is still considered to be a demonstration of bad manners.

This third Catalyst honors your body as the playing field in which to explore the gymnastics of breathing with a vast variety of aerobic rhythms. Learning to whisper/breathe with the *Eight Primal Energies,* invigorates the breath of life as the prime mover of all inspired action.

Oxygen Starvation

Dr. Otto Wareberg, a Nobel Prize Laureate, has said that all degenerative diseases and debilitating effects of aging are caused by oxygen starvation. Oxygen starvation! Pathogenic viruses, bacteria and cancer grow fast and remain strong in a low oxygen environment. Muscular tension restricts the free circulation of oxygen. As tissues grow more rigid, the pumping action is diminished and carbon dioxide builds in the bloodstream. All this adrenaline flooding the system keeps the body in a state of constant stimulation, which is the cause of so many health problems.

The adrenal glands, thinking the system is under attack, work overtime and become exhausted. With barely enough life force to meet the demands of a fast paced lifestyle, the body becomes the breeding ground for the common cold. Heart disease is rampant, high blood pressure is epidemic and autoimmune diseases are on the rise. Thus begins a vicious cycle of physical and mental decline. The habit of holding the breath was instilled in us at birth. Most hospitals still conduct unnatural birth practices that sever the umbilical cord before the baby has discovered its natural breathing rhythm.

Your next breath will contain more than 400,000 of the argon atoms that Ghandi breathed in his long life. Argon atoms are here from the conversations at the Last Supper, from the arguments of diplomats at Yalta, and from the recitations of the classic poets.

-Harlow Shapley
Beyond the Observatory

Imagine having lived nine months in a fluid world where all needs are provided and be met in this world with a slap on the behind. Feeling the pain, the baby gasps for air in fear of its imminent death. A gasping breath pattern that reflects fearful insecurity is often the result of such harsh treatment.

Most of the breathing techniques we learned as children come out of a quasi-military context. How many times have we heard teachers exclaim, "Suck in the gut, shoulders back, stomach flat, and BREATHE!" The strain of effortful breathing divorced from our feeling nature has created a world of shallow breathers. Cut off from gut-level feelings and living a stressful lifestyle, Asthma is growing at an alarming rate. A gasping breathing pattern creates muscular tension that tightens its grip on the walls of the chest. Adrenaline that is intended for emergency conditions is released.

Cancer is the result of oxygen deprivation in the cellular structure. Vital breathing habits unites the body to the emotions and the spirit to them both.

-Szent-Gyorgi

Addiction means a desire that can never be fully satisfied. I personally feel that cigarette addiction is an unconscious desire to get more breath. When drawing in smoke, there is a rush of pure air that charges the body with energy for one brief moment, and at the same time, diminishes oxygen by loading the lungs with toxins. When oxygen levels remain in a low state, depression or hypertension grows strong. Without sufficient oxygen charging the system, life itself becomes shallow, boring and flat. Is it any wonder we crave substances to make up for the deficit. When free-spirited breathing is regained, addictive tendencies often fade because what is being craved is being satisfied.

Suppression of emotional energy is what most cancer patients have in common. Conscious expression of invigorating life force charges the immune system.

Fun Breathing

One day, when watching my twin boys playing with their toy airplanes, they audibly breathed with flowing gestures that were in congruent harmony with the action. Seeing what fun they were having, I picked up one of the planes. Giving my breath permission to take me on adventures supreme, a spontaneous life force swung into action. In seconds, the invisible power of breathing expression guided my every move with brilliant execution. With a daredevil attitude, I became a fighter plane shooting bullets, *Pppppp! Pooop! Pow!* And in another moment, I gasped for breath, having escaped being blown to bits. The simple pleasure of playing with the infinite diversity of breathing aerobics is just pure fun.

Almost no one dreamed that the quiet rise in carbon dioxide could eventually induce a kind of violence that rivals even nuclear war.

-Ed Ayres,

While teaching a creative movement class that evening, I expressed that life force integrates the physical, emotional, and spiritual dimensions of our body and all of life into wholeness. To demonstrate, I encouraged everyone to fly an imaginary airplane while breathing with full sound effects. Instantly, gestures joined with the rhythmical expressions of their breath. Needless to say, a dazzling display of life force burst into bloom. When I asked everyone to lock their knees, this entire playful activity came to a jarring halt. Without the body's fluid support, the process of breathing is instantly curtailed. Shallow breathing turns any activity into a shallow experience.

You sense yourself closer to the living primal matter underlying all phenomena when you portray a child breathing like the wind.

-Donna Lions

A shift in breathing rhythm can wake you up as if you had two cups of coffee. Imagine breathing in peace and calm in order to get a good night sleep. Free-spirited breathing can move you into a euphoric state any time you please. You are never more than a breath away from the play of it all.

Physical Density

Billions of dollars are spent on methods of losing weight or gaining weight. Starving ourselves with cardboard food is a sad plight. What is worse, most dieting makes us feel edgy, tired and unhappy. The rub is that 98 percent of the people who lose weight gain it back. The theme running through this manual is that we possess a natural genius, which balances our weight in tune with our specific body type. Due to early trauma and unnatural conditioning, this extraordinary inner wisdom lies buried under layers of physical density.

If a sponge is shrunken and dry, it is not capable of absorbing much liquid. Tightly bound muscles can neither absorb nor distribute in creating oxygen.

-James Kepner

Several years ago, a doctor helped me set up a class for a group women who struggled with losing weight. These women taught me a great deal. While spending time embodying these women's body language, my back arched, my belly distended, and my jaw pulled inward, giving me the appearance of a double chin. Feeling physically heavy, I knew if I maintained this posture, I would start to gain weight.

The image of a bottle filled with a lifetime of unexpressed emotions and impulses came to mind. The dense holding patterns in the posture acted as the stopper on the bottle. When weight expands from the buildup of emotional energy, there is an unconscious need to inflate and blow-up as big as a house - or burst! When the primal power of emotional energy is continuously repressed, circulation of oxygen radically diminishes. This means there is not sufficient internal movement to keep weight in balance.

Few people stop to consider the fact that smoking is dependent on the breath for its effects. One does not enjoy the physiological lifts from a cigarette if it is put in your ear, between your toes or just held in your mouth!

-Philip Smith
Total Breathing

From this insight, I coached these women to amplify their weighty posture - the force that weighs them down. As they waddled around the room, I asked them to consider what their weight was protecting. Most of these women agreed it was the pain of unwanted feelings. Whatever we resist, persists. All the padding in the world does not make unwanted feelings go away. They just fester and build in size in the underbelly of the body.. Blocking the urge to eat intensifies the urge to eat. What we call an urge is an emotion urging us to come alive to our authentic feelings. Rather than being victimized by their weight, I taught these women to move with fluid dexterity while audibly breathing and humming with different emotive energies. Igniting the breath from the floor of their pelvis while moving their body in undulating motions, created an ecstatic high that was breathtaking. This amazing mechanism takes in oxygen from the environment and expels waste gases from the body, including access weight!

No matter what the size of the body, making the play of breathing a euphoric experience renewed these women's sensual nature. Feeling great moving and breathing with profound pleasure uncovered a realization that their emotions are not the problem – it is the 'weight' of massive negative thinking that continuously stirs up stories of trauma, victimhood and denial from the past. This chronic habit of mind blots out all the passion and bliss that the life force is designed to provide. When having fun flowing with the breath as the prime mover of intelligence, the intellect lightens up, and obesity of form is no longer needed to entrap the feeling heart. When humming with feeling through the day, negative thinking habits ceases to be an issue.

I've found out how important oxygen was to burning fat and how much it affected the way I looked and felt. Yes, to that skin, those eyes, that healthy glow, are all directly connected with oxygen.

-Susan Powter
Stop the Insanity

Moving fluidly with ecstatic pleasure circulates more oxygen that burns fat and keeps it off. Breathing with playful enthusiasm ignites a chemical aphrodisiac in the brain that stimulate a 'natural high' without the use of drugs.

Peak Performance

Without sufficient oxygen, we end up by 'playing dead' as though our greatest problem were to survive until the danger - living - was over. We don't try to free ourselves from this grim trap because we aren't even aware of being prisoners.

-Therese Bertgerat
The Body has its Reasons

Most peak performers experience superhuman forces that literally propel them to victory. It has been discovered that most of these athletes have little idea of how to consciously draw on this bigger than life power when they're lagging behind in performance. When I recall the different athletes I have worked with over the years, I am always shocked to hear that the dynamics of breathing is barely mentioned in their training programs. How odd! During any sports activity, it is the animating principle of oxygenated life force that fuels quick-witted instinctive power.

The coaches I have talked with about this issue assume that proper breathing happens automatically. This is true when children are supported to sustain a fluid body language and free-spirited, emotive breathing capacity while growing up. Conditioned to hide or disguise the sensations of feeling, the habit of taking tiny gasps of air and holding it during physical activity is a chronic habit.

Most painful accidents are the result of this primary split that rages between the body and the mind. Tense muscular action is required to hold a world of unexpressed feeling from being seen, felt and heard. When dense muscular holding patterns are overlooked in an athlete, awkward mistakes in timing become commonplace. Knowing how to tap into the reservoir of primal energy via breath play can catapult us all into victorious fulfillment of fit health throughout life.

Breath Olympics **catapults any sport, exercise or movement activity into new Olympian possibilities by providing the instinctive edge and unlimited flows of energy that nothing else can provide.**

Bracing yourself to feel strong in action is only one of the many possible responses to take. Breathing into these tense places feels as if a weight has been lifted from your spirit. In this moment aerobic strength takes you victoriously over the finishing line.

-Ted Arnold

Easy Does It

While unleashing the rhythmical diversity of your breathing capacity, at first, you may become a little dizzy or experience some lightheadness. Hyperventilation may result from breathing so deeply that you have more oxygen in your blood than you can handle. This condition is not dangerous. It is simply an indication that your system is starving for oxygen. If this happens, shake your body like a rag doll. Pause for a few seconds and breathe with long flowing breaths into your belly. This loosening procedure uses up the excess oxygen and deep breathing centers your energy.

When asked to take a deep breath, a convulsive gasp is often heard. The shoulders are pulled up. The stomach muscles tighten and the chest is thrust out. Breathing is perceived as effortful and no fun. Being fluid in motion rather than muscle bound in tightness, a cellular world opens up that ignites the expressive vitality of breath play you had as a child. If you recall, there was no intense effort or muscular exertion while using your breath to enhance any activity. So don't try so hard!

How come I can't get my second wind? You are not using the full capacity of the miracle of energy-producing oxygen that is your breath.

-Paul Bragg

Breathing through the different emotional energies is designed to be an artful, exciting activity. Your breathing rhythms reflect every emotional feeling and every disturbance of feeling. It may be a little scary when repressed emotions and traumatic memories rise to the surface. I find it helpful to think of buried material as sediment that has gathered at the bottom of a glass.

When breathing with feeling, toxic, emotional buildup moves up and out of the system. Be thankful that this stuck energy is finding a safe way to the surface, rather than creating tension and pain in your body. If you begin to huff and puff or find it difficult to speak, slow down the rhythms of your breath and pause at the end of the exhalation. Pausing grounds your energy and brings you home to your center.

As your system gets used to taking in larger amounts of oxygen, uncomfortable symptoms will vanish. Reclaiming this natural instinctive prowess lets you know when to speed up and when to slow down in your activities. Playing with your breath in a variety of ways can change your mood because at the molecular level there is really no distinction between the mind and the body.

From lovemaking to sports, breathing with the dynamics of emotive expression stimulates the stamina and endurance to go that extra mile and reach amazing ecstatic states anytime you wish.

Unlike other nutrients that feed the body such as vitamins, minerals and proteins, oxygen cannot be stored within the body and must continually be replenished.

-Philip Smith
Total Breathing

Activations

In this day and age, endless advice is given how to breathe the 'right' way. Contrary to popular belief, there is no correct way to breathe. Below all these imposed breathing methods, the fluid pulse of life is moving so swiftly, only the dynamic, primordial power of free-spirited breathing has the instinctive genius of supporting all action. Like a talented musician who can play many different kinds of music, exploring infinite ways to breathe with emotive feeling is a practical means to restore health, vitality and mental alertness.

Breathing through the nose is relaxing, and breathing through the mouth is energizing. Breathing simultaneously through the nose AND the mouth is a 'duo' way of breathing - the ultimate relaxing/energizing activity.

Was a soul something like a breeze: something you couldn't picture or grab but could only feel like the wind off the Gulf when the day cooled down.

-Coleman Hawkins
Body and Soul

Breath Sensing: Play with expanding your awareness of your breath patterns while lying down, sitting, standing and walking. Pay attention to 'where' and 'how' you breathe instantly drops your awareness into your body. In this moment endless repetitive thoughts can take a long needed rest. Explore this now. Follow your breath as it moves through your torso. In the act of breathing, the upper part of the torso acts as a bellows mechanism, with the ribcage, lungs, and diaphragm functioning together like an air pump. Does your breath feel labored, jerky, smooth or mechanical? As you breathe, do you feel any movement occurring in your ribs, belly or shoulder area? How fast or slow do you typically breathe? Notice if it is easier for you to inhale or exhale. Which lasts longer? If you are in the habit of not fully exhaling, it effects your body's natural inclination to relax.

PC Pump: The puboccoccygeus, or PC muscle, spreads out like butterfly wings on the floor of the pelvis. You clamp down on this muscle to stop the flow of urine. The 'bushy tail' ignites the flow of feeling expression and the PC pump unleashes life force to travel through the core of your body. Drawing up the PC muscle into the center of your pelvis and releasing it in the process of breathing gives you amazing personal power and full-bodied strength. Breathing from the floor of your pelvis drops you into your body and transforms breathing into passionate involvement with life.

There is a breath that fills and a breath that empties. Between the filling and the emptying, there is a divine, indescribable moment of total fullness.

-Harlod Dull
Watsu

Yawn Sigh: Having the freedom to open the mouth and fully breathe with audible expression is often a challenging task. The habit of shallow breathing, the body's wisdom forces us to yawn in order to absorb more oxygen. Sighing releases withheld tension. Conscious yawing and sighing can thoroughly relax your whole face, neck, and throat. While focusing on the PC muscle as an elevator, ignite its power by opening your mouth like a mighty Hippo! Sigh out the air while encouraging the muscles of your face to relax.

The air, once the very medium of expressive interchange, has been displaced by the strange new medium of the written word.

-David Abram
The Spell of the Sensuous

While engaging in this highly relaxing/energizing activity, yawn once more while feeling the coolness of air moving down your throat and notice how the air warms up your throat when you sigh out. Another powerful image that opens your throat is imagining a huge ball of oxygenated helium in your mouth pressing the roof of your mouth up and sense it rolling down the throat.

With all this oxygenation, your eyes may tear and natural yawns may take over. This is a sign you need oxygen!

Pregnant Pause: Most of us never full exhale. So many toxins are stored in the body as a result of this habit. Relaxing at the end of your exhalation is a simple way to clear all this toxicity. Letting go of the compulsion to breathe is the shortest meditation in the world – a heaven-sent feeling that renews peace of mind in any chaotic moment. Resting in the quiet space between the breaths is the 'melt down' that helps you absorb more oxygen while refueling your inspiration with a zest for life.

The womb of the moment, lying within the pause between the two breaths of life and death, is a world of infinite possibility, waiting to give birth to a new cycle of humankind.

-Reshad Field

The Accordion: Vitality is a profusion of life force that synchronizes all your body's motions into coordinated expression. When the breath is the prime mover of any activity, the movements flow in harmony with the activity. Imagine a little accordion in front of you. Hold this imaginary accordion with your hands. While audibly inspiring and expiring, move your hands in tune with the activity. This means when you audibly draw in air, expand your hands outward, and when you audibly release air, draw your hands inward. Explore playing the accordion with different speeds. Long, flowing rhythms relax you and snappy percussive rhythms stimulate a 'get up and go' feeling.

Vowel Breathing: Trained to mask emotions, our facial expression loses its elasticity and animation. With wave-like currents of motion, whisper through the five vowels; a, e, i, o, u. Each vowel enlivens your face in a specific way. Merge the vowels into a preverbal language that increases the dynamics of feeling expression. An expanded breathing capacity activates each and every vowel in order to unite all languages with the flowing feelings of life force.

Opening up to novel breathing patterns can stretch, tone and firm your body from the inside. Light-filled buoyancy transpires.

Turn yourself inside out. Let yourself be guided by the the spirit of life itself, the holy breath.

-Unknown

The Holy Wind

The Holy Wind is the breath of God individualized in all that exists. This invisible wind within us and the swirling, spiraling wind that surrounds us– being one and the same– is the first language of creation. The invisible, sacred power of the holy wind envelopes us, caresses us, and fills us with constant nourishment. It is only by means of wind that we talk. Flowing from a single, inexhaustible source of aliveness, breathing as the prime mover of all inspired activity is the doorway into altered states of consciousness, super health, and remarkable feats of mind.

The spirit of life force loves adventure! With childlike innocence, become a turbulent, howling wind breathing renewed life into the inner universe of your body. Breathing with dazzling kaleidoscope of oxygen charged possibility sweeps up toxicity that may be lurking in the shadows. With growing momentum, continue to build and subside your breath power until it explodes into a blinding sand storm! With long, flowing sighs, return to peaceful repose. What remains are wildflowers blooming in your inner landscape with colorful profusion.

Enacting the Soul of Inspiration is a powerful way to know more clearly what inspires you. Breathing as the wind opens up multiple dimensions of inspiration and the adventuresome discovery of novelty.

Breathing as some awesome wild creature radically shifts shallow breathing habits into primal energy that knows no bounds.

-Jack Johnson

Magnifying the fast and slow dynamics of your breath may create some dizziness and numbness in your face and hands. Simply slow down your breath and rest in the 'pause' at the end of your exhalation. Now here is the fun part, with the Soul of Inspiration as your divine companion, blow out a hundred birthday candles while pumping your PC muscles in rhythmic measure. Breathe as a Mexican jumping bean popping open tight shoulder blades. Breathe as an exploding firecracker into your over-worked brain. With utter enjoyment, breathe as a jet propelled laser beam clearing tightness in your spine. Wiggle your bushy tail while becoming a wild monkey hungrily seeking food. Sniff the air. Pant with excitement as a delectable feast appears before your eyes. Meet up with a scary tiger and gasp with fright! Sigh with relief as this creature turns the other way.

End this wild foray its helpful to lie down and breathe with long flowing waves that generate peaceful feelings. Imagine you are resting in a dewdrop glistening on the petal of a rose. Remember, you are learning to tolerate more and more oxygen. Regardless of what you have been told, you can breathe all day long with the wildest dynamics of breath and never get dizzy again because you have rejuvenated the life force as your most precious gift of life. More vital intake of air is the key in linking the body and the mind. More dynamics of air in the system changes the chemistry of consciousness.

Breath is the holy air that holds together the entire universe and gives it life.

-Anaximenes
Sixth Century B.C.

When my children would turn into a cyclone of confusion, I would forcefully whisper, "Go to your breath!"

Physical Activity

The image of the gymnasium was for the Greeks a metaphor for creating a more fit and healthy lifestyle. To be fit with life force was the evocation of creative, emotional and spiritual muscles that could help them respond with inspiration to the needs of the moment. When daily activities are perceived as a 'gymnasium of creative possibility,' you are transforming not only the way you carry your body through space, but also your whole way of being in the world.

The wind does not have words, the unwritten pages spread themselves out in all directions.

-Tomas Transtromer

Work becomes uninspired when one goes through the motions with no life force fueling the activity. Turn mundane activities into a great fitness workout by using your breath as the prime mover of action. You may need to set time aside to choreograph the simple motions of reaching, bending, twisting and carrying a heavy object with the liveliness of audible breathing. When leaning over and picking up a heavy object, you may notice you hunch the shoulders while holding your breath. There's a tendency to hold the legs straight rather than bend the knees to absorb the extra weight. The most common habit is immobilizing the musculature in the belief that this action provides stability and strength. The more intense the action, the more expanded your muscles need to become. Why? There is more spacious room for oxygenated energy to equip you for the task.

We are beings of unimaginable breath of consciousness, propelled from the heart and mind of God.

-Deborah Koff-Chapin

The more fluid your body becomes, the more the breath can effectively travel to all your cells and rejuvenate them with high-quality oxygen. So, when turning a tight bottle cap, for heavens sake don't remain silent! Grunt out with primal power to give you that added strength. Sounding with the dynamics of any task sustains awareness of the present moment. When you are caught in rush hour traffic, or in any situation that makes you feel anxious, breathe out your frustration and anxiety. As tense patterns come into awareness, renewed inspiration is released to breathe with a fullness of feeling.

When cutting vegetables, picking up a young child, lifting a heavy bucket or cleaning the floor, you will exert far less muscular effort when rhythmical breathing becomes the prime mover of the activity.

Listen to the air. You can hear it, feel it, smell it, taste it, be it. The holy air renews all with its breath.

-Lame Deer

Walk Primal

In ancient Tibet, people had to cover great distances and rugged territory as a daily occurrence. In order to successfully accomplish this feat, they developed the ability to breathe as if the dynamics of the wind motivated their actions. This enabled them to absorb huge amounts of oxygen and gain the needed endurance and stamina to tackle the job. With the lightness of free-spirited breathing and a fluid body language they could glide over the ground and fly down the side of a mountain with weightless abandon.

We all possess this fluid, free-spirited gift of aliveness. As Black Elk so aptly said, "Grownups can learn much from children how to walk down the path of life with a carefree spirit." It all starts by honoring your breath as the spirit that is interconnected to all that is. Pause for a moment and take a meditative walk about the room. Visualize your entire body as massive lung that is continuously circulating flows of energy into all aspects of your life. While inhaling and exhaling intend that your movements we filled with a sense of lightness, ease and balance. Rather than churning out endless thoughts you've heard over and over again, flowing with the wave motions of your breath gives your mental mind something to focus upon.

When the respiratory process is freed, our breathing spontaneously responds to changes in activity, body position, temperature, noise, and, of course, stress.

-Donna Farhi
The Breathing Book

In other words, the sound of your audible breath keeps the intellect from the creation of constant chatter. While focusing attention on your mouth, imagine shaping your throat an empty vessel continuing down through the organs. While shaping vowels with your audible breath, notice how each vowel shape widens, lengthens and deepens this vessel into a spacious chamber.

For instance, when inspiring the vowel Ah, the upper ribs expand. When inspiring vowel Eah, the lower portion of your ribs expand. The vowel Eeh stretches your ribs in a lateral direction. Inspiring the vowel Oh expands your ribs in all directions. Playing with all vowels as a language of feeling that opens the mid-section of your body with pleasurable sensations.

Mirroring the Soul

This expressive arts performance before the mirror begins by contrasting your free-spirited, breathing essence with your predicable breathing pattern. Recognizing your body image, particularly the way you ordinarily breathe, changes the blueprint of your structure. The first step is becoming aware of and appreciate your body image as it is now. Your breath expresses every nuance of feeling you experience. If you have kept a lid on your feelings, your breath will reflect this state of mind. In spite of massive control that limits the range and intensity of our breath, this natural auto-pilot feature of breathing continues to do its amazing job.

The air element carries every color ray of the cosmos. Walking in the pure, fresh air while breathing in a rainbow of colors is revitalizing.

-Janet Armond

Take extra time to contemplate this information. The breath of human consciousness is a shared activity. We all breathe the same air. About 20,000 breaths are breathed per day, totaling an average of 5,000 gallons of air. Something like 100 million breaths will have passed through your system in your lifetime. Your lungs have 300 million grapelike sacs with a total cellular surface area the size of a tennis court! And that's not all. Every day of your life, you absorb atoms from the air that exploded forth from the Big Bang. This means we are the breathing cells of a vast living organism that sustains our life.

May we remember that our breath is the same breath that is intertwined with the whole cosmos. May we be empowered to breathe as the thunder roaring across the sky and come alive as never before.

A wind sweeps my life energies into a harvest, a quantum wave. I ride this momentum beyond what I can know.

-Carolyn Mary Kleefeld
The Alchemy of Possibility

With approximately sixty thousand miles of capillaries, how much inspiration are you willing to draw into your body? How much Olympian breath power are you willing to release out into the world? Protective boundaries have little meaning with the knowledge that your breath interacts with everything, making you a divine facet of the entire living Earth.

When saying your name in your normal way, notice how you typically breathe. Notice any tendency to tighten, deflate or lift your chest. Holding patterns like this dampen energy and build stress in the body. A popular breath pattern is taking a quick gasp of air and while suspending the breath while speaking. In other words, it's very rare that the breath supports our speech. A mind filled with toxic buildup is one reason we go blank or stumble over our words when attempting to convey an important message.

Born a champion of life force, reclaim your primal heritage! As a *Sacred Actor,* expressive arts practice before the mirror is celebrating the free-spirited breath of life before the whole world as witness.

Another name for Soul is the life force that sustains the breathing universe containing all that is.

-Peter Guralnick

In preparation for your performance, invoke your *Primal Name*. Consciously magnifying the life force with the dynamics of inspiring energy, limiting patterns of breathing fall by the way side. Let go into the flow of your breath by breathing life and more life into the very heart of this magical name. Within this one word, inspire the breath of spirit to flow.

Play with expanding the shape of the vowels in your *Primal Name* with the powers of the Great Wind. Oxygenate the cellular code of the DNA located in the heart of this magnificent new name. Intention is everything. The phenomenon of 'entrainment'– the process that synchronizes and links the personal and collective life force with universal

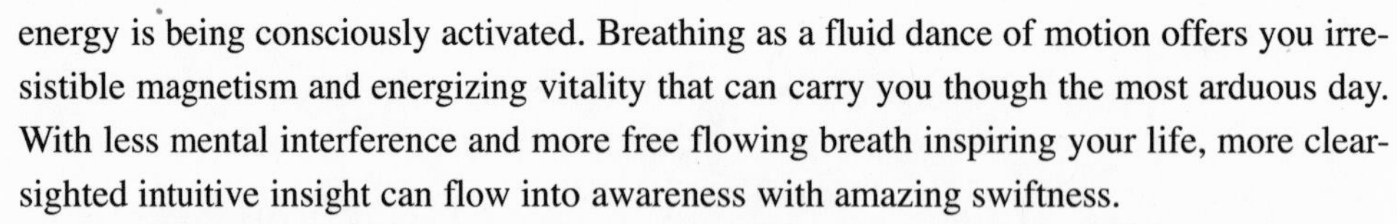

energy is being consciously activated. Breathing as a fluid dance of motion offers you irresistible magnetism and energizing vitality that can carry you though the most arduous day. With less mental interference and more free flowing breath inspiring your life, more clear-sighted intuitive insight can flow into awareness with amazing swiftness.

Life force is the breath of God breathing through you.

-Heraclitus

Mastery of *Primal Energetics* is the ability to produce any feeling or state of consciousness and shift it at will. Consciously shifting the way you breathe is a simple way to accomplish this feat.

Picture of ageless vitality taken March, 2007

Breath Olympics on Mount High is about to begin. The air is fresh and alive. Witness yourself stepping up to the arena where the games are being played. Sense a crowd of thousands waiting for you to make your appearance. You have come not to compete, but to demonstrate the universality of the life force in embodied action.

As the spotlight brightens on your face, you have one minute of clock time to unleash the wind-swept energies of primal power. Shift into a fluidity of being by softening your knees and spiraling your ankles. Take a deep breath and send a wave of vitality to flow through your belly, heart, mind and spirit. In the essence of your childlike nature, surrender to the irrepressible surges of spontaneous impulse. Breathe as the first womb giving birth to creation. Breathe as the fountain of youth gushing forth a kaleidoscopic display of inspired rhythms that make a 4th of July celebration look pale!

As great rushes of windy life force and hissing air-sounds travel through you, slow down your pace of breathing into long flowing breaths. Consciously rest for a few moments at the end of your next exhalation. In this timeless moment, see the entire audience breathing in unified harmony with the spirit of life. Through all the tumultuous, shocking, and surprising events that are happening all around, witness people everywhere breathing renewed life into the future health of the ecosystem. In this desire to secure sustainable, balance with nature, see us all working with every possible resource to purify the air – the divine breath of God. May the recovery of our breathing body enable us to come into lasting relationship with the life we have been given.

The filling and emptying of breath is the rhythm of the universe,
sending waves of energy to ignite the root impulses of your primal nature.

-Ajit Mookerjee
Kundalini

Mother Hum

Inner Voice of Feeling

There is no sound so simple, so pure, as humming.
This is the ultimate language of love - but can any one express it?
He who has savored it once, knows what joy it can give.

--Kabir

All of life is vibrating and it's all humming! Every atom and particle in the solar system is humming its own resonant tone. Call it God, spirit, divinity, or wholeness; the 'truth' is in the tone. Like great cathedral bell that rings far and wide, the Mother Hum of the universe ceaselessly drones out vibrations if feeling throughout creation. In his book *Music of the Whole Earth*, David Reck said it best: "Harmonious humming vibrations are so all-encompassing that everything seen and unseen are filled with it. This sacred sound is what is referred to as the 'music of the spheres."

The sacred humming vbibration will lead humankind to the spiritual domain from which we came.

-Robert C. Lewis

The Fourth Catalyst attunes you to your inner voice of feeling made audible. Like a whale's sonar language that can travel for hundreds of miles through the ocean, humming with the dynamics of emotional energy can penetrate the atoms of your cells more effectively than any ultrasonic machine.

Every child hums its feelings through the day. The only problem is that this miraculous activity has not been given sufficient value. Humming a little tune in an unconscious way is a pleasant thing to do, but humming with primal power unleashes massive overtones of vibration. Humming with pulsatory waves of energy is a simple an highly effective way to sustain health, vitality and freedom of response. In other words, stimulating abundant vibrations is about developing greater tolerance to experience heightened excitement and pleasure.

Swiss scientist Dr. Hans Jenny has experimented with projecting humming sound waves into liquid substances. The patterns produced by these sounds reproduce the essence of everything from a seashell to a spiral galaxy. For instance, ultrasonic machines can detect the exact tone of your liver. When this tonal frequency is projected in a gelatinous substance, an amazing likeness of a liver appears. Since our bodies are mostly water, humming can effectively restructure the cells of the body. What is even more astounding, humming does more than affect matter – the ultrasonic vibrations of humming tones *create* matter. Imagine what we can do to influence our own health and vitality when attuned to the Soul of Vibration that can ignite the transformative potential to change whatever ails.

Personalizing Tone

The inner voice of feeling is my inner companion I call *Humma*. To me, she is the feminine voice of God, the Soul of Vibration that quickly lets me know what is true. Humma is a friend for life. She gets up with me, goes to sleep with me and never abandons me. As I write these words, I notice a subtle pain in the neck. An image of a hardened seed of the Redwood comes to mind. I muse that all the wisdom exists within this seed to grow into a mighty tree, and yet a stubborn shell can thwart it! Vigorously humming into the center of the pain while giggling my neck helps to loosen the density of pain from the inside out. As my neck relaxes, a conflict is being uncovered that is giving me a pain in the neck! Attunement with Humma sustains my youthfulness of spirit and original innocence.

With the discovery of the superstring theory, musical metaphors take on a startling reality, for the theory suggests that the microscopic landscape is suffused with tiny strings whose vibrational patterns orchestrate the evolution of the cosmos.

-Brian Greene
The Elegant Universe

Humming with different emotional energies can be used to quiet the mind, diminish pain, synchronize brain waves, improve motor skills and shift debilitating moods into the pure presence of being.

Recently, I have had good success in helping people with asthma. The unfortunate habit of gasping for breath makes people feel as if there is not enough air to survive. Tense abdominal muscles always accompany this fight or flight breathing pattern. Humming with the full range of mighty, emotive power focused in the belly naturally deepens breathing, thereby reducing anxiety and stress.

New research reveals that humming is being used to help people deal more effectively with schizophrenia. In one study, there was a 59% reduction in auditory hallucination when people hummed a short time at different intervals of the day. This is understandable because it's almost impossible to think when you're humming! These pulsations stimulate delta brain waves that also generate a deepened peace of mind. Another study has discovered that Alzheimer patients, who can barely talk, can hum and sing favorite songs from the past with no trouble at all.

In the clamor of modern life, 60 million Americans suffer with hearing loss that is caused by exposure to noise pollution. Irritating noises, from a screeching motor to a screaming child, won't sound so bothersome when you can take a minute and resonate in harmony with the bothersome tone. Humming with these radically different tones enriches your repertoire of colorful expression

Artist, musician, physicist, doctor - all are approaching the paradigm of the fundamental vibratory essence that underlies their work. The ancients knew it, our bodies know it. The emerging physician, the new doctor of balance, fullness and resonance, rests on a new understanding of the physics of harmonies and the powers in sound.

-Don Campbell
Music and Miracles

Audibly or silently humming is a meta-language that sustains between-the-lines communion with others. This wordless language establishes a link between what is being communicated and what is being felt below all words.

Meta-Language

In fact, a simple hum is found to be the most consistent sound uttered by people in the helping profession. I am not suggesting you drown out your conversation with humming. It is about interspersing more feeling into language with the richness of resonant, vibrating frequencies of emotional energy.

Language are for those who have forgotten how to communicate.

-Kedren Bryson

Mara, a client of mine, was about to end her marriage with her husband. Her main complaint was that he showed no interested in anything she said. She doubted if he had any truly loving feelings towards her. I put on the video camera and filmed their interaction. I asked her husband if he was interested in what his wife was saying. He said he was, but after viewing the video, I brought attention to his controlled, stoic facial expression, unyielding body language and serious vocal tone. He confessed that he was taught to believe that any show of feeling was girlish, weak and unmanly.

I asked if he was open to explore a new idea that might enrich his relationship with his wife. He agreed. I coached him to gaze into his wife's eyes while she talked. Once he was comfortable with this challenge, I asked him to periodically hum to indicate he was hearing. I stressed that he did not need to agree or disagree with what was being said, only to communicate 'interest' in what she was saying. As he explored doing this, his wife jumped up and hugged him! What a revelation – it takes more than words to communicate with meaning.

Truth rings true in the tone, as does the eye of wisdom, that can see into the heart of the matter.

-Wowza

Being on the same 'wave length' with anyone's vibration lets them know they are understood and stimulates more intuitive responses from the heart.

Activations

Before we begin, I recommend wearing earplugs for the *Activations* that follow. This simple device creates a sanctuary inside your mind, which heightens your ability to feel the vibrating power of humming with greater ease. For instance, put on earplugs and place your hands on your upper chest area. With some vigor, hum a long sustained tone. Notice how the vibrations from your chest are radiating energy into your hand. As you vigorously hum again, open your mouth while making an 'ah' sound. Notice how quickly the vibrations diminish. This experiment indicates that sound projects tones outward and humming projects tones inward.

Being out of tune is always irritating because the energy you put into your efforts doesn't get you anywhere. Coming into sympathetic resonance with vibrational harmony puts you on the same wave length with your intentions.

-K.C.Cole
Sympathetic Vibrations

I suggest humming while you read through this material. Allow your eyes to float over the sentences while humming as a language of feeling. When an idea resonates with you, listen to the feelings that are generated. With practice, you'll be able to 'photo read' the most complex material by glancing over the printed page while humming. Your conscious mind will protest that nothing is understood; yet your sub-conscious mind can easily understand and retain what you are reading.

Humming tunes up neurological capacities, balancing the sympathetic and parasympathetic nervous system with resonant harmonics. Humming with a unified bodymind puts you on the same wavelength with what rings true.

Sonic Brain Massage

The following Activations are designed to awaken dormant areas in the brain. Being a part of a headstrong culture, it's astonishing that so little of our potential brain-power has been accessed. Note that the brain consists of 100 billion vibrating humming neurons. Each neuron forms up to 10,000 connections with other cells, thereby creating the potential for more combinations than there are stars in the heavens. The nervous system can be perceived as one long extended brain that 'thinks soundly!'

You may see in your daily life, work and relationships, your tone of voice can influence the outcome of all communication.

-Kay Gardner

To start, shape your mouth into a fluffy pout and pulse out humming tones that sound like a motorboat! Encourage your lips to flutter in the breeze, which makes them tingle with energy. Once your lips are vibrating, visualize these vibrations traveling into the center of your brain. With clear intent, visualize the neurons that compose your brain being regenerated. Humming in this playful way produces multiple wave states in the brain, which generates clarity of mind.

Humming on your inhalation and exhalation stimulates healthy supplies of oxygen to flow into the brain. This requires a relaxed, open throat. With your fingers, gently wiggle your Adam's apple to loosen tension in your neck. As you hum on your inhalation, draw your tones directly into your head with the intent of vigorously massaging the tight sutures in your skull. Roll your head in figure eight motions while circling your humming tones around both sides of your brain. Explore this action a dozen times as you encourage your eyes to roll with the curving motions. This practice of balancing the hemispheres of your brain while working at the computer, releases eyestrain, neck tension and stimulates more innovative ideas to flow.

Emotions have sound and vibration for they are actually a multi-level phenomenon which include neurological patterns within the brain.

-Kenyon & Essene
The Hathor Material

In a world requiring rapid pace thinking and quick decision making humming is the best acoustic tool for enhancing emotional and mental clarity.

Overtone Humming

The body is an orchestra of bio-chemical vibrations that form a complex symphony of overtone resonance. Overtoning involves the creation of simultaneous, multiple tones on one note. For instance, when the string of an instrument is plucked, a single note sounds which instantly sets off a series of overtones. A focused display of overtones charges the entire nervous system with renewed resonance.

Begin by elongating each one of these syllables for as long as your breath lasts. The syllables are – *Mea mm, Mee mm, Ma mm, Mo mm, Mu mm.* While toning each one, direct your tones to flow inward rather than projecting them outward. Hum while shaping your lips into a pout. Stretch your jaw as if you are about to gargle. Imagine your mouth is the amphitheater, your tongue is an exotic dancer and your humming tones are a laser beam activating healing energy. With a small lip enclosure, encourage the exotic dancer to undulate through the upper palate of your mouth.

The MMM consonant has a rich buzzing noise like a bumble bee that can bring great balance to our emotions, diminishing our egotistical side by slowing down the lesser, moving mind and tapping into higher mind.

-James D' Angelo
Healing with the Voice

Overtone chanting is a profound spiritual practice that sounds two or more tones simultaneously. With deepened awareness every tone is heard containing within it all other tones.

Experiment with changing the shape of your mouth while blending the syllables together into a long drone. As overtones occur, your sinuses will start to tingle. Humming while shaping the vowels *eeh* and *err* and back to *eeh* is another means of increasing overtones. Slide your tongue on your upper pallet while shaping these syllables. The harmonics resonate most within and between the syllables. With practice more embellishments can be added to create an amazing array of harmonics. Some of these include: shifting your tongue on the upper pallet, lip and glottis trills, vibrato effects and pitch shifts. A body in motion is self-arousing. Hum while pulsing your PC muscle in rhythm with your tones increases energy to flow through your spinal column.

The greatest lesson of the Overtone is to resonate with all, to know all, and be silent.

-Wayne Perry
Overtoning

When humming on your inhalation, tilt your tailbone back while slightly arching your spine and head into a curve. When humming on your exhalation, tilt your tailbone downward while rounding your spine and head. Coordinating humming vibrations with spinal movement generates increased circulation of excitement to flow. Enlivened excitement streaming from the tailbone supports the health and vitality of the spine.

The thymus gland holds powerful energies of rejuvenation. This area is known for its ability to dissolve pathogens and sustain the health of the immune system. Without sufficient emotive activation, the thymus shrinks in size, as we get older. Imagine your chest is a drum. Turn your hands into fists and 'lightly' drum your chest. Thumping your chest like Tarzan while humming with vigor thrills the nerve endings and acupuncture points in the heart area.

The elements of nature are vast and impersonal. When you become an element you have complete freedom that cannot be experienced in any other way. You are free to be the element as you feel it.

-Moni Yakim
Creating a Character

Fuel yourself for fast-passed action by pumping up the volume of your tone. Massive tingling sensations set off a blazing fire through your nervous system that stimulates passionate power to take action. Speed up the rhythms to energize yourself and slow your rhythms down to tranquilize your heart rate. Rattling instruments while humming creates high amplitude acoustic stimulations in the central nervous system. Humming while lightly tapping your skin all over your body soothes frayed nerves while creating visible changes in brain wave activity.

As we grow older, calcium and protein diminish in our bones, making them brittle and more susceptible to injury. Once again, I emphasize that intent is everything. With the intent to renew the vital strength of your bones, humming throughout your skeletal system is an excellent means of warding off osteoporosis. Trace your hand across your skeletal system while directing the overtones of humming to flow into the very marrow of your bones. This technique is the essence of magnetic healing that is often referred to as 'laying on of hands.'

Humming is most readily comprehensible to the soul, to the immediately sensitive realm of human feeling.

-Rudolf Steiner

Humming with intent acts like a built-in vibratory beam that offers directional guidance towards achieving superior health, vitality and presence of mind.

Elemental Humming

Like the sonic radar of dolphins, the whistling of summer winds and the gurgling of mountain streams, we live in a harmonious, humming world. In ages past, sun, moon and stars, river, sky and forest were looked upon as sisters and brothers of humanity. When we behold the suffering Earth, air, and water of the modern age, it is obvious that this brotherhood is no longer felt.

Research is underway involving the speeding up of the human voice by two octaves. The result is that our voice sounds exactly like chirping birds. When sped up to eight octaves, our voice sounds exactly like crickets. Slowing down the voice by three octaves makes it sound like the speech of dolphins. Slowed down by eight octaves, our voice will sound like ocean waves. Orchestrating the elements of nature like a symphony conductor directing an orchestra reveals nature's song that is always humming. With a symphony of vibration circulating through your being, physical, emotional and mental maladies are being continuously cleared from your field. As the poet Gary Snyder wrote, "As the crickets' soft autumn hum is to us, so are we to the trees as they hum to the rocks and the hills." Your experience will be enhanced when using environmental music that reflects bird-calls, rain, wind, creature sounds and ocean waves.

Humming with the five elements keeps you attuned to the feeling sensations of the potent Earth, the oceanic waters, the buoyant air, the fire of passion and the pure etheric substance of the pregnant void.

The human voice is able to focus and project intention during sound making better than any other instrument.

-Jonathan Goldman
Healing Sounds

The Earth element represents the grounded support of our intrinsic nature. Being environmentally aware of the ground as your expanded identity, hum with potent power deep in your belly. Dropping into your low, resonant range develops cellular strength and brings more vigor into your organs.

The Air element represents the buoyant life force that inspires a youthfulness of spirit. Humming as if you are communing with a small child or a kitty cat stimulates that lighter than air feeling. Hum as effervescent champagne bubbling through your tones clears the sky of your mind.

The Fire element represents the arousing intensity of the blazing sun. To be on fire is to be full of excitement about life. Humming filled with staccato impulses of dazzling enthusiasm sustains that 'get up and go' energy to accomplish difficult tasks.

I hum through my tired, overworked brain with the power of a cascading waterfall filled with healing energy.

-John Dunbar

The Water element represents the flowing continuum of feeling energy that sustains health, vitality and intuitive guidance. Hum as a flowing river that builds into mighty waves rolling towards the shore. Hum as a rain of tears nurturing a parched land.

The Ether element represents the spacious, unending void, the mystical emptiness and peaceful repose vibrating through all of life. Quietly hum while extending one long tone in your middle range. Hum as a luminous beam of light that moves you beyond all belief.

The resonance of crystal stones has been measured to hum/vibrate up to 500,000 times per second, and atoms and stars hum/vibrate 1,000,000 or more times per second. With your super conscious sensibilities, hum with the resonance of crystal stones, atoms and stars! With heightened vibrational feeling for each element, blend them all together into a humming language.

Truth is in the Tone

Living in a mental state of confusing contradiction makes it difficult to feel the impulses of intuitive information informing your movements. Being separated from the truth of gut level feelings, the intellect is not equipped to make sound decisions. Instead of simple instinctive action, value judgments get in the way to complicate the matter. Under these circumstances, even manifesting a parking place can create a traffic jam! Before you learned words, a nonverbal tone and gesture came forth to indicate what you wanted or didn't want.

A measure of wellness is flexibility, the individual's ability to move with the elements. Illness suppresses the the primary element of expression.

-John Beaulieu

Making sound decisions via humming can quickly indicate what choices 'ring true.' Listen to the feelings that your tones are eliciting. Trust that these feelings are telegraphing information into your mind that will be intuitively understood. Let's say you're in some form of conflict and you can't make up your mind what to do. Here is a process to help you feel out the answer with your humming tones. Bring your hands out in front of you and put one possible decision in one hand and the other possible decision in the other. Now you're holding the conflict in the palm of your hands rather then creating confusion and conflict in your brain. As you hum back and forth between your two hands, listen to the quality of your tones. An enthusiastic hum is signaling *yes*. A groaning tone indicates *no*. In other words, the auditory channel transmits innovative impulses of intuitive knowledge.

***MMM. What a great idea*! All the information you will ever need is encoded in the cells of your body.**

Humming performs a micro-massage upon your organs, releasing stress and restoring balance.

-Ted Andrews
Sacred Sounds

Recently, I've been working with an investment group and teaching them to use humming to intuit the stocks, which will give them the highest dividends. The basis of intuition is non-intellectual, so spontaneous, creative ideas, insights, and actions come alive from your inner voice of feeling. With this information, I coach the participants to hold two stocks in their hands while relaxing their body into a fluidity of being. The next step is to have them imagine humming into the very molecular structure of each stock. As they hummed back and forth between their two hands, an affirmative tone inevitably appeared that indicated the proper choice. Needless to say, the results of their success with this technique were very inspiring.

Tonal Meditation

Each of us possesses a unique, sonic signature that reflects our divine essence. Little infants often make up a simple melody that they hum over and over again. Without validation for this beautiful skill, they quickly forget the indwelling melody of their song. Humming is singing with your mouth closed. If you wish to connect with your essence song, sit and listen to the great all-encompassing silence – the silence that carries you beyond outer noise and inner discord.

Humming with a lullaby affect dissipates stress, and depression.

-Don Campbell
The Mozart Effect

Humming is true prayer in action. Visualize a luminous circle surrounding your body. With long extended humming tones, see the shimmering light from this circle spreading out into the farthest reaches of the universe. Imagine the universe is humming your song to you. A variety of different melodies may stream into your awareness. Be patient. Allow this melody of melodies to take form and substance. Once you hear the melody with your inner ear, place it in your heart and hum it with feeling.

When you have difficulty falling asleep, hum your essence song as a gentle breeze that floats across your body. A cocoon-like chamber of quiet is created that transforms hypertension into peaceful relaxation. Perceive your essence song as the immortal splendor of your soul that can nurture you through any painful state. Hum as nocturnal moonbeams filling you with effulgent light. Hum into 'a nameless rapture of a thousand dreams' cradling you in love. It is reported that Socrates slept soundly the night before he was executed. When asked how he did this, he said a sweet humming tone streamed through his body and kept his mind content.

The entire planet sings and dances to the humming music of God.

-Mozart

For expectant mothers, place your hands on your belly and create a special lullaby for your baby. Direct this lullaby to flow into your baby's heart as a prayer for its continued well-being. This little soul feels your humming vibrations; so don't be surprised if it starts to kick with the rhythms of the melody! As you welcome this magical being into the world, hum its lullaby. When your baby is distressed, hum this lullaby. Watch how this melody soothes the pain and brings swift healing. You can do the same for your inner child. When your fragility threatens to overwhelm you, hum this lullaby to the child within your heart and feel its spirit come alive with joy.

Years later, children have been known to recognize songs and lullabies that had been played to them while they were in utero.

-Don Campbell
The Mozart Effect

Hum of Healing

I'm reminded of a client of mine named Bridget, who was suffering with a tumor the size of a basketball in her belly. She was preparing for surgery, but was still open to explore different alternative methods of healing. She had heard that stored emotional memories are often buried inside the cells, but nothing she had tried could reach the core of their tenacious power.

Some part of her knew she had created the tumor and there was another part of her that could un-create it. Being a very shy person for as long as she could remember, making sounds was a very intimidating prospect. Humming with emotional energy did the trick. In this simple way, she had the courage to express her feelings without having to dwell on dredging up painful memories.

Once she felt comfortable recognizing and expressing the energy of emotion via humming, she was directed to go inside her body and pay a visit to the tumor. I encouraged her to sense the sensations in this area and amplify them with her humming voice. Once inside the tumor, fearful trepidation appeared on her face. I asked her to fully express the fear and panic with her humming voice. As she did this, her sounds soon turned into a confusing chaos. She indicated that a childhood memory had arisen, but she thought that this early experience was healed in therapy. I coached her to let go of the memory for now and simply hum out these chaotic feelings. As she did this, I asked, "What emotion lies under the confusion?"

I offer humming as a prescription to clear confusion, anxiety and transform negative thinking into responsive action. Humming brings emotions, mind and body into joyous alignment.

-Fredrick Bell M.D.

She blurted out, "Anger!" I exclaimed, " Drop all past judgments about this energy. Simply hum out its primal power." As her humming voice deepened into a roaring rumble, I directed her to use this big and bold power to explode her tumor to bits! With humming blasts of fiery emotion, her body finally relaxed into a peaceful state. At the end of the session, we gave thanks for a primal power that knows perfectly well how to sustain health.

The biggest realization that emerged for Bridget was that talk therapy had brought understanding to the issue but speaking the language of emotional energy is what help clear this blockage in her feeling nature. Unfelt feelings create addictive compulsions. For instance, if you're consumed with an addictive urge for a second desert, hum with the energy of unrequited desire. As a *Sacred Actor,* pick up an imaginary dessert and gorge yourself with its deliciousness. As you lick your fingers, hum with total satisfaction. Heightened oxygenation traveling through your system can often satisfy any craving. A good question to ask is, "What else can fill me up in this moment? What else can satisfy this craving?" Hum with any emerging feelings and listen to the tones that emerge. Who knows, humming with more sweetness may satisfy what all the desserts in the world can never satisfy.

If you want to permanently release an issue – pain, illness, tumor, disease, addiction, whatever– you need to go to the source and regenerate the mind/body at that vibrational level.

-Wayne Perry
Overtoning

I derive great fun when sitting down at a fancy dinner party and exclaiming, "Why, it's absolutely a crime not to hum over good food!" Within minutes, a table of sober people begins humming up a storm as they savor their food - probably for the first time in ages. No longer 'enslaved-in-boredom,' hum/trace around the clock, the curtains and the door handle. Hum with your dog's bark. Hum to the spin of the dryer or to the rush and swoosh of the vacuum cleaner. Hum in sympathy to your child's cries. Hum while scrubbing the toilet and discover that purity exists everywhere.

Go through your day humming as a beautiful flower, a favorite animal, ripe fruit, a vibrant color that is brightening your mood, or any symbol that resonates with the beauty of your soul.

The voice of feeling is indeed the organ of the soul –the eternal fountain, forever flowing from the heart.

–Longfellow

Walk Primal

Walking while humming is becoming fully in the moment. You may notice when focused on the flow of your humming tones that shapes and colors become more acute. Where you place your attention energy will follow. Humming with awareness of rolling your feet across that pavement, the bending of your knees with each step, the swing of your arms, the bobbling of your head and the blinking momentum of your eyes, is meditation in motion. Awareness of walking in the unified field of creative possibility can encourage more diversity of tone to enrich your experience. From buoyant lightness to bursts of firry intensity, every quality of mind can be hummed with each step you take.

Walking is a excellent time to practice the art of 'overtoning,' the creation of audible combinations of partial tones, while at the same time humming a lower fundamental tone. Articulating vowels with your mouth partially closed can be done even while walking through a busy mall. This process can do so much to dampen the effects of noise pollution. When hearing sounds that are irritating, humming with a similar intensity of tone can greatly minimize any unhealthy sound. While exploring the power of overtoning, visualize a halo of light radiating over your head. Hum again while imagining this halo of light transforming into lotus flower bursting into full bloom. Feel its divine nectar absorbing all negative vibrations into light.

I believe the essential unity of life hums through us all.

-Ghandi

Mirroring the Soul

In this ceremony before the mirror, say your name in the usual way while noticing the posture, attitude and familiar vocal style. Say your name a few times more while listening to the tone being expressed. Whatever you discover, hum out this familiar tone. Does the tone move in straight lines or is their some wave motion in it? Is the tone warm, cool or cold? Do you like or dislike the vibration of your voice? Your task is not to fix or improve this part. Simply heighten your awareness of what you hear, which instantly offers you more choice in the matter.

The future is created out of an active, rich imagination. Solo performance before the mirror brings the creation of your dreams into actual form.

As a *Sacred Actor,* you have been chosen to embody the Soul of Vibration,. which can help people everywhere awaken awareness of their inner voice of feeling. Through this process, the social role is making the shift from self-centered awareness into the essence of whole-centered awareness. In preparation for this performance, invoke your *Primal Name*. Encode this chosen name with the different vibrating qualities of nature. Intend your humming voice to become a lazar beam igniting the resonant frequencies of the Earth, water, fire and air. By sharpening awareness of the superconductivity of

Countless millions set out to meet at sacred sites around the world to resonate with one another. The mass media was mystified. Why are all these people humming? It seemed there was a natural impulse to hum the same tone, to hear the same sound, to speak with one voice, singing, breathing as one body. We are one . . . we are love . . . we are whole.

-Barbara Marx Hubbad

Humming with spiritual intent arouses the vibrational channels in the body, To freely hum with love promotes a liberation of the human spirit.

-Daren Johnson

vibrational tone, you are no longer fixed in any limited pattern as your sole identity. An unknown source once said, "Angels voices bending space and time, calling all heaven's bells to chime; the sacred hum."

Standing at the expanding edge of the horizon, honor the stupendous knowledge that you are a free spirit living in the vibrating flow of a coherent universe. From atoms to galaxies, amoebas to neurons, the evolution of your consciousness is humming its way into a future world of whole-beingness.

Your performance begins by imagining you are the original child of creation in the womb of the Great Mother. Gaining substance, gaining form, let your tones pulse and throbs in the liquid home in which you dwell. As your amniotic home begins to shrink in size, hum tones that build with greater and greater intensity.

With startling impulses of tone, feel your tailbone pushing you through the birth canal into the miracle of new life. As the pure radiance of your being emerges, hum through the invisible umbilical cord that reconnects you in sympathetic response to the entire cosmos. Feel the energy of a newborn baby in your heart. Feel your vulnerability, your purity, and your original innocence. Honor the intent to be born into an exciting new life. Celebrate your newness by humming up a storm!

The collective is only as great as every individual. In the twinkling of an eye, see people everywhere becoming the change they wish to see in the world. Out of this restoration of spirit, witness humming languages of unbridled enthusiasm take hold to build new frontiers of understanding between all people and all nations. By inhabiting a transparent body reflecting the external landscape of creation, the world itself is perceived as an 'open system' vibrating with the radiance of love – in divine concert with all that is.

Gaia began to hum a lively tune that came up from the depths of his soul to proclaim for all the world - his joy in living, humming on this Earth of abundance and harmony.

-Jean Hudon

Song Talk

The First and Future Language

The language of early man, as it is with young children now, was sing-song in nature and perhaps closer to birdsong in inflection.

-James D'Angelio
Healing with the Voice

We are born with uninhibited vocal powers filled with a vast reservoir of feeling. Before any words are known, a baby sings out its needs and desires with singing tones rich in resonant expression. Unfortunately, all this spontaneous outpouring of melodic feeling is short lived. As cultural patterns determine specific language tones and verbal rhythms, the musical quality of our feeling nature is driven underground. With enormous emphases on the development of the mental mind, our speech reflects this mechanized tendency. As Otto Jespensen, a linguistic scientist has written, "The mental mind of advanced civilizations moderate the expression of passionate feeling. In contrast, the speech of uncivilized people passionately express their feelings as musical song."

It is in song that the world rejoices. The Fifth Catalyst reactivates the melodic song essence in our speech, which can motivate our lives towards more harmonious interaction with others and the planet.

Tone shapes consciousness. As the world is getting smaller, we are coming into relationship with people very different than ourselves. As a future language, *Song Talk* opens harmonious pathways for the enhancement of telepathic and empathetic communication with others. What is required is the realization that emotions are music. Each emotional frequency vibrates through our being with its own melodic, rhythmical signature. Once again, I quote scientist Candace Pert, author of *Molecules of Emotion*. She writes, "If we could hear the music of the body with our ears, then the sum of these sounds would be the music that we call the emotions."

The body itself is intrinsically music, right down to the DNA that make up our genes. If we were imaginative enough to think musically as well as alphabetically, this just might allow us at long last to escape the tense tyranny of machine thinking.

-Larry Dossey, M.D

The ability to change our tone to reflect anyone's vocal style enhances deepened understanding of the diversity of human nature. In fact, nature intends for the voice to expand musically with each passing year. As we wake up to the vast healing potential of sound, cultural styles of speaking will expand to include the lyrical harmonics of emotional energy.

The First People

One late evening on my eighteenth birthday, I watched a television program on an early tribe of people. The film started with a man enacting his escape from the clutches of a wild beast. Without any known words, he displayed his fear by making sporadic gasping sounds and trembling his body from head to toe. In the next moment, he transformed into the wild animal that was growling and clawing at his own flesh. Collapsing to the ground, he quickly crawled into a cave to escape being killed.

The most abstract system of philosophy is, in its method and purpose, nothing more than an ingenious combination of natural sounds.

-C.G. Jung

The next scene of the film showed the tribe members performing the actions they had just witnessed. With full-bodied sounds and dance-like movements, one group enacted the wild beast, and another group enacted the hunter's battle with the beast. It appeared to me that these ritual performances were an embodied schooling that prepared these people to venture out into a frightening new world with more creative options. When the film was over, I wondered why all this rich vocal expression was set aside in order to speak a word language.

The next day, while taking a stroll on the beach, I mirrored the high-pitched, warbling tones of the birds flying above me. While exploring this soaring language, I heard a message resound deep within my soul, "Let your spirit take flight, sound out your truth and be free." As I walked down the beach, I saw an old uprooted tree and droned out a crotchety sound that reflected its gnarled shape. In that instant, the old, withered tree came alive with shimmering beauty. As I drew closer, I heard the old tree respond to my attention. A gnarly voice exclaimed, "Beauty of soul exists everywhere. It exists in you and in me. Thank you for noticing and expressing my song. "

Let us be more conscious of our present, sonic environment and learn to resonate with what we have created. Life will be easier, more vibrant, magical and childlike.

-John Beaulieu

Before I left the beach, I looked out at the ocean. The scene was so profound; I stretched out my arms to embrace it all. In that timeless moment, I spoke as the *Mother of the World* communing to her children to honor the inner beauty of their true nature. As I walked home exploring my new found language, the song of the birds, the whispering winds, the roar of the cars and the tapping of my feet on the sidewalk blended into one vast symphony of rhythmical music. When a stranger stopped me to ask for directions, my words sang with a melodic quality that I had never heard before.

Silly Babble

Expressing my inhibited feelings through a made up language was my therapy. This profound process would never fail to drop me into my body. Like magic, my gestures and expression would magically come together in coordinated harmony. When shifting into my normal style of speaking, tentative awkwardness would return with a vengeance. Whenever this way of speaking did slip into the conversation, my friends or family laughed at me for acting so silly. At the time, I had no logical explanation to offer for this unusual form of communication. With no support for my sonic discoveries, the pleasure of speaking a made up language soon faded from awareness.

In the early part of the babbling stage the infant combines the consonants and vowels to make its own language according to the music of emotion and instinct.

-Paul Newham
The Singing Cure

Many years later, I attended several acting classes in which teachers used preverbal language called 'gibberish' – a form of silly babble – to break the ice and loosen up inhibitions. When witnessing how much spontaneity was instantly released, I knew this process was anything but silly. Much later, I discovered that certain Christian congregations practice Glossolalia, which means 'speaking in tongues' – the ecstatic utterance of the Holy Spirit. This definition clearly resonated with my own discoveries. What would it take to free Glossolalia from past traditions and empower ourselves to speak with total freedom of expression as a sacred gift from God?

The Persona

The origin of the word person is 'per-sound,' a person whose material substance is composed of sound. The word 'persona' represents a vocal mask that was originally used in Greek drama to imitate different character archetypes. Identified with our social role, we speak through a mask designed to project different emotional attitudes. Being hypnotized to assume cool voices, smart voices, nice voices or shy voices, an authenticity of expression is rarely heard. How many men do we know who have forced their voices into their bowels in order to sound manly? How many women do we know that learned to speak with a light voice to insure their feminine nature?

The chronic habit of speaking in a high or low tonal range inhibits our feeling sensibilities. Encapsulated in a narrow range of expression, it's a scary thing to sense our voice trembling with shyness, quivering with fear or failing us all together. What an eye opener it is to wake up and hear the abstract intellect saying, "I broke up with my boyfriend, I got a great promotion, and our dog died" - as if reciting a grocery list with utter detachment.

Identification with a predictable tone of voice can numb us all from ever participating with the vast symphony of sonic music playing inside. Dr. Albert Mehrabian of UCLA conducted a landmark study on the 'three V's' of spoken communication - verbal, vocal and visual. What he discovered is that people only hear 7% of our verbal interaction. The vocal, feeling element; intonation, projection, and resonance accounts for 33% of what people pick up in the communication. The visual element - what people see - the expression of the body and face when speaking, adds up to 55% of people's overall focus. This information startled me. All through school, it was the verbal message that almost all educators focused on.

Tone influences us greatly because our bodies are sound sensitive. A shrill voice can produce involuntary muscle tightening and constriction of blood vessels in the person and in the listener. A thin, whispery voice is tiring because it's a strain to hear what is being said. An aggressive, abrasive voice sustains these same feelings in the nervous system and can keep others at a distance. Sounding 'cool' can disguise feelings so well that everyone who hears it responds with the same disinterested detachment. A voice projecting childish naivete makes it difficult to assert oneself and be taken seriously by others. A voice resounding with painful trauma projects a victimized personality, which supports the trauma to continue.

There are more words for diseases than for health. There are more words for conflicts than joy and love. There are more words for control than for freedom. In this regard, the words we use shape the reality of our experience.

Liberating Speech

While offering a self-expression workshop at Esalen Institute, I introduced *Song Talk* as a harmonious means to express emotional energy in a safe and healthy way. When using this preverbal means to dialogue a fully range of feelings to others, telepathic understanding increased. To those of us who where naturally attuned to the creative right brain, *Song Talk* is easy. It is not so easy for people who are identified with the logical side of the brain. To solve the problem, I created a system of 'quick

People have a tendency to speak in cliches, in stereotypes. It sounds like a dull routinized series of chopped-up, all-too-familiar segments of sound, usually placidly inconsequential, wholly lacking in depth, originality, or wit in short noise.

-Ashley Montague
Growing Young

What you consider as a normal speaking voice, others may hear as angry or annoyed or withdrawn.

-Arthur Lessac

Suddenly, a channel opened between my throat and my heart and unrestricted emotion welled up in me and filled out the sound of my voice. It possessed my voice, and completely opened wide the long unused passageway of my throat. In that instant I felt healed at the core of my being.

-Tracy Gay Holliday

essential languages' that make it fun and easy for anyone to speak. Through the expressive power of these simple sound languages spoken with a fluid body language, the sound barriers that inhibit their feeling expression were effortlessly released. When I directed participants to shift back into their normal speech habits, awkward laughter filled the room. Contrasting the free flowing body language that supported *Song Talk* with a conditioned style of speaking and static body language was a shocking experience. All the spontaneous dynamics of expressive energy was usurped by mechanical, clipped utterances spoken with little feeling in the matter.

When the body/mind becomes attuned, it becomes capable of hearing the voice of the unknown. The sounds heard in such a state do not belong to any particular language, religion or tradition.

-Swami Rama

Our vocal potential can span over four octaves of tone. It is rare that an octave of tone is ever explored in a lifetime, except under extreme duress.

Activations

The communication of thought through words is the main object of speaking in most schools across the country. Language is an abstraction of sound expression. When speech is deliberated from the mind of thought, the tone tends to move in straight lines. With little melodic feeling running through the dialogue, we are less 'moved' in response to what we hear. Speaking with the feeling tones of free-spirited aliveness opens the creative right brain, which inspires more wave motions into speech.

A shift from eye to ear would be consistent with the shift from analysis to synthesis, from rational knowledge to intuitive wisdom.

-Fritjof Capra

The *Activations* that follow uncover this natural gift of vocal expression that is often lost in the process of maturation. Restoring the primal energies back into language can extend your sonic range beyond gender and cultural considerations. Through this process you will have at your command a practical ability to shift into the essence of any quality of tone with artful expression. Embodying the melodic rhythms of original languages will set in motion the expression of emotional truth.

Unlocking all the registers of tonal color liberates the voice from restrictive categories called alto, soprano, bass and tenor. Now all qualities of vocal expression can be used to express all that you are.

Move your Vowels

The vowels are the word's soul, and the consonants its skeleton. They are living portals, doorways that allow the tonal language of feeling to be expressed into the atmosphere. Skimming over the vowels while speaking words is a clever way to disguise what is really being felt. Embodying the unique qualities of different vowels opens up a resonant energy state that supports the melodic expression of emotion without mental deliberation. As voiced tones, vowels support the singing quality of the voice.

Keeping your vocal instrument in tune allows it to be played harmoniously by the vibrations that constitute life itself. It may well be that it's the symphony of life we were born to orchestrate.

-Steven Halpern

Below are five vowels with specific words that emphasize their unique qualities. As you sound out these different words, listen to the unique tonal qualities of the vowel and how you shape it with your mouth. There are many different ways to translate each vowel's meaning. Here is a map of the territory to get you started. With a rich palette of vowel expression, the 'sonic geometry' of sculpted sound provides you with the inner power to express the inexpressible. To develop facial flexibility, relax your jaw, separate your teeth, wiggle your tongue and articulate a series of vowels with gradual enlargement of the lip opening. As you repeat the different vowels, create a forward, stretching action of your cheeks and mouth.

The vowels facilitate the most open passageways to uplift and inspire the soul's purpose – to sing the Source of all into manifestation.

• The Ah vowel represents inspired aliveness. Articulating the shape of this vowel expands the upper palate of your mouth into V-like dome. As the corners of your mouth are uplifted into an inspiring smile, sound out *Ahhhhhhh* with a bright enlivening feeling. Coordinate your gestures to move in harmony with your expression. Play with bringing out the uplifting, light-hearted nature of the Ah vowels in these words - *heart, sky, light, child, smile, high, star, shine, love, life*. The shadow side of the Ah vowel is a social role that projects a consistent happy vocal expression designed to deny any feelings that don't match this image.

The vowel element is the soul playing music through the word.

-Rudolf Steiner

• The Oh vowel represents the wholeness of soul, the great circle of life. Rounding out the shape of your mouth while gesturing with rounded arms supports the intrinsic depth of the Oh vowel. Bring out the fullness and clarity of the Oh vowel in these words – *whole, home, core, tone, voice, open, joy, source, flow, tone, roar, warm, soul*. The shadow side of the Oh vowel is identification with a dominating, authoritarian tone of voice that is often used to control and intimidate others.

The range of sonics found in the human voice can go from the growl-like depths of the Tibetan monks to the birdlike qualities found in South American Indian tribes.

-Jonathan Goldman

• The Aaa vowel represents your instinctive 'Animal' magnetism that resonates deep in your belly. Release your jaw and drop your tongue behind your bottom teeth. This particular shape creates a gutsy, sensual quality that brings out the 'pizzazz' inherent in this vowel. When exploring the Aaa vowel, encourage your bushy tail to pulse with feeling. The words are - *animal, passion, sensual, sexual, breath, dance, nature, zest, magic, crazy, express, yes*. The shadow side of the Aaa vowel is a voice that projects a gruff vocal quality that works to disguise vulnerable feelings from showing.

• The Uoo vowel represents vulnerability, 'Uoops.' This vowel shapes your mouth into a kiss, which naturally sounds more childlike and sensuous in tone. Notice how the energy of this vowel flows vertically through the core of your body. Softly sway your body as you explore these words, – *tune, true, beauty, blue, loose, juice, fuel, fluid, ooze, move, moon, you*. The shadow side of the Uoo vowel is identified with a fragile tonal quality, which sustains a victimized identity.

• The Eee vowel represents freedom of *feeeeling*. This lateral vowel shape spreads the vibrations through the cheeks of your face. Explore spreading out your arms while exploring the Eee vowel in these words – *free, glee, see, be, clean, sweet, dream, beam, squeeze, please*. The shadow side of the Eee vowel is projecting a shrill, nervous voice of anxious concern.

So the whole natural world can be conjured up for the ear by human voices speaking the expressive consonants.

-Marjorie Spook

Consonant Containers

Vowels allow the uninterrupted flow of breath and consonants interrupt the flow of breath in order to make words more intelligible. As the skeleton of the word, they enhance articulation, and produce rhythmical patterns, melodies and tonal colors. Take each letter of the alphabet and bounce it, strike it and punch it out with varied pulsation. Once you have a feel for the different letters, take any word, such as "PASSION," and articulate the consonants with rhythmic gusto. Now say this word with monotone inflection. Feel the difference. With a balanced interplay between vowels and consonants, a harmonious framework of nourishing tonal action is created.

There are eighty-four reflex points on the upper palette of the mouth. Accentuating rhythmical combinations of consonant/vowel patterns engages the neuro-simulators of the brain with energetic stimulation.

Developing the powers of sound is a profound holy act. Emotional expression appears most spectacularly when verbal expression fails altogether.

-J. Ruesch

Quick Essential Language

The creative play of sound is so effective in moving us beyond confusing definitions and dualistic meanings. With permission to express an unlimited range of emotional energy in imaginative, artful ways, the voice naturally becomes more colorful, melodic and playful. To reclaim the feeling sensations in nonverbal speech, remember a time when you communed with a baby or a pet. Imagine this communion happening right now. Notice how your facial expression and vocal tone lightens up with increased aliveness.

Each one of these languages exercises your tongue, jaw, and lips in new and different ways. For instance, Bae, Bee, Bah, Bo, Buh smacks your lips together like a soft drum which reverberates energy throughout the entire skull. Dae, Dee, Dah, Doh, Duh, flicks your tongue on the roof of your mouth, which stimulates the neurons of the brain. The gutsy sound of Rae, Ree, Rah, Roh, Ruh strengthens the nervous system and Zay, Zee, Zie, Zoh, Zuh juices up the immune system. Explore this now. Make up a Quick Essential Language with Lea, Lee, Lah, Low, Luh. Play with resonating the sounds of these languages in your head, chest and belly.

In the future we will not need words to communicate from the heart of all matter. A hidden language will be revealed that will express volumes simply with the expression of sound.

-Wowza

The *Eight Primal Energies* in the last half of the manual will be expressed with a simple language that consists of a letter chosen from the alphabet and supported by five vowels.

Articulating the consonants and vowel shapes with rhythmical, feeling variations prevents 'mumbling' the syllables with no meaning. Once you become more practiced, mix up all the syllables into a universal language that offers untold freedom to express the full range of your feelings. When first making up an original language, try to make sense of what you are saying. In other words, speak a known language with pre-verbal sounds! For instance, create a question such as: "Boba dora mute?" Now create another phrase in answer to the question. Listen to what you've created and feel into any message of meaning that may be elicited during this process. Make up another phrase. Through this universal language the depths of your emotional life can be expressed with flourishing ease.

When you observe the consonant and vowel elements in speech, you actually discover a self-expression of the human being in each word and tone.

-Schopenhauer

Explore the creation of original chants. You have millions of original phrases living within you that can form the 'bare bones' of innovative chants. With unusual variations of dynamics and coloration, repeat this made up chant over and over again. Create affirmative phrases to give you strength or to give you the courage to overcome any limiting behavior or conflict. These phrases that are musically orchestrated by your creative genius have enormous power to bring your dreams to fruition. No longer depending on outside forces to help you succeed, your inner power is used to unfold your true purpose in life.

From deep-grounded sounds to sharp, driving sounds, use all your sonic powers and more to support your grand voyage through life.

Musical Expression

As the first and future language, *Song Talk* resounds a musical intelligence of harmonious expression that is so needed in our world today. Like music, it is a language that offers total freedom of expression that is devoid of any value judgments. Making up original languages springs from the most primal parts of our instinctive nature. The tones are motivated by a flow of feelings that speak without the need of known words.

The echoing song of creation turned the world into the dance of life, forever singing the blessings and praises of the Creator of creation.

As Ken Carey, author of *Starseed,* expressed so eloquently, "You will sense the vibrational frequencies upon which each plant, each animal and each mineral functions. You will sing the songs that will cultivate the garden that is this world, songs to regulate her climate. You will remember the songs of wind and rain, songs of the seasons, songs of evocation and blessing, songs of love. And within you will arise the songs that will brings forth new creatures and species to bridge the life forms of today with the life forms that will carry biology to the stars." These words form the essence of *Song Talk.*

Musicalizing language unifies speaking and singing into one continuum of expression. Like a beam of light, strong and vulnerable feelings can be concentrated or diffused to animate speech. Below are statements that emphasize the specific qualities of five vowel archetypes. Relish and savor the musical melodies that lie below the words.

The Aaa vowel: *Sensuous, passionate pleasure animates my animal nature.*

This Uoo vowel: *Soothing music moves moody moods to newness.*

The Oh vowel: *Open the bold voice of roaring, potent wholeness.*

The Ah vowel: *Child of light and love, shine as stars high in the sky.*

The Eee vowel: *Feeling peaceful and free, sweet dreams sing me to sleep.*

Singing out your words is different than bringing more melodic tone into your known language. Sustaining singing tones would be somewhat intimidating in normal company. Creating more wave motion in your language is bringing more feeling tones into speech. If self-consciousness still exists, do anything different with your voice except trying to sound good! When singing a familiar song, become a different character Dare to sound through a sumptuous mouth shaping a radically different vocal style than your own. While listening to different singers, capture the essence of their style by singing along with made up words.

The new sciences are proclaiming that the brilliance of sound to cure is the most profound non-chemical medication there is.

Sound Healing

We possess a genetic blueprint for healthy well being. When the mental realm controls the feeling heart, symptoms appear to let us know we are out of balance with the healing source of our being. Amazing curative abilities are intensified when your voice recovers its expressive diversity. Today's medicine is using ultrasound to observe babies in the womb. The fetus is very sensitive to sound. Certain sounds make its body contract or expand. Sonic mammograms are used to detect breast cancer. Chiropractors use ultrasound to speed the healing of tendons and joints. These amazing instruments can even explode kidney stones and remove diseased cells. By means of sound it is possible to

Why does not our humanity rear up and defend its birthright to sing and dance and be joyful before our maker and our loved ones? Why do we so easily stuff our voice, the herald of the soul?

-Bradford S Weeks, M..D

You hear a voice that wells up from the depths of her being, a voice that dwells within her from head to toe, a voice that unfolds like black velvet.

-Jean Cousteau
(speaking of Edith Piaf)

When you are truly inspired to sing, it's as if someone with an absolutely marvelous, powerful, perfect voice was singing through you.

-Joy Gardner Gordon
The Healing Voice

cause geometric figures to form on sand and also to cause objects to be shattered. How much more powerful, then, must be the impact of this force on the vibrating, living substance of our sensitive bodies?

The bristly cell quivered to the high-pitched tones of violins, swayed to the rumblings of kettle drums, and bowed and recoiled, like tiny trees in a hurricane, to the blasts of rock-and- roll.

-Jeff Goldberg

The emotional impact of sound making acts as an intuitive super food that nurtures 'sound solutions' for any health issue, and it's cost effective.

Robert Assogioli, M.D. writes, "Sound will contribute in ever greater measure to the relief of human suffering and to the harmonious synthesis of all human 'notes' of all group cords and melodies, until there will be the great symphony of the one humanity."

This vision is in harmony with the new string theory of physics that proposes the body is a glorious stringed instrument. Elementary particles are perceived as the "musical notes" or excitation modes of elementary strings. When emotions are blocked from flowing, the strings can become flat or sharp. When directing hum/sounding vibrations to flow into the numbness or pain with the intent to heal, the subatomic 'strings' increase in vibration. The sensations that are stimulated can transform dissonance into harmony.

Sound is vibratory energy. Sound touches us and influences our emotions like no other source of input.

-Joshua Leeds

Arnold Mindell, in his book, *The Quantum Mind and Healing* writes with poetic beauty: "Body symptoms are unsung songs. Illness is simply a suitcase with unpacked musical gifts. Your symptoms are not just a part of an ill body but a group of parallel worlds waiting to be sung." This means symptoms are not opponents to overcome but potential allies that are designed to wake us up in making needed changes.

Every organ, every bone, every cell in the body has its own resonant frequency. Together they make up a composite frequency like the stringed instruments of an orchestra.

When approaching the healing, transformative domain of awareness, a larger and deeper method of vocal expression must be explored.

-Rudolf Steiner

Hum while moving your hands over your body. Feel with your hands any areas that draw your attention. Listen to what your humming tones are reflecting in different areas of your body. If you're aware of a painful symptom or dealing with a health problem, moan and groan in sympathy with this condition. With your hands coordinated with the rhythm of your humming tones, stimulate the area with exciting pulsations of energy.

To intensify the healing process, visualize a brilliant golden light glowing from your hands. While focusing this glowing light into the heart of this symptom, ask what is its purpose and deeper meaning in your life. Be open to intuiting any specific information, such as specific tones and rhythms that my help to dissolve the dissonance. You may be drawn to make fast vigorous tones and suddenly feel the urge to make long flowing tones. Trust the spontaneity of the process. Know that your tones are breaking up the density and a peaceful state of mind will occur that lets you know the healing process is complete.

Music of Emotion

The rhythmical power of music has been used for centuries to heal the body, clear the mind and unlock our true nature. Music as emotional energy is designed to soothe or arouse you to take whatever action is necessary to accomplish your life's purpose. For instance, unpleasant feelings can be perceived as dissonant music cautioning you to slow down and intuit healthier possibilities. Enthusiastic feelings can be perceived as upbeat music expanding your energy outward, signaling you're moving on the right track. Even numbness can be viewed as a form of ambient music that is attempting to quiet a busy mind to slow down and relax.

Film scores, I am told, rely on sounds of which we are only peripherally aware to convey emotional tone, set the stage, and build anticipation..

-Andrea Olsen
Body and Earth

A delightful project is gathering music that varies from the primitive to the celestial. Organize this music into an emotive continuum designed to inspire impassioned embodiment. Like a magnet, this continuum of musical pieces can help you exercise a full spectrum of emotional responses. Use different pieces of music as a switch to connect you to any emotion you need for a specific purpose. For instance, fire up your creative spirit by using music with exciting rhythms, accelerating tempos, and dynamic crescendos. A rousing march can invigorate your potent power. New age music and children's lullabies induce peaceful energy to flow. Percussive drumming arouses the potent courage and motivation to move ahead against all odds. 'World beat music' combines a wide variety of musical instruments from faraway lands. This unusual music, with its sensuous, diverse sounds is excellent for heightening creative risk taking.

The true poet paints and sculpts with consonants, sings with vowels, and dances in the dramatic moods of his various rhythms.

-Marjorie Spook
Eurythmy

Selecting music for its emotional content acts as a 'super-energetic' booster that can alter your moods and outlook any time you choose.

When you're overwhelmed with pain, attuning to the underlying music of emotion helps to voice the depths of emotion without inhibition. The more complex your musical tastes become, the more capacity you have for transformation. The more you are able to respond to the resonant music of emotion, the more co-creative you become to make real changes in your life.

Walk Primal

In the beginning our bodies uttered the first sounds, Grunts, screams, sights, ecstatic laughter, yells, snorts, exclamations. "Aaah!" became the 'word' for happy. These words became the way to talk of ideas and things other than feelings in the body.

-Kate P'Neill

Walking with the spontaneous rhythms of sound in pace with your steps is becoming as emotionally mobile and physically flexible as a child. With original music playing in your heart, a simple walk is transformed into a musical improvisation that can lift the most depressed mood or rebalance a hyperactive disposition. Pick a *Quick Essential Language* that offers continual novelty of rhythmical expression. For instance, Mae, Mee, Mah, Moh, Muh is a mellow mumbo jumbo melody that soothes a tired mind into increased serenity. Jae, Jee, Jah, Joh, Juh brings out more juicy joviality. Pae, Pee, Pah, Poh, Puh increases peppy power. Sae, See, Sah, Soh, Suh opens up a sensuous, sexy quality. Imagining the ground as your personal drum beat out with your feet, any buildup of strong feeling. In a few minutes tension and stress is released into the ground.

Exercising these short languages that you embellish with dynamic rhythms is coming in tune with the swing of any activity. Pulsing the syllables into the rhythm of your steps is opens your child's heart of joy. When attuning vocal rhythm in harmony with your steps, open your awareness to the unified field that surrounds you.

Most effective is being an inner activist and a spiritual warrior of the Sound Current.

-Wayne Perry-
Overtoning

One easy way to experience this field, is to project silent vocal rhythms to extend out around you in all directions. Rather than a head filled with repetitive thoughts, sonic rhythms fill your mind with energetic power. Listen to the wisdom pouring through you in the stillness beyond the sound. An affirmative phrase, such as, "I walk with joyous jubilation!" can be silently projected into the field. Marvel how quickly the entire atmosphere of the field transforms into joyous jubilation. The emotional quality of jubilation ignites the chemical, interlukin 2 - the chemical that is so instrumental in healing serious disease. The synthetic version of this chemical is very expensive. Embodying joy is cost effective.

Walking with the spark of life echoing from the heart of your feeling nature brings you into direct rhythm and pace of your life in the making.

Mirroring the Soul

We need simply to learn to allow the song in our heart to have its way with us.

-Bradford Weeks, M.D.

The soul is your original heart of feeling singing with lasting happiness. As the Irish bluesman Van Morrison said," I wanna know, did ye get the feelin? Did ye get it deep down in your soul?" Without a soul song guiding us through life, our vocal expression often sounds flat or sharp. One could say that the 'tonal signature' of the personality is 'sculptured sound' set in stone. Once again, the stereotype of character reflects a predicable tone of voice that shapes our behavior and intellect into predictable channels.

At the mirror, once again, say your name in your usual way. Amplify the familiar tonal quality of your social role. The more you can duplicate your familiar tone as an actor would, the inner walls of resistance, suppression, and inhibition are released.

A word can be empowered with magic. The key is learning how to use this power.

-Ted Andrews

Invoke your *Primal Name*. Your task is to encode this name with a rich diversity of sonic freedom. See this name as a magical tool that acts as the container of superhuman or even supergodly powers. In other words, how would you express yourself if you had all the powers of God? Open up a whole cacophony of emotive sound-making and direct them into the vowels of this chosen name. Exercise rhythmical diversity into each consonant. Spreading your arms that rise from the unknown depths of your being let the World Soul sing through your *Primal Name*. As the great Sufi poet Rumi exclaimed, "The voice of the soul is endlessly extravagant!"

Give physical shape and vocal song to your ancient animal essence

-Paul Newwham
The Healing Voice.

Engaging in performance art practice before the mirror fires the same neurons as if you were living the actual experience.

Witness yourself walking to the center of the cosmic stage. Before you are a vast audience of beings are hoping to experience the healing, transformative power of original sound-making. Perceive yourself as the sounding board; the exquisite, primal instrument through which unique sonic rhythms, made up melodies and sound-filled languages will flow. With purity and innocence, curiosity and enthusiasm, resound the letters of the alphabet. Play with letters in dancing enthusiasm.

Without mental deliberation, open your throat to the 'dared expression. With a fluidity of being, sing out all the letters of the alphabet with feeling. Dance the letters into bursts of chaotic dismemberment! After this outrageous letter play, sing out syllables with melodic waves of feeling. With made-up verses exercise your primal tongue. Out of these inspiring syllables of expression, unleash an original language,– an ancient song language that is seeding and harvesting the evolution of your first and future destiny.

As you look out into this audience of souls, notice that your song has set a collective 'dared expression' on fire! Listen as voices of Heaven and Earth is heard resounding in harmonious interchange with the glory and beauty of life.

Aborigine creation myths tell of legendary totemic beings who had wondered over every continent in the Dreamtime, singing out the name of everything that crossed their path - birds, animals, plants, rocks - and so singing, the world burst into being.

-Bruce Chatwick

Primal Yoga

Groundwork for the Eight Primal Energies

All the primal energy of our evolutionary history exists in our body.
How to acquire the lost heritage of this energy is the science of Yoga.
-Adams Beck

Faced with the diminishment of Earth's life-support systems (which makes us all an endangered species), personal sustainability happens only when we know in our bones we are one with the elements and creatures of nature. Raised to think that we're above the animals, insects and vegetation that abound in the natural world, we have lost so much of our instinctive heritage.

***Primal Yoga* was created to support union with our feeling nature. Attuning your heart to the embodiment of the natural elements and your creature nature is one means of sustaining our future on this Earth.**

Believing we are separate and thereby have dominion over nature sustains inner and outer pollution of natural resources. I quote Jean Houston, brilliant mythologist and author of, *The Possible Human.* She writes, "The pollution of the air and water, the erosion of soil and earth, are only the dark resonance of what is happening in our hearts, our joints, our cells, our arteries. In failing to care for the ecology of our own bodies we have committed mayhem on the rest of the world."

We are all creatures of the earth. She requires that we become like the animals and live by instinct.

-Antero Alli
Angel Tech

Our body is a living ecosystem interdependent with the elements and creatures of nature. Audibly breathing with elemental energy while wiggling, undulating, writhing, rolling, slithering, creeping and crawling on different sized balls prepares your body to express, without reserve, the *Eight Primal Energies*. To enhance instinctive flexibility, rolling on a tennis ball throughout your skeletal system helps loosen tight muscular attachments that densify this native born energy. Bringing your bones into awareness shifts emphasis from a muscle dominant structure into a fluid, cellular medium.

Once surface tension is released, place an eight to ten inch in diameter beach ball on your tailbone with your knees bent. Let your spine hang down from the tailbone like a hammock. Once again, generate pulsations of movement from your tailbone. Feel these pulsations ripple up through your back, which loosens surface tightness along the spinal column and opens up more space between the vertebrae. While resting your spine on a medium beach ball, wiggle your tailbone as a fish skimming

Failing to go through the primal, evolutionary movements of our animal heritage is an inhibiting factor to both body, mind and behavior.

-Moshe Feldenkrais

From fish to apes, humans carry the characteristics of our ancestral heritage in our spines, hands, and the swing of our hips.

-Andrea Olsen
Body and Earth

There is a quality of creatureliness that I find lacking in our world today.
-Cartoon

through the water. Audibly breathe as a fish taking in nourishment from the sea. This means open your mouth and gorge yourself on oxygen! Breathe and wiggle all areas of your spine on the ball. Once you feel the coordination of breath and movement, create an original posture that represents your fish-like nature.

Shapeshifting through the different stages of the mutational process – fish, amphibian, reptile, monkey and early human – opens up more complex levels of movement awareness and extended brain development.

Imagine the brilliance that propelled a fish in water to grow limbs and crawl onto solid ground. This mutational genius still exists within your DNA. Roll over and place the ball between the pubic bone and belly area. While wiggling your tailbone, imagine growing tiny limbs as you shift into the essence of your amphibian nature. With breathing excitement, use your new limbs to push up your torso with writhing motions. The erotic motions of writhing build fluid strength without muscle-bound density.

Activating the early language of grunting and groaning to reflect the amount of pressure you're feeling on the ball, releases all stories and concepts connected to these primal sounds. When amplified, these grunting tones of pressure act as prime mover of your body's guidance system. Spontaneously following your sound rather than thoughts is the key to accessing deepened authenticity of feeling.

Create an original posture that represents your amphibian nature. Resound with a made up language that taps you into the mind force of its power. Meditate on your ability to shapeshift into different domains of consciousness in order to continuously grow and evolve in an unknown world.

Attune to the momentum of change while shifting into the essence of your serpentine nature. Become a cobra shedding its skin. Explore slithering your spine from side to side on the ball. It is as if your entire body is one long tail undulating with fluid dexterity. Slithering motions soften the bony structure of your ribs and breastbone, which regenerates sluggish, stagnant energy in your solar plexus. Out of this expression of serpentine energy, roll off the ball unto the ground.

Shapeshift into your reptilian nature by exploring creeping motions across the ground. Play with coordinating your limbs with your newly discovered legs. Wiggle all your hinges free while creating varied writhing motions. Create an original posture that reflects your reptilian nature.

Exploring a diversity of different crawling motions builds enormous flexibility in your skeletal structure. With well-oiled bones you regain the needed support to remain adaptable in any unpredictable moment.

Out of these creeping motions become an early mammal crawling on all fours. While practicing your crawling skills, reach out with a limb or leg that resembles an octopuses tentacles exploring and inquiring into a new terrain. Accompany all these explorations with an instinctive sound language. By awakening an alert, awake, aware sound language, resilient adaptation to new and different experiences is naturally strengthened. Another transition is taking place that offers greater differentiation, independence and the determination to engage with the world. With heightened curiosity and excitement, transform into your monkey-like consciousness. Infuse your face with quick, dart-like expressions and express yourself with monkey talk.

Going through the developmental journey releases fixed emotional attitudes and brings us back to the ever-changing flow of originality.

-Jack Ball

Exercising the essence of your 'creature' nature can teach you instinctive skills that can help you thrive in any urban jungle.

Take pleasure in regenerating your trigger-ready reflexes and exciting inquisitiveness by bouncing on a large Physio Ball. Feel the delight of frolicking on this ball with the pure joy of simply being alive. Notice as you bounce in the field of gravity, your arms create many unusual designs in the air. Each free-spirited bounce supports you to play at the instinctive edge of your creative potential. This is aerobic fitness at its best! Pause and create an original posture that represents the malleable and versatile traits of this amazing creature.

As a *Sacred Actor*, enact the first human making the transition from crawling on the ground to standing on your feet. Encounter the most vulnerable sensitivity of stepping into a new world of constant change. Create an original posture that reflects this early human. Stretch your torso and limbs to grasp a delicious fruit on the highest branch of the tree. Dwell in this posture while sounding out a primal language that expresses the depths of your newfound feelings. Sense the brilliance of your primal mind urging you to grow and evolve or become extinct.

When shifting back into your familiar posture, see your posture as you have never seen it before. Honor the 'Habit Yoga' you repeat day in and day out. Imagine being told by some outer authority that you must hold this one posture for the rest of your life! With that thought, bring your writhing, creative movement resources to awareness. Excite your bushy tail to wiggle free of any unconscious posturing, be it political or behavioral. Sensing any static posturing as voluntary – a shape you can put on and take off – is 'behavioral flexibility.'

Engaging in the play of movement gets our emotions flowing, and our emotions are what gives us a sense of unity, a feeling that we are part of something greater than our small and separate egos.

-Candace Pert
Molecules of Emotion

Becoming co-creators with the primal movements of your evolutionary history develops a more sensitive, bolder and graceful body to guide you into the creation of an exciting, abundantly fulfilling future.

The *Eight Primal Energizers* that follow, explore in depth, the primal power of emotional energy. Original postures will be created that acts as a safe container for the most intense feelings to be expressed. Enjoy of voyage.

How can there be peace if there is exclusion and supplication? In understanding there is peace, there is freedom. Understanding give right validation to all things.

-Krishnamuti

Diamond Mind

Radiant Peace

Ultimately we have just one moral duty; to reclaim large areas of peace
in ourselves – more and more peace – and to reflect it toward others.
And the more peace there is, the more peace there will also be in our troubled world.

–Etty Hillesum

An Interrupted Life

Short of entering a monastery, retreating into the desert or climbing to an alone mountaintop, experiencing radiant peace in a world fraught with anxious concerns is an enormous challenge. Discovering a calming energy in the midst of any disruptive activity is a true blessing in an increasingly changing world.

The first primal energizer attunes you to the Soul of Peace as the underlying vibratory power of your true being. Even the worst calamities can be absorbed with grace when identified with this radiant, peaceful power as your innermost soul.

Serene waves of energy are always flowing below the surface of our tense, anxious lives. The tranquil music of peace is the fundamental cord of our existence. The practice of embodying calming breathing rhythms and contemplative movements as a daily practice is becoming aware that you are no longer trying to become more peaceful – peace is who you are at the core of your being. Embodying the whispering beauty of peaceful energy transforms the stresses of the day into useable energy to accomplish any task at hand.

The promise of peace,
Forbidden, long hoped
for, goes on like the
hills in an infinite
dream.

-Phyllis Levin

Eye of the Hurricane

It was in the late sixties when the Soul of Peace made its appearance in my life. While attending a three-month spiritual development program at Arica Institute in New York City, one practice required us to spend three days meditating on the sounds of the city merging into the universal sound of *Om*. On the second day of the process, my mind finally quieted down enough to hear the drone of tone below the blaring noises of the city.

On the evening of the third day, one of the trainers came to my room to conduct a special ceremony. Sitting in a meditation posture, we formally bowed to each other in a salutation that honored our spiritual union. Gazing into each other's left eye we internally chanted, "We are One." After spending a few minutes focusing in this way, I felt warm rushes of energy move up my spine. All sense of time dissolved as I witnessed this man's face magically changing into a series of different identities. As the meditation came to an end, I watched transfixed, as his head lit up like a diamond glittering in the sun. In that moment, I felt as if I was being drawn into the light of his very soul.

True peace is found in this moment. Acceptance is the 1st step to inner calm.

-Swami Rama

On the way to the Arica Institute the next afternoon, I was the only passenger riding on a city bus. At one stop, a group of teenage boys got on the bus. Within minutes they were swarming around me, shouting and laughing. One boy grabbed the big woolen scarf around my neck and used it to keep me from moving. Two other boys started to rip off my coat. Each time I struggled against the attack, I felt the scarf tighten around my neck. As I glanced up, a boy was looking at me with deep intensity. In that instant, our eyes merged into a mesmerizing embrace.

In that timeless moment, he spread out his arms like a great bird taking off into flight. With utmost delicacy, the tip of his fingers brushed the shoulders, head and backs of the boys who were attacking my body. Feeling his touch, they flinched backwards in confusion. When the bus stopped, they quickly disappeared out the door like ghosts into the night.

Since wars begin in the minds of men, it is in the minds of men that we have to erect the ramparts of peace.

-From the UNESCO Charter

Still holding our gaze, we simultaneously nodded our heads, and he was gone. As I stepped out of the bus, I had the distinct feeling that I had been transported into the eye of a hurricane. The storm was still raging, but being in its center, I felt safe from harm. Overcome with tears of gratefulness, I blessed the mystery of life that was beyond my comprehension. Walking through the cold, wintry streets, everyone I passed, no matter how stressed out they appeared, seemed to be bathed in a radiant light. As the entire landscape coalesced into a giant network of life-giving light, all the sounds of the city transformed into the magical word *Wow!* Out of this all-encompassing sound, a voice whispered in my inner ear, "I am the Soul of Peace, the serene abode in the eye of the hurricane. Relax. Breathe deep. Know I am always with you."

Several days later, while hearing the wind whisper through the trees, I recalled that this whispering sound reflected the breathy voice of the Soul of Peace. As I explored this whispering quality with my own voice, I was instantly drawn into a deep state of relaxation. Dwelling in the peace of the moment, the ordeal I went through on the bus flashed across my mind. Some profound invisible power united that boy and me at a soul level. This power was so strong that it calmed me down, and in the process, dissolved the adverse intentions of the group.

Self-acceptance gives a wonderful serenity, a great moral strength and a deep sense of internal peace.

-Raberto Assagioli
The Act of Will

As I went about cleaning the house and preparing food, I explored whispering with different vowels, which I found very relaxing. When tension had me in its grip, I called forth this peaceful presence and whispered, "Slow down, relax and be at peace." This phrase became my personal mantra that traveled with me through the day.

When I went to Hollywood to earn my living as an actress, and experiencing rejection on a daily basis, I gradually returned to my tense, fast-paced lifestyle and quick manner of speaking. Occasionally, I would hear a faint whisper calling me home to myself, but I couldn't pause long enough to hear its message.

Wait a Minute!

During my acting career, I worked as a presentation coach to help people move through their inhibitions and stage fright before the camera or audience. It was ironic that Betty, who was dealing with chronic burnout, came to work with me. Betty's pace, the way she moved and spoke, was so fast and furious it was difficult to understand what she was saying. She was besieged by a series of accidents, and driven by extreme restlessness. Her nervous fingers twitched and tapped with incessant activity. In our first session, she had all the answers to solve her problems, but was unaware of the tense mannerisms and frenetic energy running her body. As Betty nervously turned her ring and spoke with ruthless speed, I blurted out, "Wait a minute!' I suggested she pour out all her pent-up feelings, frustrations and tension into this simple statement. With outrageous vocal variations, I joined her in exclaiming *Wait a minute!* to our overactive brain and all the unconscious habits that were making us both crazy. Finally, we sighed and simultaneously exclaimed, *Wow*! With the willingness to pay attention to the tension and stress that's building in your body express it with creative verve, limiting patterns let go of their hold because you are no longer trying to deny them.

The body always leads us home if we can simply learn to trust sensation and stay with it long enough for it to reveal appropriate action, movement, insight, or feeling.

-Pat Ogden

Chanting, "Wait a minute" with all the conflicting feelings you feel is an excellent way to release any habit pattern that runs you. This simple technique also acts as a 'cool down' to pause and take a deep breath.

When we are capable of stopping, we begin to see and feel the truth.

-Thich Nhat Hanh

During the session, I asked Betty to close her eyes and recall everything she felt grateful for in her life. Tears filled her eyes when she named her faithful dog that loved her no matter what. As she spoke about her dog, I brought her attention to the serene tones of her voice. I encouraged her to drop all her words and hum these peaceful sensations into her anxious state of mind.

The next step was coaching her to whisper, first to herself, and then to me, "I am the Great Peace. Slow down, breathe deep and relax." As Betty whispered this phrase for a few minutes, a quiet miracle was taking place. Her nervous gestures relaxed, and her face became beautifully illuminated with radiance.

As her eyes slowly opened, she sighed out one long whispered sound. Sitting for some time in total silence, she finally exclaimed, "Why, this is truly amazing! Enacting this peaceful presence whispering through me, I sense an inner contentment I've never known before. How can something so simple as whispering catapult me into the deepest relaxation? With this secret, I could face any audience right now with confidence."

I promptly said, "The secret is realizing the source of this emotion lives inside of you. This means you can choose to feel peaceful in any moment you choose."

When Betty left, I clearly saw the need to develop an 'emotional fitness' program that exercises the full range of emotional energy that has as its foundation, the Soul of Peace.

Activations

Just as creation hides the creator, your physical form conceals your spiritual presence. The *Activations* that follow enable you to merge your presence with the Soul of Peace. As a *Sacred Actor,* embodying this serene calm, the stress of mental conditioning can be transformed into clear-minded awareness. New age music is a helpful addition in creating a peaceful atmosphere. Be on the lookout for recordings of bells, gongs, chimes, birds and ocean waves that set the tone you desire.

The eternal sounds of etheric peace is the flowing undertone which is forever continuous.

-Hazrat Inayat Khan

To start, recall peaceful moments of quiet reflection, moments of serene tranquility in which you were at peace with yourself and the world. With the intent to receive and feel these peaceful sensations, slow down the pace of your breathing. Like a lover seeking the Beloved, bask in any peaceful vibrations that unfold from these remembered experiences. With all the time in the world, attune yourself to the Soul of Peace that is as near to you as your own breath. Now let go of the memories and simply relax. Whatever peaceful feelings have emerged, perceive them flowing from the Soul of Peace. Feel these feelings as sustained music that fills you with the calming rapture of deep repose.

Light Body

"You look radiant today," you say to a friend who exudes well-being. You are seeing that person through her or his aura!

-Kay Gardner
Music as Medicine

We are all immersed in an energetic field of glowing light. High-powered machines are revealing that an immense play of light is refracted in every cell of the body and the body of the world. When the DNA is split in half, its center glows with light. These shimmering light-encoded filaments vibrate about a thousand times per second. This is what gives us the illusion of appearing solid and separate from everything else. In the heart of this brilliant light, exists the Soul of Peace. With each breath you take, imagine your head is lighting up like a glittering diamond in the sun

Being a human beacon of light-filled consciousness, the Soul of Peace represents the ultimate holographic bandwidth of a unified intelligence.

Your *Diamond Mind* can breach vast distances. Your diamond sensibilities possess the power to reflect 'whole sighted vision' – a quantum reality in which nothing is separate from anything else. It's all about opening your bandwidth wide enough to glimpse a portion of it. One way the luminous light of peaceful calm can be awakened is opening your peripheral vision to see the whole of your surroundings — the walls, floor, ceiling and objects in the room.

Seeing the auric field unites seer and seeing as one and something more – this form of seeing goes beyond itself

-Paul Tillich

As your peripheral vision expands, focus on an object before you. Notice the details of its design. Sustain focus of the object while expanding your peripheral vision. Notice you are now near-sighted and far-sighted at once! With this broadened awareness, witness inner and outer reality joining as one continuum of flowing energy. Remote viewing, seeing across great distances, is within us all. Taking a panoramic view of a disruptive situation internal and external conflict surrenders its mighty hold on your mind. Honor this great collective power of light that can awaken in an instant. All it takes is insight expanding into far-sighted awareness..

Any disruptive occurrence can be instantly changed into a peace-making experience when turning on the light of your *Diamond Mind.*

Whispers of Wow

The word *Wow* is perceived as a modern mantra that elicits wondrous, spontaneous revelations in the moment. Unlike the mantra *Om*, which reflects a controlled, straight-line consciousness, the *Wow* mantra reflects a multidirectional awareness that encompasses all expressions of feeling as sacred. With heightened awe and wonder of life, embracing a Wow Consciousness awakens the ultimate peace – the wholeness of being.

There is no environment 'out there' that is separate from us. We are intimately fused to our surroundings and the notion of separateness is an illusion.

-David Suzuki
The Sacred Balance

The movement meditation, *Whispers of Wow* is interwoven through each of the *Eight Primal Energies*. As the ultimate 'cool down,' is magic can shift you in and out of any emotional energy at will.

The trinity of vowels that compose the word *Wow* are - Ah, Oh, Uh. The open Ah vowel expands your consciousness into the pure lightness of being. The round Oh vowel opens the soul of the word, and the vulnerable Uh vowel draws all the energy back into the core of your being. When creatively whispering with the intent of stimulating calming energy, shift into a fluidity of being by balancing on your sitting bones and gently swaying your torso.

The vital force radiates through and around us like a luminous sphere.

-Paraclsus

Imagine you are in a forest surrounded by hundreds of giant trees all whispering together in harmonious interaction. In this open, relaxed state, whisper the syllables, *Wah Ohh Uhh* as a flowing, melodic language that opens the spiritual unfoldment of the present moment. Give yourself full permission to interchange these vowels as the language your soul expresses in the moment.

With an audible inhalation, draw in pure inspiration that is ignited from your tailbone. Feel this aerated energy being absorbed into every pore of your being. Audibly exhale as one long whispered breath that clears away the stress. While audibly drawing in the air with an open relaxed mouth, notice how the air cools your throat and as you release the air, notice how the air warms your throat.

Become aware of your hands lying on your lap. See the texture of your skin, the shape of the bones, knuckles and nails. Gently open your hands while audibly inspiring the different syllables of *Wow* on your inhalation. Feel the sensation of warmth spreading through your hand. Pause in open attention. Exhale your air while curling your hands inward. Rest in the silence between the breaths. Once more, whisper *Wow* as your hands unfold like a flower opening its petals to the sun. As you breathe out, curl our hands inward, returning you home to inner quiet.

Listen to your whispering heart until it fills your being and becomes the motivational energy behind all your daily actions.

-Ken Carey

An infant explores the subtle opening/closing of its hands for hours on end. It is a profound way to relax, gain equilibrium and rest into a peaceful state of mind. You can apply this process to other areas of your body and achieve the same relaxing affect. As you inhale, whisper *Wow* into a tight shoulder while sensing its interior lengthen and widen. As you exhale, feel the breath release this tension into deep relaxation. If you start to feel light-headed and spaced out, focus your breath in your belly and breathe out the word *peeeece*. Rest at the end of the exhalation.

This wind, flowing round the Earth, would be shaped by her magnetic field into a huge, pulsating aura streaming off into space behind her for millions of miles.

-Peter Russell
The Global Brain

When *Wow* is turned upside down, the word 'Mom' appears; the original, maternal humming vibration of creation. Humming the *Mommmm* tone is a profound means of dropping into the cellular structure of your being. Start by imagining the interior of your body transforming into a holy cathedral of great beauty. Visualize the walls of this sacred temple becoming translucent, stained glass windows reflecting rainbow colors of shimmering brilliance. Gently undulate your spine while humming with siren-like waves through the limitless echoing expanses of your inner temple. With each humming vibration, surrender into a liquid pool of tranquil serenity that rocks you in sweet embrace of your being.

Embracing your body as a sacred temple that carries all matter, energy and information is to breathe, walk and talk as the embodiment of radiant peace.

Embrace the Earth

When I pay attention to the external world, I am like an arrow pointing outward. When I close my eyes and sink into myself my attention becomes an arrow pointing inward. Now, I try to do both at once--to point the arrow in and out at the same time.

-G. I. Gurdijieff

Personalizing something makes it more real. Coming into union with Earth as your home makes this concept a reality. From this expanded awareness it becomes natural to work for the welfare of the whole. In other words, when embracing the reality that Earth exists inside of us, we can take better care of it.

Identifying with the Soul of Peace, expand your peripheral vision while simultaneously whispering *Wow* for as long as you can sustain your breath. With each whispered *Woooooow*, sense the boundaries of your body becoming porous and permeable to the energy that surrounds you. Sense your energetic body expanding out into the room, into the country, the world, the solar system, and finally into the infinite reaches of the sky. Visualize your auric body is a million miles deep, tall and wide. Breathe into the immense spaciousness that you are.

Whispering *Woooow*, look down and see the Earth floating below you. Be a light bearer of peace as you slowly reach out and cradle the Earth in the palm of your hands. With praise and many blessings, send radiant peace into the hearts of all the people, creatures and vegetation. As a final benediction, *Wow* the Earth in wondrous exaltation. Listen as all the inhabitants of the Earth *Wow* back to you in appreciation for the peace you have bestowed upon them.

Only those movements which are supported with conscious, spontaneous breathing can release people's physical restrictions.

-Elsa Gindler

Expanding awareness into an intergalactic awareness, which extends as large as life itself all beliefs of victimhood vanish into the luminous light of peace.

In your mind's eye, create an invisible bridge that moves you through the galaxy, solar system, planet, country, state and back home to you. From this galactic perspective, see excessive worries and troubles dissolving with the knowledge that you can expand your energy to embrace the world as the Soul of Peace.

Retaining a peace state of mind is a never-ending process. While taking a shower or drinking tea, feel a renewed sense of peace as you give thanks for the water of life. While relishing the smells and tastes of your breakfast, send peaceful blessings to the vegetation that created it. As you listen to the birds chirping outside your window, celebrate the bird of paradise existing within your own heart. Perceive the ground below your feet being filled with fertile seeds that are growing a peaceful new world in love with all that is. When conflict and frustration emerges with family, friends and co-workers, exclaim to yourself, "Wait a minute!" Take time to share and demonstrate your newfound ability to slow down and relax. Slowing down in the midst of a maddening moment means you are no longer caught in the hypnosis of cultural conditioning. When taking that extra moment to see the billowing clouds floating across the blue sky, a wild rose by the roadside, a bright star illuminating the dark night and a sparrow chirping on a branch, conflict and struggle rest in silence.

All the pirouettes in the world cannot impress me as much as a simple movement that originates from a deep feeling of aliveness and understanding of the miracle of the human body.

-Frances Becker

Wow in Motion

Exquisite grace is not achieved with mechanical exercise, it comes alive with a fluidity of being fueled by life force. Conduct this simple experiment. Press the side of your arm and hand against a wall for about eight seconds while exhaling all your air. Release the pressure of your arm while audibly inhaling with long flowing breaths. Notice how your arm magically floats up in the air with no muscular effort.

Lighten up your other arm in the same way. For an even stronger effect, visualize your arm being magically filled with helium. After pressing your arm against the wall for a few moments, let go and witness it rising upward with the buoyancy of a balloon. Pay attention to the inner sensations pulsing through your arm. Next, press both arms against a doorway. Step away from the doorway and give them space to float upward without obstruction. With this lighter than air experience traveling through you, float your arms in spiraling pathways with whispering breath energy supporting the movement.

I move with the infinite of nature's power

-Rig Vida

Creating peaceful movements can be perceived as your personal Tai Chi moving meditation that spontaneously flows out of your original nature.

Visualize the magnificent beauty of the sun rising and setting in all its golden radiance. With humming tones leading the way, spread out your arms and pause at the height of your sun-filled beauty. Intend that the brilliant glow of the sun to inspire you with abundant health, vibrant energy and the manifestation of all your dreams. When slowly lowering your arms, hum as a golden sunset filling you with the warmest repose. Create a humming dance with the simplest nuances of impulse leading the way. With each new gesture, feel the shimmering colors of your inner beauty spreading out over an endless horizon.

Attention to sensing quiets what is compulsive in our thought, so that the mind becomes free and available for its free-flowing function of perception.

-Charles Brooks

Song Talk

An ancient Hindu quote expresses the essence of *Song Talk,* "The Great Singer built the worlds, and the Universe is Her song." The substructure of the universe is a vast intricate wave of sound vibrations in the endless here and now. The Great Peace can be perceived as the fundamental octave resonating throughout the unified field of this eternal now. Whisper singing with streaming melodic tones that build and subside with feeling is a powerful means of shifting into the substructure of a consciousness that is always singing with peace. With sounds as soft as rose petals that lightly float in the air, explore the *Wow* Language' of Wea, Wee, Wah, Wow, Wuu. While stretching open the different syllables of this sonorous language, intend your head, torso and gestures to flow as many colored feathers wafting in the wind. Keep exploring a hidden world of unsung harmonies yielding ever deepening peace.

Be a vessel through which the Soul of Peace speaks. You may be struggling with a conflict at work or are unable to find time to relax. With your pre-verbal language, speak as this serene peace offering you all the wise counsel you will ever need. Pause and rest in silence. Trust that your body, heart and mind are processing this information at a subconscious level. Be patient. A translation of what has been spoken is forth coming. As upwelling intuitive impulses rise to the surface of your awareness, your answers may come in different forms such as specific words, symbols, images or metaphors.

Humans are becoming much more sensitive to the non-human languages of the surrounding world. We are learning the tree language, the languages of the birds and all the animals and insects, as well as the languages of the stars in the heavens.

-Swimme & Berry
The Universe Story

A peaceful state of mind dissolves in midair when speaking in a rapid, harsh manner. Whispering your known language is a great preparation in bringing more peaceful repose into communication. A few minutes of whispering to yourself or a playmate is a profound away to enter into an altered state of awareness. Whisper/speak the statements that follow. Draw out the vowel tones with the melodic music of peaceful tranquility.

As the Soul of Peace, I am as near to you as your very own breaaaath.
I let go and relaaax. I have all the time in the world.
Whispering as the Great Peace I am content and fulfilled.
With serene tranquility, I have all the time in the world.
Peace, peace, peeeeeece, endless waves of peace pour through my heart.

If you listen to the tides of the oceanic pulse, you hear the music of all that's ever been.It is the lost language of unheard sound.

-Carolyn Mary Kleefeld

Walk Primal

Life has gotten so busy, time-pressured and complex that even a leisurely walk is usually spent dwelling on worrisome thoughts that dull the sensory wonders of the present moment. The habit of walking on fast-forward and driven by expectations can be changed any time you wish. When amplifying your style of walking as an actor would, awareness grows that this condition is created through limiting habits of mind.

Moving with the natural grace of the Soul of Peace, breathe as an endless river of feeling that inspires rejuvenation on all levels.

Stand in peace before you walk. With heightened peace as your intent, explore how slowly can you walk. Have you ever tried it? Taking long, deep breaths helps to fuel this process with boundless life force. Walking with the slowness of cumulus clouds floating in the sky may induce wobbly vibrations in your feet. Let this happen. Encourage any feeling that wants to be expressed. Anxious feelings may arise when first slowing down your pace. What eradicates this condition is turning on the light of your *Diamond Mind to* illuminate whatever may obstruct your path. This enlightening power can also be used to see the enormous beauty that surrounds you. It only takes far-sighted eyes to see it and appreciate it.

Let us be fully united in our hearts and speak and walk together in peaceful harmony.

-From the Rig Veda

Whatever draws your attention, whisper with a voweling language your feeling responses. Enjoy taking the time to move your spine as seaweed in the currents of water. In order to spread peace out far and wide, imagine invisible crisscross tensional forces expanding out from your body as radiant light. As you step forward out of this luminous light -filled space, radiant peace to the Earth with each step you take. Rooting peaceful energy into reality helps to center you in space.

Mirroring the Soul

It takes courage to see all of oneself in the mirror of truth. Self-love grows strong when realizing that your conditioned tendencies are the salt and pepper of your unique being. With embodied awareness behavior habits, there is no need to improve or fix them. Without awareness you are confined to the rigors of repetition, which deadens inquiry. Simple acknowledgment of your automatic reactions offers you more internal space and more room to breathe.

If we could strip the ideologies that separate us, stop the greedy destruction, and walk by the riverside, we would discover that we are all children of the same earth.

-Cahill & Halpern
Ceremonial Circle

Before the mirror, say your name as you tune into the posture, facial expression and emotional quality of your social role. How much peaceful expression is allowed in your personality? Do you struggle more with inertia or hyper-activity? When the limiting aspects of the social role are accepted, the deepest peace comes into being. As Dr. Deepak Chopra is quoted saying in his book, *Ageless Body, Timeless Mind*, "A lifetime of unconscious living leads to numerous deterioration, while a life time of conscious participation prevents them."

When I was a trainer for Arica Institute, one of the most powerful meditations that helped bridge the duality that exists between the ego and the essence was *Trespaso*. Two people would sit across from one another and gaze in each other's left eye. Internally they would chant, "We are one." Over a five year period, I must have gazed into a thousand people's eyes with rapt attention.

A universe of inner peace shines out from our eyes when we become the Soul of Peace. Breathing, speaking and walking as this unified force of relativity, everything in life is perceived with tranquil serenity.

Here is an expanded version of *Trespaso* you can do with yourself in front of a mirror. While looking into your eyes, expand your peripheral vision. Focus your attention on your face and at the same time diffuse your vision to see the whole of your surroundings. As you look at yourself from this expanded view, cover the left side of your face with your hand. Notice your impression of seeing this half of your face. Deepen this experience by gazing into your left eye for one minute. Notice any feelings or impressions that emerge.

When our brain waves resonate with those of the Mind of the Creator, our inner voice comes into direct communication with God.

-Barbara Marx Hubbard
The Revelation

Now cover the right side of your face. Notice in what way this side differs from the other side. Gaze into your right eye. Slowly go back and forth, covering one side and then the other side. Often one side appears to expand outward and the other side appears to contracts inward. One side may appear more introverted or extroverted, friendly or stern. What is it like to witness two different sides of your personality without judgment or preference?

As you focus on the space between your eyes, open your peripheral vision. With this wide view, simultaneously view both sides of your face. The magnetic poles that balance the rational and irrational sides of your nature come into harmony when opening the 'third eye,' the intuitive, wisdom center of the soul. In this moment, nothing is lacking. What shines in all its beauty is the divine essence of your soul. This is the face of your natural state. Observing the essence of our being and the ordinary notion we hold of ourselves in one penetrating look – thinking and feeling blend into the transparency of light-filled awareness.

But as for you, resolve to keep a quiet time both in you homes and here within these peaceful walls when the bells ring on Sundays. Then your souls can speak to you without being drowned out by the hustle and bustle of everyday life.

-Albert Schweitzer
Waking the Sleeping Soul

With your *Diamond Mind* lit up, any new idea, problem or relationship can be seen with greater clarity. Feeling bigger, roomier and more extended spatially deepened relaxation occurs. For instance, when an argument is brewing with a friend, quiet your mind while feeling into your physical reality. Take a second to notice which eye you are focusing on. Shift your attention into the other eye. When both sides of your friend's face come into clear relief, open your peripheral vision while focusing on the space between the eyes. Moving your sight beyond a dualistic viewpoint is seeing with all your senses awake. Attuning to your underlying connection is honoring the oneness you both share. In this expanded state, send radiant peace to flow into the heart, mind and soul of this person before you. Concentrate on the shifts of energy that are occurring between you.

Performing new ways of being before the mirror is an effective means of developing the power of inward choice and the exploration of new waves of being.

I believe that just being conscious of our ability to shift our rhythms within the fabric of a frenetic society will make our hours less anxious, our days less stressful, and our lives more complete.

-Stephen Rechtschaffen

In preparation for your performance before the mirror, invoke your *Primal Name*. Encode this magical name with the Soul of Peace. By anchoring whispered tones of peaceful tranquility into the very soul of this name, the wisdom needed for your future evolution is intuited more clearly. With this magical tool, know you have the power to shift out of any debilitating state and create what is right for you in the moment.

Before the mirror anything is possible. Imagine the mirror before you is transforming into a movie screen. As a *Sacred Actor,* you have been chosen to embody and demonstrate peace in action at the United Nations. A large group of weary people are sitting before you. They are overwhelmed with the enormous task of keeping global peace. It is obvious that they are doubtful that anything can change their heavy disposition. As you feel all eyes focused upon you, invite them to chant, "Wait a minute!" Give them full permission to pour out all the emotional buildup that devours their energy. Feel the empowerment of creating real change in a group by honoring and expressing the truth of emotional authenticity.

That which is within and that which surrounds one is the great peace and it is holy. Live in the peace, be this peace.

-Navajo Chief

The symbol for your performance is the White Dove, the winged messenger that spreads the essence of divine harmony throughout the world. With a flowing breath ignited from your tailbone, expand your arms as the great wings of this magnificent bird. With each rise and fall of your wings, intend the energy of peace to fill everyone's heart with gladness. With each intake and release of breath, sense the healing, transformative energy of renewal regenerating people's spirit.

As deepened relaxation fills the room, invite everyone to open their peripheral vision while gazing into each team member's third eye. Ask participants to acknowledge that below the surface of the public persona the Great Peace is alive and well. Like the young child that still lives within their hearts, invite them to whisper as the wind. As the energy in the room builds with oxygenated life force, draw everyone into the circle to *Wow* each other in mutual admiration for being instrumental in bringing about world peace. Perhaps, for the first time, see these people let down the guard and look deeply into each other's eyes with no value judgments obstructing their view.

The Soul of Peace comes into view when the separative boundaries of the ego merge with the boundless breath of being.

The above scene is meant to be a permission giver. With play practice before the mirror, you are developing the power to affect real change in people's lives wherever you go. As you exercise the physiology of real peace, it is obvious that this unmistakable quality is now recognized in everyone, whether they know it or not. When walking into the presence of your family, friends or co-workers, regardless of any mental condition or mood they are identified with, call forth the Soul of Peace and witness this condition dissolving into equanimity.

And above all, let us daily send the radiance of peace into the hearts and minds of the public experts who are dealing with issues of nuclear war, toxic wastes, acid rain, rising rates of radioactivity, expiring species of plant and animal life, loss of topsoil and forestland, dying seas, the growing misery of half the planet's people. They need, more than ever before, a holistic power that can break through the illusion of separateness and rekindle peaceful co-existence in the world.

Peace is a daily, a weekly, a monthly process, gradually changing opinions, slowly eroding old barriers, quietly building new structures.

-John F. Kennedy

Whatever your practice, the most important things is taking the time to reach the God force of peace within.

-Bob Cranmer

I tasted you, and now I hunger and thirst for you. You touched me, and I am inflamed with the love of your infinite compassion.

-Saint Augustine

Heartbeat

Compassionate Love

*We must become all eyes like the narcissus, and once having become all eyes,
the Beloved is seen in every eye.*
-Sant Darshan Singh

The starvation of millions of people today, the wars between nations, and the poisoning of the environment reflect an overwhelming loss of love. How do we connect with this inborn love on a personal and global scale? A new worldview is required that extends our awareness beyond our personal boundaries and dualistic notions of reality. When regaining genuine love for ourselves, all of humanity becomes the expression of our extended family.

The second primal energizer connects you with the Soul of Love as total freedom of expression made sacred. Exercising the physiology of this loving presence with breath, sound and movement is the healing balm that sustains an open heart through the many trials of living.

We are made in love. Love is the heart-felt expression of the Great Peace. Awareness of a limitless reservoir of love and expression of this generosity of spirit to others is the secret of lasting happiness. Embodiment of the Soul of Love is opening the realization that you were born wonderful, remarkable, lovable and unique! As a spiritual being, you have greatness of spirit. You have inner strength and power and a glorious capacity for living, loving and giving.

Loss of Love

So many of us have experienced the trauma of being abused, abandoned and hurt by people we love. These people are only reflecting their own lack of love that has been perpetuated from generation to generation. All human sickness stems from the absence of love. The insidious belief that we are not good enough to be loved forces us to act subservient to other people's wishes. Acting like a deprived victim is a strategy to gain other's sympathy and soften their critical assessments of our character.

The last time I saw him, he was walking down Lover's lane holding his own hand.

-Fred Allen

With a loss of love, it is only natural that our intellect goes to work and builds elaborate systems of defense to protect our fragile, wounded heart. Remaining isolated behind an unfeeling mask is to remain unfulfilled, dissatisfied and deprived emotionally as a human being. Being encapsulated in this painful condition, unceasing internal voices endlessly build shame and blame about what's wrong with our appearance, performance and our right to be alive. On and on the litany goes: "My breasts are too small. I'm not smart enough. I don't have what it takes to succeed. They will judge me if I show them who I really am." With messages like this, there is a tendency to become very abusive to our body. We force this amazing vehicle to work overtime, beat it up with mean words when it gets tired, and starve or stuff it into sickness.

Even the lowliest shadow self has a purposeful and holy function; that somehow, having to hit bottom is a sacred ritual, an integral part of the creative process.

-Jacquelyn Small
Embodying Spirit

Gaining excess weight, twisting and contorting ourselves into unnatural poses, slumping into oblivion, acting invulnerable and choking our voice into a monotone are strategies to avoid the pain of this great loss of soul-felt love. Enduring the strain in our eyes, we can no longer see genuine insights that give meaning to our lives. Our spine can become so contracted; it rebels with chronic back pain. Our heart can feel so neglected that it attacks us. Can you blame it? A heart that is continually mistreated and its wisdom unheard burns out and finally mumbles, "I'm out of here!"

As I write, I am reminded of Dora who spent much of her time living in an iron lung. Some friends brought me to see her in hopes that my work could lift her spirits. In our first session, Dora reflected the same loveless scenario that I have been attempting to heal in myself. Believing that self-love was a vain, conceited and selfish idea, she had many doubts that our healing process together would work.

Rejoicing in the wonder and awe of love is an embarrassing idea for most of us. Immediate associations of egotism, vanity, and selfishness often fill the mind. Egocentric behavior only arises when self-love is absent.

Together, Dora and I created a ritual in which I coached her to breathe and hum as the embodiment of the Soul of Love, and to dialogue with the wisdom of this compassionate power. Her final task was imagining the seeds of a beautiful garden of flowers existed in her heart. By turning her loveless beliefs into compost, the garden would spring into bloom.

Love occupies a majestic place in healing. Lying outside space and time, it is a living tissue of reality, a bond that unites us all.

-Larry Dossey, M.D.
Healing Words

As I approached her two weeks later, I knew from the light shining in her eyes that something had changed. Dora reached out for my hand and exclaimed, "Oh, Elisa, a magical change occurred when I personalized the Soul of Love as Musica. I've been lying here not able to move a muscle, but when Musica hummed through me with love, I felt as if I was dancing from the inside out." With a long, thoughtful sigh, she said, "I'm beginning to understand why I got so sick. My inner voice kept bombarding me to wake up, but I no longer knew how to respond or trust my feelings. All I could do was numb them with drugs and alcohol. Only when identified with Musica, could I forgive myself for the creation of a loveless life."

Love might be called the holy emotion because it unites the body with the spirit in an unbounded process of wholeness.

-Sephano Sabetti
The Wholeness Principal

Activations

The Activations that follow exercise the power of self-love to grow strong in your heart. One of the key issues that can impede our loving nature is the inability to forgive ourselves for our past actions and forgive those who hurt us. A lack of forgiveness is resistance to change. If the strength of our will remains in resistance, we stay dependent on what we are resisting. Alignment with the source of love offers boundless opportunities to step away from the pain of these experience love without limits. Being the embodiment of love in the depths of our being, the loveless part is embraced with open arms. In the twinkling of an eye, compassion is stirred to 'forgive those who trespass against us." I offer this quote from Dag Hammarskjold, "Forgiveness is the answer to the child's dream of a miracle by which what is broken is made whole again, what is soiled is again made clean."

Self-love is a sacred act. With an abundance of self-love, daily confusions and hurt feelings can be redirected through a loving heart rather than churned out in endless mental deliberations in the head.

The heartbeat of a person with depression is unusually steady. Ideally, you heart rate sould be variable - your heart can respond appropriately to the different tasks it's called upon to do.

-Dennis Charney MD

Heart of Compassion

This extraordinary heart that beats within us pours out its fluid vibrations into every infinitesimal aspect of our being. Contemplate this astounding information. Your heart pulls blood through the body as the moon pulls on the tide. Your heartbeat, being fully attuned to the rhythm of life, thumps 100,000 times a day, approximately 40 million times a year, and within 70 years, supplies the pumping capacity for nearly 3 billion cardiac pulsations! And that isn't all. This amazing organ pumps two gallons of blood per minute. One hundred gallons of blood per hour flow through your vascular system. When unraveled, your heart spans about 60,000 miles in length, which corresponds to more than twice the circumference of the earth! The incessant beating of your heartbeat echoes in the Great Heart of that reverberates throughout all creation. This is the true meaning of unconditional love that throbs in rhythmic measure in every moment of your life.

Opening the heart in relationship to all that you are sustains self-love and compassionate service as the greatest task there is.

Original Innocence

When I was going through an old scrapbook my mother left me, I was most touched by my baby pictures. As a young infant I appeared so joyous, so open and loving. No matter what expression I had on my face, the light of love radiated through me. As I turned the pages of the scrapbook, I noticed some other pictures that were taken of me a few years later. In these pictures, I saw a shy little girl hiding from the camera. My head was tilted to the side, my chest was concave and my eyes were cast down. I was struck with the undeniable fact that I was born in love and this love was hurt and went underground. A belief got established that I was too stupid and ugly to be loveable. This belief forced me to mask my pain by hiding behind a shy persona believed to be real.

From love you are made. Before layers of cultural conditioning curtail their spirit, the original innocence of unconditional love shines from every young child's eyes.

Are there ways you could treat yourself better?Do you treat yourself as well as you treat others? Is it time to throw a party to show your appreciation?

-Anodea Judith

Very few of us were lucky enough to have retained the open heart of a baby. We have had to adopt various behavioral strategies designed to get the love that we need. These conditioned tendencies create a distance between the head that runs our social role and the heart that runs our feeling nature. It is obvious that your head and heart have important roles to play, but if the head rules, the inner voice of feeling fades into the background.

That which fills the universe I regard as my bodyAnd that which directs the universe, I see as my own nature.

-Chang Tzu

Here is an opportunity to connect with the pure presence of love that shone from your eyes as an infant. To start, I invite you to find a baby picture. If you can't find one, draw a picture of the baby you once were. Gaze into this baby's eyes. Let the innocence of this infant touch your heart with renewed love. Feel the life force of this baby cradled in your heart. Contemplate which people, pets, images or natural elements have touched your young child's heart. Bless and praise them all for helping you keep the flame of love alive. Clear your mind of these experiences and simply bask in the afterglow of the loving feelings that have been activated. Drink deeply from this inexhaustible wellspring of love living in your heart.

Now look for pictures when you are a little older. Self-consciousness can dramatically limit how much love we can feel. From the time we are small children we are being conditioned to judge ourselves harshly and to think of ourselves in negative terms. And if we didn't conform, we are branded as naughty, lazy, stupid, bad and a disruptive influence. Look for any pictures in which you start to disguise how you feel or attempt to hide from being seen. For instance, notice the posture and facial expression of self-conscious concerns. You chin may tuck into your neck or you may wear a 'chip' on your shoulder.

Getting a handle on some of the negative beliefs that get instilled in the mind, more times than not, healing gifts are revealed.

Why not fall in love with the body you've been sleeping with all your life?

-Stewart Emery

Let an early memory to come into awareness. Don't focus so much on the story but on the feelings that arise from reviewing the memory. What belief was formed out of this experience that may still separate you from fully loving yourself? What kind of walls got erected to protect your heart? For instance, if you felt unlovable, say this limiting belief out loud. Listen to the sound of your voice. Drop the words and express this sound with full voice. To release a belief that can rule your life takes volume! Turn this sound into the compassionate language of humming. Allow your body to move as needed to better facilitate release. As resonance occurs with the belief, hum love into this disharmonious belief. While humming, imagine these loving frequencies composting this belief into fertilizer to grow renewed love in your heart. Affirm that this negative belief has served its purpose and is now no longer needed.

Love's Body

No door that enough love will not open. No gulf that enough love will not bridge. No wall that enough love will not throw down.

-Cloud of the Unknowing

The molecular system of your body stretches back to the origins of life on the planet. This means the wholeness of your body is not a thing or an object. It is through the body that love is felt and expressed. Being the container of this infinite love, every cell in your body is very sensitive to vibrations of loving feelings and affirmative thoughts. It listens to everything you say and responds accordingly.

Developing self-communication with the Soul of Love living in your heart is the greatest insurance to promote good health and a powerful sense of self-worth.

Your body enjoys and appreciates recognition. Communing with love to your body sustains divine assurance in the intrinsic power of your being. Picture a mother humming with love while softly rocking a crying child into calmness. Mother and child deeply understand this language without words. Sending humming vibrations of love through your body can quickly free up tension and open the way for more heart-felt love to flow. Place your hands on your shoulders with tender regard. Greet your body by humming out this meaning, "Hello Body! How are you feeling?" Listen to your body with full acceptance. Embrace it with your hands. Touch its softness, depth and wisdom. With deepened appreciation for this astounding gift of life, exclaim, "Dear body I shower you loving gratitude for all that you are." Pause for a moment and sense how your heart feels when receiving loving tones of genuine appreciation.

The power of love to change bodies is legendary. Love moves the flesh, it pushes matter around. Tender loving care has uniformly been recognized as a valuable element in healing.

-Larry Dossey, M.D.

Bridge the gap from your body to your mind. Hum with the message that exclaims, "Hi Mind! Blessings and praises for all the enormous thinking demands you endure." As you give your head a humming hug, allow it to express itself through movement. Let your hum indicate where and how it wishes to be moved. Know that this intelligence in your head knows perfectly well what it needs to disperse tension.

Hum into your pelvis while exploring its powerful interior. Hum into these large bones and muscles that contain gut level knowing. Thank your pelvis for the grounding support and sensuous pleasure it provides you. Greet your shoulders, belly, knees and feet in the same way. Hum with love into deeper levels of your being. With humming tones, encourage these parts to express themselves in movement.

The emotional expressiveness of lovie directly affects the immune system, and people are less likely to develop serious diseases.

-Dr. Bernie Siegel

Each one of the many systems of your body has a mind of its own. Together, they contribute in different ways to the quality of your movement and expression. Hum through your endocrine, skeletal, fluid, immune, cardiovascular and nervous system. While humming praises and blessings into your muscular system, communicate how appreciative you are of its strength and power. While loosening your bones and shaking loose tight hinges, thank your skeletal system for the flexible, structural support it provides you. With a brisk touch, hum/tap your hands all over your skin and feel your nervous system come glowingly alive. This simple activity is a powerful means of warding off psychosomatic symptoms of disease.

Once, when humming love to my liver, it started firing tiny impulses like a Morse code. When I asked what was wrong, it said, "Give me more water! How can I keep moving out all this junk without sufficient water?" While praising my feet, I asked them to forgive my lack of care. Instantly they curled up in a fetal position. I laughed when sensing how shy and self-conscious they felt when receiving so much loving attention. One of my clients reported her eyes started blinking and squinting when she hummed to them. When asking what was the matter, they said, "The glasses you're wearing are wrong for us! Get new ones and we will be a lot happier."

Tender Touch

Touch speaks louder than words. When we are moved to tears, when our emotions are deeply affected, we say we have been 'touched.' To touch and be touched is the ineffable language of the heart made visible. Studies show that healing is speeded up and fewer drugs and surgical procedures are required when tender, loving touch is administered to a wound. An infant who does not get sufficient touch yearns to return to the womb. Just like a plant that needs the sun's energy to thrive, we need to touch and be touched to keep the light of love alive. As a massage therapist, I became an expert at giv-

The phrase "I just want to be held" is heard in every tearjerker from Sister Carrie to As the World Turns.

-Byron Scot

ing loving touch to others, but soon realized how unfamiliar it felt to touch myself with loving attention. As I noticed my habit of slapping on cream in a coarse, haphazard fashion, I heard the voice of my mother exclaiming, "It's not nice to touch your body." I couldn't help wondering how many young children were instilled with that unfortunate belief. Enough is enough!

When the animals talk to you, will you know what they are saying? When the planet sings to you, will you be able to wake yourself up and act?

-Gary Lawless

Your hands are healing instruments. Magnetize them with energy by vigorously rubbing them together for at least thirty seconds. Varying the intensity of rubbing creates more friction. Slowly move your hands apart and notice any tingling sensations that are vibrating through them. These sensations stimulate 'Oxytocin,' the love chemical that is used to treat depression, schizophrenia and obsessive-compulsive disorders.

While rubbing your hands together again, intend this 'love force' to beam from your hands. As tingling sensations grow, remember times when you were touched by the beauty of nature. Sense the warmth of the sun bathing you in its warm glow. Stroke your face with hands that are filled with the warmth of sun-kissed beauty. Intend your hands to transform into fluttering butterfly wings. With dancing fingers, pulse flickering touches across your cheeks. Humming with simple affection cradle your head as a mother cradles a newborn baby. If a smile occurs, intend this smile of happiness to spread through your body.

It is only the heart that can tell you what reason cannot know. Being in touch with a love that is without boundaries is to become a transmitter and receiver of unconditional love.

When labels are put aside, pain is an intense sensation that is signaling you to pay more loving attention to yourself. Pain forces us to grow whether we like it or not. When we attempt to deaden pain by contracting the body and ignoring what we feel, we deaden the potential insight this pain has to offer. Almost everyone has experienced car accidents, falls, and surgical incision that disrupt our body with wounds, fractures, and sprains. Focus on an area that has been abused, injured or deeply hurt. Hugging and humming into a painful area in your body is a regenerating healing balm that thaws out old wounds.

When cells are loaded with traumatized memories of the past, they lose their responsiveness. Personalizing pain as the home that houses an abandoned infant brings more heart-felt feeling into the matter. This infant cries to be hugged and loved. With your humming voice, direct loving feelings to vibrate into the heart of this little infant. With each outpouring of humming energy, visualize vibrant, healthy cells and tissues, resonating in harmony, With a loving generosity of spirit, spread your hands open while stroking your entire body with long flowing touches.

So take it as your duty to give those around you permission to love. Encourage their affection by showing it yourself, without regard for what you may get in return.

-Deeoak Chopra

Loving Connections

Walking through life with a loving heart is the most powerful magnet to which other people are attracted. Regardless of what protective mask or defensive role a person may be projecting, a loving heart is the 'melt down' that gives permission for the toughest mask to soften. Let face it, deep down, we're all waiting for our feeling heart to be recognized, appreciated and freed to be expressed. As O. Fred Donaldson writes in his book, *Playing by Heart*: "As playmates, our quest is to increase the playmates within our personal and collective playgrounds. In this way the source of love flourishes"

Scientists have measured this whole-body state of loving awareness radiates a magnetic field that can be measured up to eight feet away from the body!

The next time you enter a room full of people, test this theory out for yourself. Consciously radiate loving energy into the entire space and intend this love to enter into the hearts of everyone present. When you give someone a hug, spend an extra moment humming into their heart with feeling. In this simple way, heart to heart connection is made. Above all, let us respect our right and everyone else's right to express their uniqueness, free from ridicule or condemnation; Let us never seek to impose what we believe on anyone else. Following this simple philosophy we cease to be a slave to imposed thought and behavior. By choosing to open our hearts and 'be love' here in this moment with all the human beings that cross our path, we give ourselves the gift of fully experiencing it.

Love evokes the true self to emerge and be seen and felt in full glory.

--Janet Zuzzerman

Song Talk

Being born with an infinite supply of love, a baby can freely voice its true feelings without inhibition. Enduring years of conditioning NOT to be ourselves, the dynamics of our vocal power lies buried in layers of muscular tension. When a lack of self-love is felt, more times than not, a social role is developed that conveys a sentimental, sweet tone of voice. A contrived vocal style designed to convince others that we are a loving person, can deaden authentic feelings of love from being seen, felt and heard. Being identified with any consistent manner of speaking, the colorful kaleidoscope of tone that expresses the full range of heart-felt feeling is concealed in a mask of pretense.

Identifying with the Soul of Love is reclaiming the immense depth and richness of love's varied tones of expression.

The present moment embodies pure love.

Goethe

Infants become blissed out when they hear their language mirrored back to them. When we talk to babies in adult tones, they become confused and act out their frustration in unpleasant ways. Pause for a moment and express yourself as an infant seeing the world for the first time. Play with simple syllables that rise up and down in tone. When playing with the light-hearted musicality of this pre-verbal language, notice the way your body responds. With sing/song involvement every gesture reflects the spontaneous truth of your moment-to-moment feelings. Now shift back into your known language and speak in your normal way. Do not be dismayed if you hear more constriction of spontaneous feeling in your voice. Conscious recreation of your normal voice opens the way for greater warmth and musicality to flow into your verbal expression.

Imagine you are greeting the infant that is still living in your heart. Exclaim, "Welcome dear child. I love you! Dear one, I shower you with joy! Praises and blessings to the beauty of your soul. I rejoice in your pure loving presence. I will always cherish you and will never forsake you. If you fall down, I will be there to take your hand." As a *Sacred Actor,* be the Soul of Love speaking as a great old sage that is revering your life's experiences. Drop your tones into your tailbone and let them reverberate through your spine. In other words, Loving tones reach to the very core of your being.

Healing and growth occurs when we can express ourselves creatively in sound.

-David Darling

My God loves your God. Beyond our comprehension, being creative in the expression of love effortlessly arises when recognizing God in all beings.

Below every painful mood, lurks an 'inner child' who is lacking in love. Subtly mirroring a friend or co-worker's tonal quality tunes you into the feelings below any masked attitude that is being projected. For instance, if someone projects a strong, cool or predictably nice personality, truthful feelings remain hidden behind the personality. If the tone is depressed, anxious or cold, subtly mirror this quality with your humming voice. Humming love into this person's heart can help shift the toughest mood into authentic expression. Mackenzie Jordan wrote in her book, *Say What You Love*: "As one million people begin to say - and I want to add -feel and express what they love unconditionally, every human being will begin to spontaneously and effortlessly live what they love, and the world will be forever changed."

But so much seems to depend upon the way any human is received into this world. Does the brand new body feel welcome, loved. Does it feel lost, rejected? The emotional climate enveloping earliest infancy seems to lay the foundation of a human's self image.

-Trudi Schoop
Will you Join the Dance

Walk Primal

We are each an aspect of this universal pattern of unified motion. Like an invisible all pervasive spider web, the magnetic power of gravity is the uplifting, supportive force that carries us in balancing harmony throughout our lives. Tune into the gravitational force by exploring where you feel the most support and ease in walking.

Gravity is a powerful metaphor for love in action. This force field holds us all in its eternal embrace.

With every step you take, be a conduit of the Great Love. Sending loving regard to the world and feeling the world send loving regard to you is walking in a primal way. Imagine your body is a hollow reed that quivers with joy when the breath of love moves through all the cells of your body. With your head rising upwards into the sky, feel the holy air embrace you with love. Loose, adaptable ankle joints encourage greater articulation in your feet. Accentuating the heal, ball, toe roll creates more wave motion in your feet. With tender flowing steps, feel your feet touch the ground like a lover caressing the beloved.

Rather than relying on a visual image of correct movement, let a sense of ease be your guide. For instance, a large stride develops more muscle-bound definition that often rigidifies hinges and joints. A shorter stride supports your pelvis, torso and head to move forward in a more effortless, balancing manner. Hum through your legs while imagining them as luminous energy supporting the buoyant flexibility of your pelvis, torso and head. With balancing momentum, hum while rocking your pelvis as a hammock that is rocking a baby with undivided pleasure. When experiencing any tightness in your muscles, hug them with humming love.

Near your breastbone there is an open flower. Drink the honey that is all around that flower.

-Kabir

When your pelvis is free to swing in any direction the very core of your being is free to move in any direction that serves your purpose.

With your *Diamond Mind* lit up, humming love to the four cardinal directions can sustain a 'web of relatedness' in those times you feel lost and confused about when and where to go. Being apart of this web of relatedness also acts as a protective shield that keeps you safe from adverse harm. One day, I walked past a field of poison oak. I spontaneously exclaimed, "Hi Poison Oak!" How are you doing? Without deliberation, a guttural humming language spoke into my inner ear that seemed to acknowledge my presence. In that moment I saw and appreciated its red blooded beauty glimmering in the sun. It's interesting to note that I oftentimes hike through fields of poison oak and I'm never affected by its poisonous power. I like to believe that a certain respect has been received and given – and in making this connection – I am held in safe keeping with this potent force of nature.

Genuine Power is equivalent to joining the human race. We need only lift our heads to see somebody always within reach of our hands whose sparkle will meet our eye.

-Cllaude M. Steiner
The Other Side of Power

Mirroring the Soul

As you stand before the mirror, witness your personality as your most brilliant creation. As you have already discovered, creating some distance from this familiar part helps to loosen up conditioned responses. Playing out your public persona with unconditional love a deeper mystery is revealed - the ego and the essence are seen to be mutually connected. From this inclusive vantage point, embody your social role as a *Sacred Actor* playing your part on the world's stage.

Say your name in your normal way. For most of us, a shallowness of breath limits the voice from its full expression. As you repeat your name a few times, notice what aspects of your persona are open or closed, active or passive, aggressive or depressed in attitude. If judgments occur, repeat them out loud. Create an illogical 'pattern disrupt' by singing out a negative statement with love!

True performing requires unconditional love for yourself and your audience as your extended self.

When experiencing stage fright know you are still identified with your social role. Fear of other people's judgment means you stand in judgment of yourself. All separation from your true self vanishes when merging with the Soul of Love. When all labels are put aside, stage fright is simply heightened energy – a massive shot of adrenaline to support bigger than life performances. With an open heart, the audience is no longer the enemy bent on judging your every flaw. They are all aspects of your sub-personalities that are here to celebrate the abundant love you are awakening in their soul.

In preparation for your performance before the mirror, invoke your *Primal Name*. Encode this chosen name with the breath, sound and movements of love made manifest. In this way, this word of words becomes a magical implement that can help you stay connected to the heart of all compassion. With your true identity primed in love, the guiding force of your nature can sweetly move you through the darkest impasse. As the mirror turns into a movie screen, imagine everyone you have ever known or will ever know in your future is sitting in front of this screen. They have come to receive a renewed gift of love. This same life force that turns the planet on its axis causes the tides to rise and the sun to set is the Beloved living in your heart.

Your performance is to love yourself in appreciation for the eternal soul that has breathed you into being. Your body is the vehicle to reveal the Soul of Love in action. In the midst of the whole world watching, gently caress your body with humming love. Cradle your head with reverence, for what you hold in your hands is the most intricate medium in the universe. Caress your beating heart. Sigh out a long extended *Ahhhh* into the love that Bask in the touch of love. Stroke downward to ground your energy and stroke upward to revitalize your energy.

Entwined in your own embrace, look out at all these beautiful people and say, "This is me. This is my body. This is where I live. I love being me." Feel what it's like to proclaim love for yourself before all of humankind. With deepened trust and faith in your own loving impulses and feelings, share these simple words with the world at large, "I love you. I bless the love we all share in common." As your proclaim this truth, visualize a great luminous web that murmurs, whispers and tugs at your heart-

You walk with a light rhythmic gait as though you were hardly walking at all. It is as if you were sitting in a rickshaw, carried along by its motion instead of your own.

-Gertrude Enelow
Body Dynamics

Connecting with loving energy, is something humans have to be open to and talking about and expecting, otherwise the whole human race can go back to pretending that life is about having power over others and exploiting the planet.

-James Redfield
The Celestine Prophecy

Speak in the mirror each day and proclaim, "You gorgeous body, I love living inside of you. Thank you for being mine!"

-Beverly Toney Walter

strings. This vast network of original intelligence is an infinite web of relationship that underlies and interweaves all experiencing, all knowing.

And then all will live in the harmony with each other and the earth. And then everywhere will be called Eden once again.

-Judy Chicago

Behind the cosmic play of life, all conflicting parties recognize their interdependence with each other. When the antagonist and protagonist join forces, true love is made manifest in our heart.

Today, a new kind of life is arising. The loving heart resides in the simplest blade of grass. Nothing can or does exist without the connecting power of love binding all that is into oneness. it is awareness of this truth that calls it forth into activity.

In Corinthians 15:51-55, "Behold I show you a mystery: We shall not sleep; but we shall all be changed in a moment, in the twinkling of an eye." Imagine now, as one being awakens, more and more beings are awakening in the Great Heart of the Beloved. In the twinkling of an eye, witness everyone, without any deliberation, reaching out to hug their neighbors as their lost brothers and sisters. With the divine essence restored, a pledge is being made to listen to the body's own needs and processes, pains and pleasures. With unconditional acceptance, all the many paths to spiritual wholeness are accepted as illuminating spokes on the ever-turning wheel of love.

There is no difficulty that enough love will not conquer;
no disease that enough love will not hear;
It makes no difference how deeply seated may be the trouble,
how hopeless the outlook, how muddled the tangle, how great the mistake.
A sufficient realization of love will dissolve it all.
Loving fully from the heart is the greatest power on earth.
Emmet Fox

Shake Out the Crazies

Order in Chaos

Eccentricity of expression allowed in a society has generally been proportional to the amount of genius, vigor and moral courage which it contained. That so few now dare to be eccentric marks the chief danger of the time.

-John Stuart Mill

All around us barriers are crumbling, values shifting, and life itself is more dramatically unpredictable than ever before. In the blink of an eye, the San Francisco earthquake hit, the Berlin Wall came down, Russia's political and economic environment turned inside out, the Middle East blew up, and New York's World Trade Center collapsed. Hurricanes, floods, fires, droughts and epidemics continue to send shock waves through our spine. On top of all this, how many times have we squirmed in anguish when suddenly faced with the bedeviling frustration of losing a job, having an accident, or watching a thirty-year marriage fall apart? And what's even worse is having few skills to deal with it.

Call them weird, call them wacky. Eccentrics may be unusual, but they're healthier than the rest of us and having a lot more fun!

-Jordan Elarably
Island of Strangers

In spite of everything we've been taught, there is nothing more insane than being sane all the time! This third primal energy unleashes a little madness to prevent the big madness. Short bouts of spontaneous, chaotic expression effectively open unbridled creativity and a 'new order' of clarity.

Quantum physics is demonstrating that the energy of chaos does not operate in logical, regular, and predictable progression. Yet, under the surface of this seeming confusion exists a swirling fractal pattern of exquisite order. This unpredictable energy reveals itself to be a coherent, evolving and fully interactive intelligence that has the power to organize data with the speed of light. Surpassing our most advanced computers, every one of our trillions of cells in our body knows what every other cell is thinking.

Power of Disruption

The disruption of order to create something new is, at first, an odd concept to grasp. Being raised to retain a stabilizing style of living in a world that is becoming increasingly more chaotic, is a crazy-making experience. As the fear of losing control builds to the breaking point, our brain has to work overtime to prevent us from making foolish mistakes. Living in a cataclysmic world, a both/and experience is in order. This means the power of disruption to create something new depends on some amount of convention.It is becoming more elastic in both mental and creative arenas.

Living systems are drawn to the edge of chaos because that is where the capacity for information processing and learning and therefore, growth is maximized.

-Dee Hockl
Founder of Visa Card

The crazy antics of chaotic energy are found in quarks and galaxies, water and music, and in you and me. Creating dazzling extravaganzas of crazy shakeouts for a few minutes a day, means there is no difference between you and a supernova!

Embodying the lightning quick impulses of chaotic energy with breath, sound and movement is the most efficient means of loosening self-imposed prisons of behavior and redundant ruts of mind into being unashamedly alive. As a mover and shaker of spontaneous impulse, the creative art of 'risk-taking' is perceived as a highly practical way to live in an uncertain world.

Chaotic energy forms the very foundation of children's play. When young children feel the slightest tension, they instinctively bobble and wiggle all over and make lots of noise! Within minutes, the frustration transforms into renewed calm. The game 'peek-a-boo' thrilled us with sudden, brief distortions that jolted us awake with surprising joy. Being unexpectedly tossed in the air and caught just in the nick of time was heaven on earth. This disruptive energy has been labeled as silly, frivolous and sometimes, downright naughty. Beliefs like this are still influencing people to conform to overly serious, highly controlled, inappropriately nonchalant and self-righteous roles that are devoted to work as the end result of living. The art of play may be a potentially the way everything operates at a subatomic level. As the early nineteenth century poet, Friedrich Schiller is quoted saying, "Man only plays when he is in the fullest sense of the word a human being; and he is only fully a human being when he plays."

Take supernovas as your models. When they had filled themselves with riches, they exploded in a vast cosmic celebration of their work.

-Brian Swimme

Instinctive Genius

How many of us have been taught not to trust our instincts. Trusting and following this chaotic energy inside our gut would surely get us into a lot of trouble. Lacking trust in our own insides, we can no longer trust what we feel and how to respond to their wise counsel. Mistrusting our instincts, we are forced to look outside ourselves to discover what is true.

Our instinctive genius has been obstructed at birth. A Danish study discovered when a baby is born and placed on the mother's belly, like any creature; it will eventually find the nipple and feed itself. When the baby is taken away from the mother, even for a short period of time, and placed back on the belly, the impulse to feed itself is gone. In fact, the baby would starve without intervention.

Full blown artistic creativity takes place when a skilled grown up is able to tap the source of clear, unbroken play consciousness of the small child within.

-Stephen Nachmanovitch
Free Play

Be not seduced by second-hand knowledge. Instinctive intelligence reflects the natural genius to live life as nature intended.

In spite of social repression, our instinctive intelligence continues to guide us forward towards greater innovation and adaptability. An inspiring example of instinctive genius was Thomas Edison who was believed to be completely crazy. He was fascinated with an idea of lighting up the world and had no idea how to do it. He played with over 10,000 materials to create a light bulb. Once he put a current through a spider web, and even dabbled in lighting up Limburger Cheese! Being a 'live wire' connected to the instinctive source bubbling in his gut, he knew that the light bulb existed. Some uncommon impulse directed him to combine wildly different ingredients that no one in their right mind would ever dream of doing. He was compelled to explore his most passionate desire - to light up the world - and he did it. The point is that Edison went beyond the school of incremental thinking and acting in straightforward, logical, linear ways. He exemplified the instinctive play of genius, which allows radically different ingredients to come together to form something new.

Order and chaos are mirror images of each other. Particles and waves are spontaneously interlaying together in a creative universe.

The aspect of the clown holds the fun house mirror up to our 'fallen' state. The grotesque, hidden, and unacceptable aspects of personal life are unveiled and shown to be universal.

-Hal Lingerman

Holy Fool

Sitting with my family in a cafe in Key West, Florida on one of those hot, humid days, I got to witness a human being using chaotic energy to transform a miserable situation. In the middle of lunch, the air conditioning went off and everybody started grumbling and complaining. A couple of kids at the next table began throwing lumps of bread at each other. Their exasperated parents tried their best to calm them down, but to no avail. A moment later an old lady got out of her chair, and stumbled into the waitress who's tray of food went flying in the air and crashing to the floor. As the owner of the cafe was about to have a heart attack, out of nowhere a little old man stood up and burst out with ***Cock a Doodle DOO!!!***

As quickly as he stood up, he sat down, and continued eating his lunch and reading his newspaper as if nothing had happened. Needless to say, our jaws hung open and we were stunned into silence. Suddenly all hell broke loose in that sweaty little restaurant. Excited talking, uproarious laughter, and joyous smiles filled the room. The kids next to us started drumming spoons on glasses and their parents joined them! It was by far the most amazing shift in mood I had ever witnessed.

***You should be ashamed of yourself for acting so silly! Oh really?* Conditioned to resist change, it takes guts to brave the forces of tradition and not feel guilty.**

So often in my life I have been afflicted with the belief that I was inferior or inadequate in some way, shape or form. Falling short of my own personal standards of perfection would leave me depressed and agitated. When studying universal archetypes I learned that the *Holy Fool* represents the chaotic energy of creation. When contemplating this archetype the little man in the restaurant appeared before me shouting, "*Cock a Doodle Doo!*" Identifying with the *Holy Fool* helped me play with my habit of self-belittlement and strengthen trust in the power that lies hidden in my instinctive impulses. Seeing my deficiencies by frankly admitting and broadly enacting them I no longer had excruciating fear of making a fool of myself!

I will never forget bouncing on a big ball and humming with delight at a fitness club, when a woman approached me and said, "What possesses a grown woman like you to act so silly?" I paused and confided in her that in the past I was stricken with extreme inhibition, but I discovered inner resources that helped me move through this painful con-

The fool's wind scatters things and meanings yet in the confusion reveals glimpses of a counterpole to spirit; nature with the purposes and intelligence of instinct, which, like spirit, cannot be accommodated to rational understanding.

-Willism Willeford
The Fool and His Scepter

dition. She surprised me by wanting to know how I did it. I told her about the great gift I received when identifying with the *Holy Fool* archetype -I was no longer paralyzed and influenced by the mental mind's critical assessments of my uniqueness. I could see on her face, that my words had deeply affected her.

A return to a childlike perspective is not giving up the 'adult,' It is a renewal of flexibility, imagination and freedom of expression.

-Liv Ullmann

She confided that her family had continuously belittled her when she expressed her spontaneous feelings and creative impulses. A belief was uncovered that she might go crazy and act out in violent ways without strict control holding her emotions in tact. With a belief like this, it was only natural she always felt upset and intimidated when in the presence of uninhibited people. After all was said and done, I invited her to bounce on the ball and see what it would be like to freely express herself as if nobody was looking. Needless to say, in minutes she was bouncing and laughing like a young kid.

When the fear of losing control is well established in the nervous system, we work very hard to be 'right' in the eyes of others rather than be happy with who we are. All it takes is renewed realization that you are an original whose uniqueness can never be duplicated by anyone. Enjoying being human by making fun of self-imposed inferiority magically dissolves the illusion of being inferior to anything. The point is, expect family and friends to be somewhat intimated when you start making new changes in your behavior. Even humming down the hall might raise some eyebrows.

If anyone in your midst thinks you're acting like a fool, for heavens sake don't argue. Broadly smile and exclaim, "Yes. I'm glad you noticed! I am all that you say and MORE!"

Subatomic paticles seem to know instantaneously what decisions are make elsewhere, and elsewhere can be as far away as another galaxy!

-Gary Zukav

Chaos as Healer

Exercising chaotic energy is a healthy, healing and wise thing to do. Studies indicate that most Parkinson patients have developed stringent control over their emotional life. In my experience in working with these people, the nervous trembling that often develops can be perceived as a radically intelligent means of releasing long standing muscular rigidity. Conscious trembling while vibrating the cells with humming tones sets off concentrated tiny motions that spread increased circulation into rigid muscles.

Recently, I worked with a woman named Louise who had developed Parkinson disease. She was a librarian who had spent her life maintaining a quiet, reserved atmosphere. Louise was stricken with embarrassment about the trembling motions that were getting increasingly worse. During our first session, I suggested that she intensify her trembling motions as a means of releasing energy. Struggling desperately to stop the shaking, this suggestion was met with resistance. I asked Louise how she prevents the shaking motions from occurring. She just shook her head and admitted she had no idea.

Let us arive as children to this huge playground: the universe.

-Francisco Alarcon

After mirroring Louise's body posture, it was a total revelation for her to realize how she squeezed her upper back, pulled in her ribs, drew in her chin and clenched her arms to her sides in an attempt to stay in control of her feelings. Becoming somatically aware of her tense physiology, Louise was willing to play with irrational shaking as a new healing energy attempting to break through her steel-like control. The next step was teaching Louise how to use her humming voice as a high-powered, ultrasonic machine. Humming with trembling vibrations while shaking her hands like a rag-doll touched a deep cord in her soul. A story emerged that told of the tragic death of her child and her fight to hold in her grief. As she finally shared her long lost tears, I brought attention to the fact that her trembling hands were now lying quietly in her lap.

A revival is in order of the natural ability of the body to continually exercise energy of varying strength, intensity, nuance, and dynamic that reveal the exuberance we knew as children.

Activations

Embodying the unpredictable sound and movement rhythms of the Soul of Chaos is the focus of these Activations. Making erratic motions may feel strange for some of you who are used to mechanized, straight-lined exercise. There is a hunger for yet fear of physical freedom of expression. Tension is trapped energy. Change creates change. By shaking loose everything that no longer serves you, is opening to a new order of energy that does serve you!

To awaken from the habit of sleep walking is a life long task. Occasionally, we have to take our shoes off and improvise in the moment to what life asks of us.

-Ann Brook

The real craziness is the need to be perfect and denounce anything that may upset this self-righteous self-image. Trying to be perfect in an imperfect world obliterates spontaneity. In other words, be not taken in by your own masquerade.

To start, recall moments in your life in which you tasted the exhilaration of spontaneous freedom. Bring forth memories of courageous risk taking in which you responded to life without thoughtful control. Dwell on situations in which you followed the pure impulses of the moment. If, for whatever reason, nothing emerges, make up a story of being outrageously alive, free to express yourself without any inhibiting influences getting in the way. Let go of this event and simply dwell in the free-spirited energy that is moving through you.

With each gentle bobble, sixty trillion body cells are pitted against the earth's gravitational pull. This interaction strengthens every cell in the body while saving strain on its muscles and joints.

-Dr. Morton Walkerr

The Bobble

The first motion that excited us as children was bobbling up and down to our heart's content. When learning to stand, we held ourselves up in the crib and bobbled up and down through the day. As we got a little older, we bounced on the bed or the couch until a grownup yelled, "Stop!" Reclaiming the playful bobbling motions made by every child is the most fun and efficient way to free tight muscles that sustain chronic tension. Bobbling on a small trampoline has been called the most efficient form of exercise because it aerates the cells, bones, organs and fibers of the heart with renewed vigor. Everyone from Olympic athletes to aging and ailing seniors is responding to these rebounding devices. Bobbling on a Physio Ball or the floor in a fluid, relaxed body can accomplish the same thing.

The biggest argument that block its worth is, "It looks too simple to be any good." Every great truth is always simple in nature.

Bobbling motions defrost frozen bodies quicker than anything I know. These lateral movements recreate the subtleness we had as young children.

-Wowza

If you're not aware of tension, it's difficult to change it. Tightening and releasing different parts of the body while bobbling loosens up stress in quick order. Intensifying, and then relaxing any holding pattern is a powerful 'isometric' exercise that intensifies awareness. To begin, put on some fun music with exciting rhythms and abrupt changes. Pulse your knees with light, bobbling motions while imagining a fountain of radiant energy shooting up through the arches of your feet, uplifting your body with ease. Once you're comfortable bobbling, tighten and release different parts of your body. For instance, keep bobbling while tightening your neck hinge. Notice how this imposed tension rigidifies your head from responding. Holding the head in a set position is what gives us a pain in the neck. Once you are fully aware of the tension, consciously release it. Bobble again and notice how effortlessly your head responds without muscular effort.

We impose control to free our fears of chaos, but this seeming chaos in us is a rich, swelling, singing, laughing, shouting, crying, sleeping order.

-Chistopher Alexander

As one hinge loosens up, all the other hinges loosen up too. Tighten your shoulders while bobbling and feel how this one holding pattern affects the rest of your body. Honor your ability to release a tension pattern at will. Let go and feel your shoulders relax, which loosens your arms into shimmering relaxation. Tighten your belly muscles and let the go. Transform a tight ass into a fluffy butt by tightening and releasing tension. Shake out one leg and then shake out the other. Let your foot dangle from the ankle and your lower leg dangle from the knee. Encourage your whole leg to loosen right up to the pelvic hinge. Bend and jiggle your body sideways. Play with making lop-sided bobbles.

Bobble freely again while imagining someone you care about coming up to you and judging what you're doing as silly, improper behavior. What is the first thing your body does to inhibit your expression? In other words, what parts of your body stiffen or contract when hearing this insult? Whatever you find, amplify this tendency by contracting or stiffening this body part. Using an accordion image, build and subside this primary tension in varying degrees. Pause and shift into the *Whispers of Wow*. Sense the flows of renewed energy flowing through your body.

This flood of energy that moves through your body wants to enliven you and connect you to others, but it is most essential for you to relax and let go for this to happen.

-Barbara Marciniak
Family of Light

The Wiggle

We need to wiggle more. As an energy medium, every cell in our body wiggles. One of the reasons children are 'high' naturally, is because they are constantly wiggling with spontaneous energy. This energy is not inert matter, it thinks and creates without words. Living in a sea of energy it behooves us all to know the language of energetic design. The exploration of wiggling waves refires the pumping action of the heart. Imagine you're a little puppy shaking off icy cold water. These lateral motions reflect serpentine movements that wiggle your spine from side to side.

Wiggling motions compose the physiology of the DNA Just like ocean waves that carry information about storms far out to sea, wiggling generates waveforms of information that spread out in all directions.

The primal force consits of wiggling movements that produce a sense of flow and wellness.

-Chuang Tsu

While focusing your attention on your tailbone, wiggle through this area with the excitement of a child at play. Wiggling from the tailbone can loosen your entire back with shimmering, vibrating energy. Keep wiggling while bending your head down towards the floor. Dangle your head and take time to allow it to fill up with fresh blood. Pause and breathe deeply. Slowly, oh so slowly, bring your torso up, vertebra by vertebra. As you come to a standing position, notice how easily your head is balancing on your neck.

While bobbling and wiggling, shake your bones free from tight muscular density. Take an extra minute to become all bones rattling with pleasure! Trust me, you won't get flabby if your muscles shake like jello. In fact, your muscles will look more streamlined with extra-added circulation traveling through them. Bobbling and wiggling motions sustain the youthfulness of your spine at any age.

Song Talk

Ultrasonic technology uses multi-rhythmical pulsations of 'chaotic sound' to disrupt disharmonious patterns of dis-ease. The profusion of chaotic rhythm is the only means found to effectively break up dense patterns of energy. We can accomplish the same thing with our voice – and it is cost effective. Making odd sounds with disjointed rhythms shifts dissonant patterns into harmony. In other words, it is novelty of tone that balances imbalance. Opening the magnitude of sonic power can shock a shaky and thin, quiet or shrill voice into renewed resonance and warmth of expression. And best of all, you don't have to think about how to do it.

When exploring non-structured sound, it's a good idea to start with the truth of what you're feeling. Intend unlearned impulsion of sound to guide you into a new landscape of uncommon happenings. Experience the pleasure of sounding with extreme levels of pitch, rhythm and intensity that shoots out of your mouth from anywhere and nowhere. With an eccentricity of sound effects, encourage your body to shiver, cower, flinch, shudder and tremble while babbling, hissing, croaking, twittering and growling with gut-level delight! These chaotic tirades open up the realization that communication is more than just saying words; it involves all of you.

Caught in the habit of intellectualizing your experiences, release a stream of verbalization with no deliberate thoughts getting in the way. Take a deep breath and become a high-powered electron with no time to think or plan what you're going to say. Your only job is to keep the current of words popping non-stop.

Release imposed control over the uncontrollable. Exercising this nonconformist strategy releases more innovative ideas and a new order of organizing power.

The trick is to expurgate everything that crosses your mind. This is radical honesty. With ingenious swiftness that speaks volumes in minutes, know that a new arrangement of healing possibilities are occurring that is blowing up an antiquated verbosity of mind. When entering the silence, be open to receiving 'sound advice.' And most important of all – not giving a *hoooooooot* what anybody thinks about it! As this pandemonium of vocal alchemy is being produced, become an alien speaking with a language only you can understand. Periodically shift into the *Whispers of Wow.* Unconformity needs conformity to survive. It's a great gift to consciously change the direction of your energy. Contrasting chaotic energy with peaceful repose is the key that brings order in chaos. Developing some repetition helps us acquire a regime of learned skills and structured knowledge.

When the rational aspects of the brain merge with spontaneous creativity, a holistic mindset is birthed. When resounding spontaneous emotional energy through language, any calamity that befalls you can be expressed with feeling tones. This means you can be a fast-talking whiz-bang with one person and a soft-talking, mellow soul with another simply by changing the frequency of your tone. Energy, determination and wisdom are inflamed to take positive action when your words are filled with feeling. So have a dialogue with the Soul of Chaos. Be open to sparks of 'crazy wis-

Being in the whole surge of energy "I" am immeasurable old; my forms are infinite and their comings and goings are simply the pulses or vibrations of a single and eternal flow of energy.

-Alan Watts

Our spontaneous sounds are one of the ways we express emotion, discharge energy, and bring our body and psyche back into balance.

-Robert Gass
Chanting

As their numbers may be legion, one is awed by the billions of sounds that one has set into motion by one's own sound that now appears so miserably dwarfed!

-Hazrat Inayat Khan
Toward the One

dom' that open a radically new way to look at any disturbing problem or frustrating relationship. Shift back to your familiar voice when you reply. In this simple way, your sonic identity is made strong.

Whole civilizations have disappeared because they did not know, until it was too late, that the way they lived was unsustainable.

-Ed Ayres
God's Last Offer

Walk Primal

I recently read an article about a group of women who decided to 'walk for peace.' After walking two miles they came back feeling exhausted. It was noticed that their styles of walking reflected gritting their teeth and pushing themselves with effortful determination. Their coach encouraged them to walk as if they were five year olds having all the fun in the world. This time they walked five miles and came back invigorated.

Turn your hallways into expressways! It really doesn't matter how you walk just walk differently! It is difference that makes all the difference.

All the universe, all the microcosmos and the brain act similarly, constantly switching on and off in multiple interconnectedness.

-Bob Toben
Space Time & Beyond

Inside every step we take, there is a powder keg of untapped creativity. Let chaos rule as you stride across the floor of your living room! Honor your ability to be adventurous, creative and imaginative. Walking with unexpected jolts of madness lightens up the dreariness of 'sleep walking' through life. Chaotic breathing and humming while going through your chores supports your personal diversity to flower.

As the *Holy Fool,* relish and savor the sheer joy of unbridled creativity inspiring your steps. With uncensored irreverence, waddle, clump and mince, pound, strike and shuffle. Prance and skip, become splayfooted, pigeon-toed, knock-kneed and bow-legged. With blasts of inspiration vibrating through you, widen your legs and lumber from side to side.

Project eyes out the back of your head and walk backwards! This is a sure way to let go of the impossible craving for certainty and significance. In the bizarre endeavor of walking backwards, there is only one recourse to take – being in the moment with what is behind you, around you and before you. If extra confidence is needed, walk as a rock star being wildly applauded by hundreds of fans! If awkwardness still has you in its grip, become a tin soldier or burst into a rag doll bobbling down the hall.

Remember how Groucho Marx bent his knees and Charlie Chaplin turned his feet out? Exaggerate new and different walks as a clown would. For instance, contract your energy body as small as possible and expand it as big as you can. Shift back and forth between these two extreme qualities.

Gaining practice walking with chaotic energy prevents accidents. It's almost impossible to take a nasty fall because you are becoming refined in using your ankles and feet to create hundreds of new movements. With fully adaptable feet and ankles, you are more able to meet any unobstructed roadblocks. So walk towards your most cherished desires as a whirlwind on a stormy day! Breathe as a typhoon breaking through any barriers that stand in your way. Skip and leap down the street triples your circulation. Take a deep breath and give thanks for successful accomplishment of your desire.

Mirroring the Soul

Before the mirror, look into the eyes of this being called YOU. Notice who is looking back at you in the mirror. The social role aspect of your nature is generally more preoccupied with the self-talk that occurs in your brain. Your primal essence is more attuned with the flow of life force that thinks without words. When confusion exists, recall the distorting mirrors in the circus. See the mirror before you as a distorting image you carry of yourself to the extreme. By skewing the tight edges of your social role, the integral balance between any conflicting forces come into balance. Seeing through the illusion of separateness, the *Holy Fool* celebrates the equality by which all things are related.

As a craftsman of chaos, your job is to lovingly disrupt and turn upside down your own disguise. Intend that all fears of looking foolish dissolve into making postural distortions with pleasure!

Express the kaleidoscopic range of social manners. If you're inclined to be nice, create an insipidly nice stance. If you've been trained to act smart, outsmart yourself with a posture that means business. If you struggle with perfectionist ideas that all this play is beneath your dignity, build your high status into full out superiority. Play out the respectability, the honorable status, the hard-earned attributes, the deadly serious attitudes that have tried in vain to protect you from feeling the wounds of past.

This is the paradox of chaos: extremely different qualities blending together, yet each quality retains its distinctive nature. With all this practice in recognizing your social role, capture in a word what your self-image is projecting. With this one word, create a name for your social role and a posture that reflects your 'habit yoga.' Consciously exercising this posture on a daily basis can click you into what this posture is hiding below the surface of the mask. This embodiment process will help you move through the dreary layers of forgetfulness that keep you mired in passivity and trapped in inertia.

Without the energy of chaos, nothing will grow. In this expressive arts performance before the mirror, demonstrating a little madness real sanity returns.

In preparation for your performance, call forth your *Primal Name*. Encode it with impulsive freedom of expression. Blow your mind and dazzle your soul with novelty! To enact the energy of chaos is to embrace all levels of expression at once without judgment. Focus diverse elements of feeling into this magical name by mixing up the consonants and vowels in many varied ways. Become the original Jazz singer crooning this magical name with outrageous rhythms that draw order out of chaos. Now that your instrument is tuned up, imagine that all of humankind and the sub-personalities that make up your extended identity are all sitting on the opposite side of the mirror. These parts of you have spent most of their lives trying to meet outer expectations and it's a losing battle. Disenchantment with life rules the day, and massive tension and mental anguish are growing by leaps and bounds.

Feeling the chaotic power of a spiritual force guiding my choices, I went full throttle into an acting career without a care in the world.

-Leo James

Sometimes I think it is like this; God has a TV set and God watches us on it. Whenever I think I'm being watched, I always sing and dance and do a commercial for myself.

-Jane Wagner

Every limit placed on what we call the universe is eventually broken in chaotic dismemberment.

-Osho

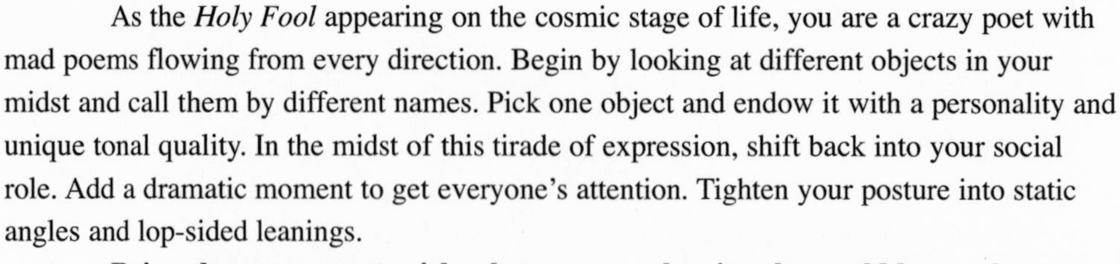

As the *Holy Fool* appearing on the cosmic stage of life, you are a crazy poet with mad poems flowing from every direction. Begin by looking at different objects in your midst and call them by different names. Pick one object and endow it with a personality and unique tonal quality. In the midst of this tirade of expression, shift back into your social role. Add a dramatic moment to get everyone's attention. Tighten your posture into static angles and lop-sided leanings.

Self actualizing people have the wonderful capacity to appreciate again and again, freshly and naively, the basic goods of life, with awe, pleasure, wonder, and even ecstasy.

-Abrham Maslow

Being the consummate risk taker, you are showing the world how to leap over the cultural bounds of normal behavior into the original play of creation.

Imagine a puppeteer pulling different strings attached to your head, shoulders, elbows and knees. As the puppeteer pulls on a string, that part of your body instantly responds with spastic, disjointed, angular movements. Without warning, all your strings go slack. One by one, head, shoulders and torso plop down with a thump! In a robotic style, sound with an abstract, metallic mental tone that reflects a computer, satellite missile, ground zero or a nuclear bomb exploding out of barbed-wire bondage. Shift into a fluidity of being. Move with fluid unstudied grace. With acceptance for what is static and fluid within you, witness the social identity of humankind more able to tolerate ambiguities, unresolved situations and behaviors that do not have a common response.

Surrendering to the instinctual exuberance of your eccentric nature is entering the playground of God in which everything in the universe is at play and there is nothing to be afraid of.

Be Eccentric!

The mental mind is inclined to label a flourishing eccentric nature as egotistical exhibitionism. This kind of self-righteousness is in itself an ego trip. Freedom of expression in others often reminds people who have become overly serious of their own repressed emotions. Life is too important to take it seriously. Repression of expression is a form of self-deception that compartmentalizes unwanted emotions with the belief they will leak out and disrupt the peace of others.

The role I played was bigger than life. I didn't know any body like that. I ran into this guy in Brooklyn, hung around him for awhile and it sank in. I woke up and played the part of a crazy fool with no trouble at all.

-James Caan

I want to add that developing a more eccentric nature is not about letting it all hang out and being insensitive to what's excessive in the presence of others. Regurgitating our worst thoughts on anyone who will listen is boring! No one has the right to dump strong feelings on innocent bystanders and call it freedom of expression. The true eccentric nature we were born with needs a revitalization of spirit.

True eccentricity is a flexibility of mind, initiative, inventiveness, and social effectiveness. It is the ability to consider alternatives beyond the conventional modes of thought. Accessing these resources requires a freedom from repression.

To be eccentric is daring to be fully alive in a world in which most people are desperately trying to preserve the status quo. To be eccentric is to be diverse and different, adventurous and creative, magical and funny, primal and passionately present in the moment. To be wildly yourself is expressing the novelty of your being without shame.

The expression of natural genius is eccentric. It is tapping into the unending flow of energy and using this energy to accomplish cherished goals with spontaneous abandon. Daring to take a stand for a lust for life, despite the seeming fear of doing so, develops greatness and courage of mind. To have the willingness to fail and even to look foolish when wearing a colorful garment in a room of grey suited people keeps the dynamics of vital energy circulating. And even more important, it's learning to costume yourself to meet your growing tastes in the moment. The more we improvise with new and different behavior that does not squelch other people's behavior, the more richly we live.

Perhaps the greatest pain of all is coming to the end of our lives with the realization that we have not fully lived out unique potential.

Blots, defects, mistakes, accidents, exceptions and irregularities are the windows to other worlds.

-Bob Miller

In what ways can you punctuate your eccentric nature today? Enjoy exactly where you are right now and appreciate the present moment as the container of all that is. Multi-tasking is the ability to focus on more than one task at a time, comes from trusting one's native impulses of sensation. This fabulous trait is often tagged as having a 'short attention span' rather than the natural genius of moving through multiple activities with passionate excitement. When relying on the innate energetic continuum of our inner guidance, this kind of healthy eccentricity needs no approval from anyone. I quote Theodore Rozak in response to the mental mind's tendency to squelch unguarded moments of pure spontaneity, "When the divine absurdity of life is perceived, we taste the sanity of spiritual madness, and become, for as long as the joke lasts, fools of God." When all is said and done, your final reward may be that dogs, children and saints will recognize a special glow about you, which they can immediately identify as holy human.

A special kind of wisdom is loose in the world.
This wisdom is difficult to codify or categorize and it refuses to be institutionalized.
It is called crazy wisdom. And so it is, both crazy, and wise.

-Scoop Nisker
Crazy Wisdom

The purpose of fear is to save your life, to catapult you into the 'now' in order to take action. However, when you hold onto fear as a lifestyle, and when you broadcast fear of life, you shut down your body and kill your vital life force.

-Barbara Marcinak

Earth

Guardian Angel

Fear Alert

Use your fear as a guide to help you understand and prepare for a challenge,
not as an excuse for abandoning it. Every important risk involves fear.
Don't run from your fear. Don't pretend to be fearless.
You just want to recognize danger and learn to adapt to it.

-David Viscott, M.D.

Emotional Resilience

With billions of years of instinctive skills at our disposal, we would not survive as a species without life-preserving energy that can shock us awake in an instant. With the slightest threat of danger, the Soul of Fear triggers staccato sensations of feeling that warn us to stop, look and listen. Befriending and embodying the physiology of this life supporting ally, as our Guardian Angel is essential in moving into an unknown world with fearless power.

The fourth primal energizer exercises the percussive energy of the fear response to shock all your systems awake with exciting vitality. As life becomes more complex, riveting stimulation is needed to keep us alert, awake and aware to the mysterious demands of the moment.

Scientists have discovered that new brain cells grow when the 'startle reflex' mechanism is stimulated. We can do the same by exercising the reflexive action of the body's flight-fight response with percussive breath, sound and movement. Even after a few minutes of this activity, there is heightened blood flow in the muscles that provide instant energy and instinctive readiness to successfully respond in any unpredictable situation.

Fear must surely be the one emotion most likely to succeed dramatically. Since the beginning of time, the human race has carried on a tempestuous love-hate affair with fear.

-Robtera Nobleman

Shark Scare

Having received so much ridicule at a young age, I often pushed myself into crazy acts of bravery. I worked hard to project a fearless attitude and invincible behavior that I believed would win people's respect. My daredevil antics came out in full force when selected to swim in an aquarium tank with sharks for a bathing suit ad. I was told not to worry. I want to add, this kind of thing is outlawed today, thank goodness.

They convinced me that the sharks would be fed and tranquilized, which would make this task perfectly safe. As I approached the edge of the pool, my skin became clammy; my muscles grew tense and my heart started pounding to the bursting point. Icy cold trembling sensations pulsed in my chest and belly. A frantic voice whispered in my ear, "This is crazy, don't do it!" When I looked up and saw the whole crew ready to

Until you get that wake-up call, will you continue to hide in fear? Expressing your feelings in the present moment is the healthiest thing you can do.

-Karina Schelde

Visualize a deer, frozen in its tracks in the middle of the road, eyes wide, body stiff. This image is a perfect metaphor for how people frequently look in the initial state of fear.

-Jo-Ellan Dimitrius. Reading People

shoot the scene, I forced myself to go through with the contract. Clenching my whole body with determination I dove into the tank with all the energy I could muster. The pressure from the tank was so great, I popped right back up to the surface. Even the water was resisting my efforts. Fins were suggested to solve the problem. I had never worn fins before. With this new propulsion, I shot right down to the bottom. When I opened my eyes, I found myself in the middle of a mocked-up shipwreck covered with sharp barnacles. As I pushed off to make my ascent, my foot got caught in the open portal of the ship. With all the strength of my being, I tried to struggle free, only to scrape my arm on the barnacles.

A river of blood formed a circle around me. Suddenly, there was a flurry of motion in front of me. It was a wriggling shark! Struck with absolute terror, I glued my eyes on the shark and it held its distance. With decisive clarity, I carefully wiggled my foot free. In the next instant, two men yanked me out of the pool to safety.

Enacting the fear response with breath, sound and movement is an expedient way to clear the habit of fearful thinking.

Lying in bed that night, I imagined being chased across the ocean by that shark. This horrifying state of affairs drove me to conjure up all the scary events of a lifetime that had never been processed. As feelings of panic, apprehension, dread and more terror evaporated my breath, I leapt off the bed and wildly danced out my fright. As I collapsed on the bed, massive impulses of sensation flowed through my body. It was as if I was plugged into an electrical power plant pulsing with sparks of fire. When I got up, I noticed a chronic shoulder pain was no longer there. This wide-awake energy lasted throughout the next day.

Life Saving Friend

One night I had a dream, which turned fear into a life saving friend. As I was about to step into the ocean, a little elf-like creature with bulging eyes started screaming its head off. Looking up, I gasped in horror. Sharks were swarming in a circle in front of me. Sighing with relief, I said, "You saved my life!" With a gracious bow, the little creature whispered, "I'm your Guardian Angel. That's my job." How strange, he sure didn't look like my idea of an angel!

On awakening, it dawned on me why I was so prone to accidents. Believing my instincts were not to be trusted, I did my best to numb any uncomfortable sensations from my awareness. No wonder I could no longer feel this life-preserving instinct warning me to stop, look and listen. With practical benefits like this, it suddenly made a lot of sense to feel and express my fear rather than try to hide it or attempt to get rid of it.

Real fear is energy! By amplifying the percussive dynamics of this instinct with breath, sound and movement, I felt a fearless quality of mind I had never know before.

Fear of Fear

When the instinct of fear is trapped in the mind of thought, we cringe before a thousand fears of our own mental design. The nervous system, believing we are in real danger, continuously floods the body with stress hormones. With little physical outlet to release this mounting anxiety - tense muscles, shallow breathing, hyperventilation, palpitations, asthma, ulcers, high blood pressure, digestive problems and nervous disorders make their appearance.

In the United States, horror has flourished as a major source of mass aesthetic stimulation.

-Noel Carroll
The Philosophy of Horror

Failure to assimilate and release the accumulation of fearful anxiety, breeds unresolved stress. Living in this bottled up condition, the outer world becomes a suspicious adversary that must be guarded against at all costs. With shaky personal power, we are forced to look to others to make our decisions for us. The slightest frown, cold shoulder, averted glance, or criticism from our family, friends or our boss can make us give up before we have even started. Once a meek behavior gets established, just the idea of starting a new business, going back to school or making new friends can paralyze our best intentions.

If you want to control masses of people, generating the fear response is the greatest manipulative ploy there is.

The grotesque weapons expenditure for the war business machine thrives on keeping all of humankind in fear. The media contributes to a fear-based mentality by offering us a constant barrage of dangerous people doing atrocious things. Protection will be demanded from anything we have been conditioned to fear. As long as financial greed is the highest value, enemies will be created and beautiful young men will be sacrificed to fight these wars.

The roots of doomsday beliefs are inflamed by habit of fearful thinking.

-Nostradamus

Many religions do its best in indoctrinating followers into believing, "If you don't do as you are told, you'll go to hell." The concept of original sin has given rise to fanatic religious control that keeps people alienated from their inner authority. How many thousands of 'holy wars' proclaim, "God is on my side and not yours!" It is important to note that these wars were instigated by the greatest intellectual minds in history. Through the agency of mental projection without heart, the ego ideal of a superior race has no difficulty in slaughtering other races judged as inferior.

Focusing on 'doomsday' is the only respite for a mind gone crazy with fear. As we have recently seen enacted in the world, young men can become so brainwashed in the tactics of terrorism that they will gladly go on suicide missions as the highest spiritual quest they can aspire to.

Robert Hare, a psychologist at the University of British Columbia has discovered that psychopaths, about to receive an electrical shock, show no surges of anxiety that normal people experience when expecting to feel pain. It is obvious that most of these people were severely abused in childhood. When the instinct of pain has been deadened, there is no lack of concern about future punishment. This means they are not worried about feeling pain. As a result, there appears to be no empathy and compassion whatsoever for the pain they inflict on their victims. These kinds of challenges require all of the creative resources we can muster. Creative drama and role-playing could have a much greater potential in the educational process. These skills are invaluable in teaching interpersonal sensitivity and renewal of feeling in our communication with others.

If we could read the secret history of our enemies, we should find in each man's life, fear, sorrow and suffering enough to disarm all hostility.

-Henry Wadsworth Longfellow/

Activations

The Activations that follow sharpen your awareness of the physical sensations of pure fear. Above all, these Activations are meant to be enjoyed. Remember the enormous fun you had playing scary games when you were a kid? Exercising the unique rhythms of sensation, even for a few minutes a day, can regenerate the neurons in your brain, smooth out hypertension and help clear out traumatic events of the past. Physicalizating the fear response can help you break free of fearful beliefs that unconsciously rule your life. Have you ever thought to honor this amazing primal instinct that works night and day to guide you safely through life? Most people I have asked about this say that the idea never crossed their mind.

The organism is provided with an instinctual reflex to deal with unforseen danger and threat.

-Stanly Keleman
Emotional Anatomy

The fear of experiencing discomfort is one of the reasons the intellect tries to circumvent all feeling. The key is building tolerance for emotional intensity.

When approaching a dangerous situation, the Soul of Fear produces a series of physical sensations, such as cold shivers, clammy, prickly skin and a fast heart rate. The mouth often widens, eyes bulge, shoulders flinch, eyebrows lift and the joints lock in place. When there's the threat of being physically attacked, the hands raise up to the chest to protect the body. When the cause of fear subsides, the body often remains motionless to sense more clearly what is going on.

Relive a situation in which you felt the warning signals of danger and responded accordingly. I recall driving my car on a major highway and feeling sharp pangs of sensation in my heart area. Just as I was slowing down, the car in front of me went out of control. If I hadn't recognized the pangs of fearful sensation, a serious accident would have incurred.

If you are having difficulty in recalling an experience of real fear, imagine scary things, like riding on a roller coaster that is going out of control; seeing big, black hairy spiders crawling towards you; being on a steep ledge with no place to go. Pay attention to what is happening in your body as you feel into these images. Some of these sensations may cause discomfort because that is what they are designed to do! This discomfort is a signal to slow down your pace and pay attention to what is happening in the moment.

In a dangerous situation, let your breath guide you to safety.

-Charles Commings

Fearful Thinking

Fearful thinking habits are false beliefs appearing to be real. Learned fear lives in the mind of thought, and pure fear takes place in the moment. These habits of mind derive their power from the past or future. It is essential to experience the difference between these two states of consciousness. Even when no danger is evident, fear-based thoughts keep the body in a state of constant emergency. The sympathetic nervous system and the adrenal glands do their best to pump out stress hormones, but they can never work hard

Manipulators are always looking for scapegoats so gullible people should be prepared for an onslaught of attention.

-Marion Moss
Removing Your Mask

enough to bring the system into balance. Sound familiar? When oxygen levels radically start dropping to an all time low, you can be sure blood pressure is on the rise.

Fearful thinking habits occur when each hemisphere of the brain distrusts and discounts the other. This state is mental civil war. The issue is control. it's all about choosing brain integration over duality.

Each of us has the capacity to cut through the knot of fearful thinking, self deprecation and loneliness that is a major obstacle to becoming a fully human.

-Julian Asher Miller
Breaking Through

Thinking fearful thoughts do not help us survive. These frightening patterns paralyze us by cutting off the life force. Recall a statement you often make that is fraught with fearful trepidation. Ask if your physical, emotional mental or spiritual survival is really threatened. Be aware that any story you have about this statement has been interpreted many times in your mind. In other words, fearful thoughts are based on fantasy that is being projected onto new situations. What is the core belief that holds this fearful thought in place? Express this thought out loud. What is its essential tone? Become a conscious 'tension producer!' Drop the words and exaggerate the tension that encapsulates this statement.

The use of 'amplification' is very similar in nature to the ancient healing system called Homeopathy – "like cures like" One example of homeopathy is to administer a diluted dose of venom to heal a poisonous snake bite. Similarly, by amplifying any physical, emotional or mental habit of mind helps to release our identification with it.

The minute you identify with any thought, you have all of the associated psychoemotional reactions such as "I'm afraid." And your mind will give you a thousand reasons why you're afraid.

-Stephen Eolinsky
Quantum Consciousness

If you don't trust yourself at the core of your being, you will never feel safe. In other words, it is self-doubt in your *Guardian Angel* that represents the real danger. As soon as you admit, "This is a scary thought I am thinking," – the present moment will not intimidate you quite as much. Now imagine if you were in a situation that represents this fearful thought. What would it be like to experience this situation without fear? As you imagine this, begin to feel it. Then you have a choice: you can imagine yourself being afraid or you can imagine yourself feeling safe. What you imagine you will feel.

Shock Aerobics

The primary impulses of the fear response take place on your inhalation and the relaxation response takes place on your exhalation. Consciously sniffing or gasping air on the inhalation and slowing down your breath on the exhalation strengthens this emotional muscle to respond with lightening quick swiftness. Quick doses of radical self-expression puts you in touch with the great stream of life that is always guiding you towards your soul's purpose.

Revere the language of fear that quickens your blood to flow and your heart to pound. It is this energy that sustains survival of the species.

-Wowza

This first Activation is another 'isometric' process that is highly effective in dissolving the strongest tension. Let's start by taking quick sniffs through your nose. Notice how sniffing widens your nostrils and opens your eyes. To generate even more energy, imagine you're a little creature in the wilderness sniffing out dangerous predators with hyper-vigilant energy. Add more quick sniffs on your inhalation. Sustain the air for a few seconds and slowly exhale all the tension. Pause and feel the effects.

Unconscious gasping of breath is a habit that generates uptight feelings and sustains nervous behavior. Conscious gasping on your inhalation and sighing on your exhalation is an expedient way to heal unconscious mouth breathing by bringing this tendency into clear awareness. Once you're comfortable sniffing through the nose with quick rhythms, gasp in air with an open mouth and slowly sigh out the stress. In order to bring

Under frightening conditions we acquire super powers, strengths, survival mechanisms, and insights. If nothing frirghtened us, we would not feel alive.

-Eric Morse

your whole body into the action, slightly arch and round your back while flinching your hands at chest level. All these primal movements are designed to awaken your nervous system to remain alert in any precarious situation. For instance, when you are about to fall asleep at the wheel, audibly breathing and sounding with one minute of staccato energy can keep you alert, awake and aware. To hold your breath is to lose your breath. When the intellect realizes that a greater instinctive power is taking care of you, it won't work so hard churning out frightening thoughts to keep you safe.

Tremble Dance

A more subtle way to contact the energy of pure fear is amplifying trembling motions as a spontaneous, aesthetic dance. Our body trembles and quivers with jerky movements when fearful signals are trying to alert us to pay attention. When the intellect puts up solid barriers to resist feeling, there is less sensitivity to recognize the signals of inner guidance. Bobbling in place while trembling your body is a healthy, expressive way to generate sufficient heat to thaw out everything from freezing cold to extreme pain. This simple dance produces tiny alternating, vibratory motions guaranteed to send shivers up the spine and set a sluggish nervous system on fire!

Allowing trembing room to express itself can warm your body and even thaw out a cold hearted heart.

-Joy Lord

Conscious trembling is a powerful antidote in counteracting anxiety, phobias, and panic attacks that is a direct result of being hypnotized by fearful thinking habits.

It is the quality of your attention that sets the healing energy in motion. Put on music with a fast, pulsating beat. Imagine that the room you're in is becoming increasingly cold. Visualize icy water dripping from the ceiling and running down your back! As the temperature skyrockets to freezing, amplify this condition with trembling motions that start in your knees and flow up through your torso, arms and head. Audibly breathe while trembling your body with micro-fast rhythms that build and subside. Fill your electrifying breath motions with sporadic jerks, stops and starts. Notice how this dance instantly increases circulation and healthy vitality.

When climbing the walls, digging yourself into a hole, jumping to conclusions, running around in circles and pushing your luck, breathing with radical speed releases tension in quick order.

If you are really in a rush to know what life is all about, then just do it and get it over with. You could be born, take the first breath, give one loud cry AHHHHHH - and die!

-Al Chung Huang

Speed Demon

So many of us were trained to hurry by hurried, well-meaning caretakers. Even with all the time in the world, the habit of speaking fast, walking fast and driving fast is a habit that is often run by fearful thinking. Living under this constant pressure to accomplish something in the future, our natural tempo and timing remain in overdrive. In order to feed the speed demon within, holding the breath is a common occurrence.

Rather than rushing around for the whole day, rush around for thirty seconds and get it over with! Breathing up a storm while running in place with hair-raising speed tickles your funny bone awake to renewed life.

Fearful thinking habits can turn us into 'couch potatoes.' Driven to remain in a safe comfort zone, there barely have enough energy to move. If this is you, make the weight of your body so heavy you move with the weight of a ten-ton elephant. Groan with the dense weight and effort it takes to move an inch. Now contrast this dense state with speedy intensity. Explore finding that balancing state between too much and too little. Contrasting your energy in this expressive way offers you more choice in orchestrating how you wish to feel in the moment.

Mr. Duffy lived a short distance from his body.

-James Joyce

The all work, no play mentality in our culture is exhausting! Short percussive breathing breaks do more than stimulate needed energy, they bring more playful expression into the seriousness of work as usual. It's also good to restore your energy reserves before they have dropped too low. One way is to plan your play as thoughtfully and creatively as you do your work. Take a three-minute excitement break each day. After taking this break, observe the quality of your mental processing .

Our body will do anything to keep us excited about life. As my son would shout out in our play, "Mom! Scare me again!"

Fear into Excitement

So many of us have been taught to fear excitement. How many times have we heard the phrase, "Pipe down! What are you getting so excited about?" In a culture where an attitude of 'cool' is the preferred response, exciting feelings appear to be some kind of disease, something to get over as soon as possible.

Without excitement, life becomes boring and drab. This emotive energy is the juice that motivates us to accomplish whatever we set out to do. Without feelings of genuine excitement, even the greatest material success appears commonplace and even meaningless. When a steady diet of dullness sets in, we reach for substitutes to stimulate excitement. Some of us become attracted to reading mystery novels or get involved in death defying activities to make up for the deficit. Being a 'thrill seeker' is craving the rush of sensation whenever or wherever we can get it. When rhythmical excitation comes vividly alive in our nervous system, there is less desire to indulge in terrifying daredevil antics that put our lives at risk.

Fear becomes excitement when we choose to move out of feelings of helplessness into improvising with the ever-changing moment.

-Julie Harris

The energetic response of fear is similar to the energy of excitement. Gasping with fear braces your muscles in protection and gasping with excitement expands your muscles with joyous aliveness.

Fear and excitement are most intensely felt on the inhalation. When breathing with excitement, notice that your inhalation is slightly more extended and robust rather than short and contracted. The energy of excitement connected to a clear vision, is the secret of bringing your desires into manifestation. Stimulating true excitement catalyzes arousal; a state of body alertness and acute awareness that is awakening you to living your

Living near the edge keeps a person sharp, aware, creative, ready to respond to life's surprises.

-Powers Booth

desired reality now. The trick is adding an upward curve to your gasping breath. Recalling a child seeing a Christmas tree for the first time will give you the proper expression. What desired manifestation could bring you into a state of supreme excitement? Imagine this desire is magically being actualized before your eyes. With gasps of real excitement and squeals of delight, reach out and embrace the manifestation of your desire with profound pleasure!

Fear is a very useful signal along the path to freedom. The stronger the fear, the closer you are to what you are seeking.

-Cheri Huber

The Fear Book

When your judging mind starts berating you with worry, have fun using your imagination to breathe with excitement. For instance, when racing to put change in the meter before you get a ticket, sniff with excitement while turning your shoes into roller skates that catapult you to your destination with the speed of light! Imagine a scene in which you are expecting guests and have little time to prepare and straighten up your house. Gasp in excitement while picking up as much stuff as you can and shove the rest under the rug! As your guests arrive, pause and enter your heart. When opening the door, shift into the *Whispers of Wow* while giving them a warm hug.

Audibly breathing with awe and wonder there is renewed ability to slow down and return to a state of calm anytime you wish. Remember, you have all the time in the world to come fully alive.

Song Talk

Another popular way political systems keep us under their control is by limiting the expression of our voice. A child should be seen and not heard. Emphasizing restrictions rather than motivations limits vocal expression. This unfortunate condition instigates one of the greatest fears of all - speaking up for what we stand for. Terrified of saying the wrong thing, we become tongue-tied; an excruciating condition that sustains tension in the neck, face, jaw and mouth.

Opera Singers sing with intense emotional energy streaming from the tailbone.'

-Robert Besely

Lest we should forget the constitutional right of every human being in this country is – freedom of expression.

One of my clients, who suffered from inhibiting shy, self-conscious behavior, picked the image of a mad watchdog barking his head off. He used this barking action to eradicate his negative thoughts and release emotional buildup. After spending some time refining this process, his barking antics took on exciting operatic overtones. After making up the scariest, operatic songs, he was thrilled to discover a powerful singing voice. Instead of wasting time feeling anxious with nothing to do, he signed up for singing lessons!

The irony of this journey is, there is no place to get to, and you have to walk through thousands of lives to arrive.

-Unknown

When catching yourself playing any victimized role, exaggerate your posture and vocal tone. Remember, you are not a victim; you are only acting like a victim. Once you can reproduce fearful behavior, frighten all the thoughts out of your head with grandiose, operatic singing! Become a firecracker exploding any terrifying scenarios that still hold your spirit captive.

Intuition speaks in the small spaces between our thoughts. If there were an activity or new talent you would like to learn, but still let fearful thoughts get in the way, call forth the Soul of Fear and breathe with frightening intensity for thirty seconds. Rest for a moment. Now breathe with excitement as you witness yourself successfully manifesting this talent with confidence. Bring the percussive voice of excitement into your known language. Shake loose any tension from your body.

Breathe in this nerve-tingly energy for a few minutes. Once your energy is flowing, chant this phrase with gusto, "Stop! Look! Listen!" This chant is great to do when you're about to fall asleep while driving. Another great chant chant is: "Alert! Awake! Aware!" When hesitating to take a needed risk, chant with rapid-fire brilliance, "Yes! I can do it. Yes I can!" Turn these phrases into a spontaneous song sung with operatic overtones. Exercising thrilling energy dissolves barriers that prevent you from taking confident action.

You can't live where you hide, and we hide all the time. The 'acquired voice' needs to release its pretense and scream free of all limitation.

Joy of Screaming

As a child, my son Ryan would love to run through the house screaming his head off for no particular reason. I would always do my best to calm him down. Never being given permission to scream as a child, the next time he went screaming through the house, I decided to join him. There we were, running around in circles screaming at the top of our lungs, when Ryan stopped dead in his tracks. He looked up at me and shouted, "Mommy stop! What will the neighbors think?"

Excuse me gentlemen, I have to go to the bathroom and Screeeeaam.

-Woody Allen

All cognitive functions, such as thinking, spatial perception, and memory are enhanced when exercising high-pitched sounds. A voice rich in high tones denotes a being that is not afraid to lighten up. When you're in the middle of taking a shower, raise your spirits to great heights by lightly bobbling your body to remove excess tension.

To recover your full vocal expression, screaming with pleasurable excitement clears the mind of entanglements and releases the untold vitality in your speaking voice.

Screaming with deep pleasure offers instant energy in any boring moment. This flamboyant process motivates you to act on your intentions as a thrilling experience rather than a terrifying threat that will incapacitate you. To start, warm up by humming with cascading, siren sounds that move from low to high and back to low. Infiltrate different vowels through your sirening sounds. Once your throat is open and your body is relaxed, Imagine these siren sounds becoming a roller coaster that gradually climbs upward into the sky and comes radically zooming down with a whisper! Feel these roller coaster sounds being generated from a wiggling tailbone. Encourage tiny explosions of screams to clear any lasting fears that have blocked the fullness of your spirit. *ScreEEEam* with joy!

Often, almost miraculously, our creative potential comes forth with irresistible power and intelligence when we are in a state of emergency.

-Laura Huxley
You are not the Target

Walk Primal

When sitting in any public place, we can witness a whole parade of people walking about in a perpetual state of distress. Stiffened necks and shoulders, tight bellies and locked knees and shallow breathing have become so deeply ingrained into the flesh, that tense patterns are perceived as normal. Walking through our days in a body shaped by anxious concern, panic, apprehensive and dread, narrows perception and builds suspicion of life itself. It's important to remember that your body and mind are one. Recall a fearful thought that fills you with anxious concern. Walk about and pay attention to the different changes you body goes through while dwelling on this alarming thought. Particularly notice any changes that instantly occur in your breath and posture. When conditioned to block excitement, there is a tendency to round the shoulders, lower the head and tighten the belly. The practice is to remain loose and natural while remaining shockingly awake at the same time.

With each precious step you take, let the breath fire your excitement.

-Jane Miller

Once awareness is sharpened how your negative thinking habits radically alter your physical behavior, take quick sniffs of air through your nose while lightly shaking out all the buildup of tension. With each series of sniffs, focus this percussive energy into other areas of your body. Remember, all these Catalysts can be done so subtly, that no one who crosses your path would know what you are up to.

Small doses of radical self-expression, [electrical sparks of exciting breath, sound and movement] can help sustain alertness and stamina to 'multi-task' through the day.

How is it that we all possess the competence to shape and perform emotional behavior in such profoundly aesthetic ways? Where are the gates that let the rush of feelings come though, if they are not within?

-Jack Katz
How Emotions Work

Embodying the Soul

At the mirror, look into your eyes. Looking and seeing are two different state of awareness. Seeing with the open mindedness of your essence is witnessing yourself without judgment. Looking at your outer appearance often brings up fear of exposure, which is the fear of not being enough. Becoming gullible to the manipulation of others is often the result. If we no longer feel the pangs of pain warning us that something is wrong, we can easily be swayed in directions are against our best interests.

Become a bridge between the worlds by stepping into the space between your social role and your primal essence. Living in the space between acting and being, pretense and presence, breathe with excitement. As you shift your focus on following this continuum of exciting energy, open your mind and see what you see.

Invoke your *Primal Name*. Chant this magical name with the intent of activating oscillating waves of high voltage currents that 'excites' and sustains the health and vitality of your 'startle reflex.' Chant this name with riveting excitement. Finally shift back and forth between the fear response and pure excitement. Intend the percussive energy of the *Guardian Angel* to keep you safe throughout life.

Every person is pregant with excitement yet fearful of the firghtening delight of fully experiencing it.

-Joseph Zinker

As a performing artist in daily life, your task is enacting the Soul of Fear as an instinctive ally that can help you brave the forces of unexpected calamity.

The social role fears exposure and the fearful idea of not being good enough in the presence of others. Paralyzing stage fright can keep us all from stepping out and taking the stand. Feeling tense and nervous when appearing in the public arena is probably the most debilitating fear there is. Spending life avoiding any unplanned activity, there is the lurking fear of making a mistake and being humiliated by an audience. The secret is staying in tune with spine-tingling sensations rather than torturous self- talk. These sensations that quiver through your flesh are adrenaline rushes that offer you bigger than life energy to accomplish bigger than life tasks. This scintillating energy that is designed to keep your 'startle reflexes' in tip top shape, is usually judged as nervousness, something to get rid of as quickly as possible. With this deepened appreciation of your inner power, make these performances in front of the mirror an act of sharing yourself in service of a larger purpose. On one level this process can help you gain practice of coming into bio-rapport with any audience as the sub-personalities of your own mind. As an expressive arts practice, you are learning to refine the shapeshifting powers of your multidimensional self.

What is the most interesting thing to enact is what is least known about you. The true meaning of this performance is beyond any story you can expect or imagine. As a *Sacred Actor*, you are called upon to enact the *Guardian Angel* of the world in a four star movie. The movie demonstrates how human society has been silenced with fearful ideas to prevent people from taking a stand on their own behalf. Having become estranged from the instinctive roots of their nature terror of the unknown is building in the heart of humankind. Your task is clarifying fearful thinking habits with the capacity of self-reference – moving into new relationship with the primal forces within. For this amazing feat, you will be paid royally!

That which may seem, on the face of it, like a crippling essence defect, may mask a hidden creative force in need of some drastic shock to set it in motiom.

-Robert S De Ropp

Sense the alert, trigger-like kinetic vitality of nervous energy as you wait to play your scene. With adrenaline as your ally there is excitement in feeling the build up of tingling sensations to support this bigger than life task. As anticipation approaches its peak, hear the director call out: "Action!"

For one minute, expurgate fearful thoughts that have filled the minds of people everywhere – the fear of death, old age, sickness, financial loss, stage fright, being judged inadequate and unlovable etc. When this expurgation has been exposed, shapeshift into a ferocious watchdog barking its head off! Dart about scaring out all the terrifying thoughts crammed inside the minds of humankind!

With lightening quick pronunciation shout, "Alert! Awake! Aware! As the Soul of Fear, I am the supreme protector of the life force! Befriending my power offers you genuine excitement to live life with confidence in your personal power." As the audience hears your extraordinary proclamation, fearful thoughtforms dissolve into jubilant outbursts of excitement that reverberates throughout the world.

The Adversary archetype is the agent of change which forces you to confront any difficulty because the difficulty itself is also an aspect of your identity. Adversarial energy opens you to draw upon creative forces you didn't know you possessed.

I remember when my body knew when it was time to cry and it was all right to explode the world and melt everything warm and start new, washed, and clean.

-Bernard Gunther
Sense Relaxation

Rain

Healing Vulnerability

Even the stone of the fruit must break, that its heart may stand in the sun, so must you know pain, and the cup he brings, though it burns your lips, has been fashioned of the clay, which the potter has moistened with His own tears.

–Kahil Gibran

The Prophet

Born vulnerable, we are all physically dependent on others to care for all our needs. It is sad to say that we are given little help in coping with vulnerable emotions when they arise. Our culture conditions us to avoid the expression of painful feelings as some kind of weakness, something to get over as soon as possible. How many times have we been told when growing up, "Don't cry. Stop acting like a baby!" With this kind of conditioning, how quickly our hands race to the face to hide those shameful tears from flowing. With no permission to depressurize, water builds up inside the chest. It is not too far fetched to say that we can literally drown in the buildup of unshed tears.

This fifth primal energizer coaches you to exercise your crying muscles, whether you're sad or not. Breathing, sounding and moving with the sporadic rhythms of vulnerable energy are an effective means of loosening tension and clearing out withheld pain.

While I was working on this chapter, I walked through a part and noticed an elderly lady sitting on a bench. She was reading a letter, which filled her with overwhelming sadness. As tears came to her eyes, a friend sat down beside her and started to talk. In an instant, the woman acted as if she was wiping something out of her eye. As she turned to her friend, she smiled as if nothing had happened. There is nothing so sad as wearing a happy mask while walking around holding in a lifetime of sorrow.

A child in a preschool playground protested angrily in a crying voice against an adult's intervention. He shouted, "Don't take my tears away!"

The Soul of Vulnerability cries to be liberated from demeaning value judgments that diminish its healing powers. Releasing the tears and embracing the hurt, this tender energy is designed to sweetly caress the losses that cannot return. Clearing the judgments that characterize vulnerable feelings, is an important aspect in sustaining emotional health. Dr. William Frey, of Ramsey Medical Center in Minnesota, reports that tears wash away the pain by releasing ACTH, a stress hormone triggered by the pituitary gland in the brain. If fragile feelings are believed to be unacceptable, all of our feelings tend to be guarded from being seen. To remain in constant control is to avoid being touched deeply by anything or anyone. Taking pills is the standard way of deadening pain. Being trapped in this apathetic place, our body's healing wisdom cannot operate properly. When holding in so much disappointment and grief, is it any wonder our bodies start to droop, stoop and sag down with the weight of depression.

The clouds pass and the 'rain' does its work, and all individual beings flow into their forms.

- I Ching

These unexpressed feelings do not go away. They will find any means they can to release the stress. It is not surprising that the display of tragedy and loss has become a media obsession. We are fascinated when the reporter prods a farmer about his feelings after a tornado has destroyed his home and family. Millions of people turn on daily soap operas and cry with the heroine who has been unfairly abused and abandoned. Books that make the heart bleed for the outrageous misfortune of others are a big selling item.

Deep down, there is a powerful force designed to relieve human suffering. Like rain watering a parched earth, a flood of tears can wash out the pain and moisten new seeds of life to grow.

Rain of Tears

The inspiration for this chapter is in memory of Rain, a beautiful, young child who lived next door. She had golden curls that hung around her neck in tiny ringlets. Her mother, Ella, created stained glass windows that glowed with a luminous beauty. On the way home from school, painful sounds were being expressed in Rain's house. When I saw my mother, she grabbed me weeping, "Rain had a high fever. She's gone! She's gone!"

The fistful of dust, I hold in my hands, will noiselessly pour, like a thread of tears.

-Gabriela Mistral

The shock was so great, I just stood frozen in shock. Finally, without a word, I ran to a deserted field a few blocks away. A gentle rain was falling. Feeling the raindrops run down my face, I burst into tears. As my tears merged with the rain, I knew the beauty of Rain's spirit would always live in my tears.

My mother had lost her beloved son when he was only ten years old, so she deeply understood the pain Ella was going through. Every day, for weeks, my mother would bring Ella soup and homemade bread. I would watch them sitting in the rose garden tenderly comforting each other. On returning, my mother would look as if she had been washed with gold dust. The plastered smile that was her trademark had been exchanged for a soft light that glowed from her eyes.

With the wind in my ears and the song of the wolves in my soul, I wailed and howled for two hours, down the entire length of that twisted back road. I mourned and accepted it all.

-Tracy Gay Holiday
Wailing of Women

Shortly after this terrible loss, my mother passed away. The memory of pungent smells of goulash and hot apple strudel filled my mind. As my mother made her passing into another world, I had a vision of seeing her body tied up with a rope filled with many knots. In my grief, I struggled to pull the knots loose. There was a thick knot of mistaken identity followed by a gnarled knot of insecurity that bound her into subservience and servitude. There was a twisted knot that had strangled her voice from speaking the truth. As the brittle knot that had hidden her extraordinary beauty came undone, the whole length of the cord turned into shimmering, silver threads connecting my mother's life with the life of spirit.

As time marched on, I returned to my habit of guarding my heart from hurt. Growing up in an abusive environment, I still believed that any show of vulnerable feelings would make me appear weak in the eyes of others. In truth, I had forgotten how to cry. With a miscarriage at forty-six, I went numb with shock. Refusing to believe what had happened, I walked through the day on automatic pilot. A few days later, I was sitting with a dear friend who asked, "How are you doing with the pain of this loss?" My eyes darted around the room to avoid the subject. My friend held her gaze with compassionate understanding. With a stiff upper lip, I replied, "I'm sure there's a reason for all of this, I just have to hold it together and get through it." She immediately exclaimed, "You do?"

In minutes, I collapsed into her arms and sobbed with grief over the baby I had always wanted and lost. With no words, she held and rocked me like a child, cooing tender sounds in my ear. When I finally got up and walked about, I felt relieved, yet I knew the healing process was not over.

Soon, I was prompted to pay more attention to the physical actions of crying, and especially how the body organizes itself to inhibit vulnerable feelings from being seen. Observing young children's expressions during painful experiences, I noticed when they fully express the pain of an event, there is no lingering regret. In minutes, most children start responding to whatever feelings are emerging in the moment. When the act of crying is not accepted, this energy remains imprisoned within the tight armoring of the muscular system.

Opening to the Soul of Vulnerability is becoming more permeable to your wholeness rather than defended in your smallness.

Out of this deep work, the Soul of Vulnerability opened my heart to the knowledge that everything is passing and to embrace the preciousness of the moment. As my pain began to subside, this vulnerable soul urged me to adopt a baby. All the adoption agencies that I visited said I was too old. Even my friends thought I was totally crazy to take on the responsibility of raising a child at my age. Nevertheless, I kept pursuing every resource that was available. In every conversation and workshop, I shared my desire to become a mother. With all my energy focused on this task, within a year, I adopted twin boys at birth! Even more extraordinary, I was in the delivery room and was the first to welcome these beautiful beings into the world.

If my head had remained the ruler over my feeling heart, I would never have attempted to tackle this awesome task. With the growing strength of an inner guiding power that speaks louder than words, I answered the challenge with full commitment. Yes, it's possible to dream big and manifest our dreams against seemingly impossible odds.

Perhaps your tired eyes itch because there is some loss you have not completed mourning. Never miss an opportunity to cry.

-Bob Mandel
Open Heart Therapy

So many tears are locked up in our bodies waiting for us to honor them by giving ourselves permission to cry.

-Christine Northup
Honoring our Bodies

And just when one feels the next breath will surely be the last, a rare and rainbow-colored bird settles on a delicate twig of the bush, and, with the magic of melodious trillings and beauty of plumage, charms the dying one back to life.

-Eldridge Cleaver
Soul on Ice

Activations

The Activations that follow are designed to sensitize you to the physiology of the crying response and channel this energy into creative expression. As a fitness, exercising vulnerable energy with breath, sound and movement is every effective in clearing the buildup of painful feelings stored in the cellular structure. This process is also effective in loosening rigidity in your torso, particularly the ribs and diaphragm.

Have you ever considered what physically happens in your body when you cry? Recall times of deep despair when you cried over some loss and disappointment. If you're willing, let yourself feel this experience once again. Dwell in the sensory qualities that arise. This may be difficult for many of you that have been raised to judge your tears as self-indulgent behavior or a sign of weakness. Notice particular tendencies, such as tightening your jaw or ribcage to inhibit the sensation of trembling. Are these vulnerable feelings welcome, or are you inclined to push them away and keep them hidden? Let go of these painful events and simply be with the feelings that have been evoked. These feelings are energies that are needed to cleanse and clear your system of distress and pain. As the heart opens, there is deepened trust to feel all your emotions with equal value.

In our mother's womb, the first sound we hear is the sound of her heart beating. This early experience creates an intimate connection between musicalrhythms and body rhythms.

-Janalea Hoffman
Rhythmic Medicine

The Pant

I invite you to imagine you're a great musician learning to express deep sadness with exquisite creative artistry. What it takes is being willing to explore the rhythms of sensation that evoke sadness, and follow it wherever it leads. Be prepared, real tears may start flowing. Bless them, honor them and welcome them as a newborn baby coming into the world. You will not lose your earthly foothold; instead, you will win back your lost freedom to feel life in all its fullness.

Your ribcage is the home of your heart. Tightening your ribs is an effective way to stifle crying sensations from occurring.

When physicalizing the actions of the crying response, you will notice that your chest vibrates with pulsing energy and your ribs quiver with spasmodic, trembling movements. Chronically tightening the ribs is a strategy that is used to shut down and deny feelings of sadness and pain. The more rigidity in our system, the less vital energy we experience.

Start this process by wrapping one arm around one side of your ribs and resting your other hand on your heart. This position allows you to feel the subtle pulsations of micro-movements of the crying response. Explore panting with your mouth closed. Lightly sniff the air with erratic rhythms that make your ribs flutter like the wings of a hummingbird. Observe how panting stimulates your entire ribcage from the inside out. Panting while gently arching and rounding your spine helps to loosen tense holding patterns that have guarded your heart. Explore panting with more free air.

Many people think that tightness represents strength. What it represents is the practicing of control, the chronic need to deny vulnerable feelings from showing.

-Stanly Keleman

While panting, open your mouth and shape your breath into different vowel shapes. When panting on your inhalation, pulsing motions expand your ribs. When panting on your exhalation, your ribs stretch downward. Explore going back and forth between expanding and contracting your ribs with sporadic breathing. While increasing and decreasing the intensity of breathing, intend this energy to clear out any lingering sorrow that may still be stored in the muscles, bones, tissues and cells. When exploring ay of these panting breaths, periodically pause and shift into *Whispers of Wow*. Breathing in with wonder and awe of deep peace brings your energy into balance. If your ribs feel unresponsive, lift clumps of skin up off your front ribs and breathe into the extra space you've created. Now lift the skin off the sides of your ribs while taking a deep breath. Do the same with the skin on your back ribs. Slowly breathe out your air while letting go of the skin. Notice how this simple technique broadens your ribcage, which helps to expand the power and depth of your breathing capacity

Rain! whose soft architectural hands have power to cut stones, and chisel to shapes of grandeur the very mountain.

-Henry Ward Bercher

Another effective technique to loosen ribs is imagining an elastic band connected to your ribs and elbows. When you move your elbows out, imagine this elastic band pulling out your ribs. As you draw you elbows in, your ribs respond in the same way. Play with this coordinated action. Imagining your ribs as an umbrella or a venetian blind opening and closing creates more flexibility in the midsection of your body.

While exploring the panting breath, you may notice the inner corners of your eyebrows come together, and your lips may purse together in a pout. Enlarging your facial expression while delicately panting is not phony behavior. On the contrary, this form of oxygenation evokes the energy of release that thaws out tension and stress. With the inevitability of change and the need for growth, it is only through embracing sadness that true joy is possible.

Shed tears in chunks. Shed tears like pieces of skin. These tears are monolithic. They have been held within long enough to grow into works of art, solid and carefully carved.

-Lisa Yount

Sometimes it appears as if nothing can make us cry, even if we wanted to. Finding a way to express our tears whenever we wish, repression of feeling no longer rules our life.

Ceremony of Tears

One of the deepest root causes of suffering is attachment to things staying the same. Our tenacious need for security and stability can create major disappointment in a world undergoing constant change. The way out is through. Children know how to cry with abandon. And when crying is over, it's over. Shedding a rain of tears prepare the ground for a flowering spring that overflows with effortless abundance for the future.

If you have difficulty crying and would like to feel your vulnerable feeling more clearly, recall people you've loved who have passed on. Take time to sense the unique gifts they offered you when they were alive. Recall people in the public eye who have touched you in some way. Remember any pets or even objects you have loved and lost. Take time to feel the pleasure you felt when stroking your pet or fondling this object. Write the names of all the people, pets and objects on different pieces of paper or chips of wood. Add a simple blessing that expresses how they touched your heart when they were alive. Hold the paper or wood in your hands and bring it to your heart. Feel their spirit melting into oneness in this tender place within you.

The greatest gift of vulnerability is to guide you to a depth of openness where you can feel the longing of your soul.

-Kimberly Marooney
Angel Love

Turn your tears into rain and release the pain. Let the rain fall and regenerate your soul. Your tears give you their wisdom only if they are allowed to move in you and through you.

Strike a match and burn the bundle of paper or wood. As you watch it go up in flames, witness their spirits flowing upwards and returning home. If your tears are still dry, be a little child waving goodbye to all the people, pets or objects that you have ever loved. Waving your little hand goodbye, see your loved ones walking down the tunnel of light into an unknown world. Waving goodbye, see them greeted by all their loved ones.

Song Talk

Once again, our body requires a balanced diet of emotional chemistry to stay in tune. Our social role, which is ruled by the mental mind, conveys a characteristic sound frequency that projects an emotional attitude. It may be pleasant or unpleasant, harsh or quiet, cool or hot. Any voice that has become singular in tone can adversely affect the health of our body.

What others say on their knees, he uttered in tone-language all the mysteries of passion and grief which man can understand without words, because there are no words in which they can adequately be expressed.

-Franz Liszt
Story of Frederic Chopin

As 'fellow feelers,' the voice of vulnerability vibrates in sympathetic response to the trials and tribulations that befall us all. This voice is often filled with bittersweet, soft, often quivering tones, because it reflects such deep reservoirs of feeling. These caring responses are filled with stops and starts of spasmodic modulations and whispered pitches of deep feeling.

The *Whaa* sound is the first crying response you made as a baby. Become one with this baby desiring to be picked up in loving arms when no one is there. Start with a whispered *Waa.* Keep it soft for at least a minute. Let your *Whaa* build in intensity for all the times your cry was never heard. Painful memories are like the sediment at the bottom of a glass. As your *Whaa* tone builds in momentum, use these tones to clear out old wounds. Intend them to come up to the surface and drain out of your body like water.

Making a mournful cry in protest of war and the wounding of Earth has the power to heal these inhuman circumstances. If our heart is insulated with layers of invulnerability, there is no inclination to change the inhuman act of war-like sensibilities.

Global and local wars, politically directed torture and famine are common-place news. What can possibly make a dent in this unbelievable truth? The women at Greenham Common, England, wailed in political protest for the development of arsenals of death. Camping in front of an atomic plant, they wailed out against the insanity of planting missiles in space and laser warships that hurl killing gas in fruitless wars destroying countless life. Their relentless cries shut down this atomic plant. On worldwide television, the mothers in Ethiopia and Sudan were witnessed wailing together over the bodies of their young children who had perished during the famine. This picture evoked massive proaction to heal the horror of war. At a recent peace march, I broke down and sobbed as a group of masked people walked by holding bundles of cloth representing all the children who had perished in the war. Invulnerability is the source of inhuman acts against humanity and nature.

Listen to the voice of the Pacific loon, that haunting wailing tone "oh-h-h-oh ooh- ooh." Like a woman crying hopelessly, endlessly. Like a baby bear who has lost its mother. Like a mournful sigh of the wind in a pine tree.

-Theodorac Stanwe

Become a musician expressing through the universal language, the song of fragile vulnerability; full of cadence and crescendo; with torrents of faltering, stuttering stops and starts. With blurred utterances of tone, wail out in sympathy for all of humankind's unrequited pain. When identifying with the Soul of Vulnerability, you'll be more able to move through painful states as a young child does, fully and quickly. Recall a mother crooning tender regard for a child in pain. Be that child crying out these statements: " Hold me, I'm in pain." Honor your right to share your hurt and the right to ask for human closeness. Gently whisper, "It's hard for me to express this, but my heart is breaking. I feel so sad." Wrap your arms around your shoulders and give yourself tender loving care.

Ain't it Awful

When the impulse to cry is continually squelched, chronic whining and long, drawn out suffering can make up for the deficit. The habit of whining is fed by thoughts of shame, blame, regrets, resentment and bitterness that build into chronic self-pity. Precious time can be spent forever dredging up childhood wrongs; how we were used, abused, deceived, misled, undermined, misunderstood and abandoned. When this habit of obsessive thinking takes over our mind, there is little relief from the pain that is felt.

Sorrow is like a ceass-less rain that beats upon my heart.

-Edna St. Vincent Millay

One element that perpetuates our miseries is the belief that our pain makes us special in the eyes of God. As a suffering martyr, we can actually become emotionally invested in depression. By exercising the crying muscles with artful execution, you'll be less inclined to use vulnerable feelings to manipulate others to get your way.

By consciously singing out the blues, you will be more able to detect insincere whining tactics in yourself and in others.

To change your tone, you first have to recognize and acknowledge it. Consciously make a whining sound. Complain about something by adding a nasal twang in your voice. Listen to the quality of the tone and notice how this tone affects your overall feelings. You may also notice that your chest starts to slump down into depression. A life of 'woe is me' shapes you into ongoing cycles of perpetual pain.

If you catch yourself whining about how terrible your lot is, exaggerate your whine as a great academy award performance. Get on your knees and whine out all the terrible miseries that have corrupted your life. Complain how you work long hours and are not appreciated, how you constantly make sacrifices and how they backfire in your face. Whine out how nobody cares, nobody acknowledges you, so what's the use. Cry for you supper, cry for love. Wail out "Poor me. I'm feelin' soooo baaad."

I merely took the ener-gy it takes to pout and wrote some blues.

-Duke Ellington

When songs of self-pity are exaggerated to the extreme, the absurdity they hold is revealed and the spirit lifts out of the quagmire of no return. Over half of the popular songs that fill the airwaves are filled with lyrics of dysfunction. Listening or singing these songs over and over can turn these negative messages into reality. Be on the lookout for lyrics like, "Oh, I can't live without you. I'll die if you leave me. Without you I'm nothing, I can't be happy if you're not happy. I'll never love again." Ugg GGkk! Enacting these victimizing lyrics with radical, uninhibited intensity awakens mindful awareness.

Wail out the blues as the star of your drama rather than its victim. Transforming self-pity into creative artistry frees you to laugh so hard you cry, and cry so hard you laugh.

Misery doesn't come to us, we unconsciously seek it out and hold onto it and wail, "Oh, if only I could be rid of this misery!"

-From a Sufi Tale

Walk Primal

Recovering from sorrow is inevitable. Painful situations can be a positive turning point to walk down roads that lead us to healthier, more wholesome destinations. Taking time out to unleash sorrow, bitterness and despair in the midst of living is not always easy. A job needs to be maintained and kids need to be fed. Giving up the chattering mind and following the impulses of your inner feelings without comment is so unfamiliar for many of us. The fear of the unknown leaves us feeling unprotected and vulnerable to what may befall us in this new territory. Carving inroads into this vulnerable state builds a tolerance for your feelings to guide you.

Do not fall into the trap of postponing living until some vague tomorrow in which you will feel better? Going for a walk while breathing with the sporadic, trembling rhythms dissolves the remorseful thinking patterns that deplete your energy. While staying focused on your vulnerable breath, open to the realization that nature knows how to consciously die and be born anew. Seeds of new life are always percolating below the cold ground. What has grown old dies away to allow the seeds of new life to unfold. Even if you're walking in a big city, realize that every green leaf, blade of grass, beautiful flower and all the varieties of vegetation are making their ascent back into the welcoming arms of Mother Earth. Where they go, you will follow.

If you 're sad all the time but rarely get mad, or if you're usually angry instead of sad, you're probably trying to cut off another vital feeling underneath.

-Jeanne Segal
Raising your EQ

Realize that very person that passes you by has known or will know some loss and disappointment in life. No one is exempt in facing some sorrow that breaks the heart in two. Feel the balancing point between knowing the suffering exists, and not letting it crush you, or make you go to sleep from overwhelm. With amazing resilience and a capacity to survive, courage is renewed to face life and death as part of our ongoing human experience.

Where there is sorrow, there is holy ground.

-Oxcar Wilde

To know in the most desolate moments of despair, seeds of your potential creativity are sprouting in every cell of your body.

Embodying the Soul

Perhaps the greatest sadness is feeling the loss of our soul. Guilt, shame and insecurity grow strong when believing we can't live up to societies' standards of perfection. How many of us spend precious time hiding blemishes and physical defects that are believed to make us unattractive to others. The problem is not having a large nose; it is the many judgments that are heaped upon the nose that make it feel so large. What do you do to hide an assumed defect? It may be very disconcerting to realize that the enormous energy that goes into assumed flaws makes them stand out ever more prominently.

Dive me deep, brother whate, in this time we have left. Tears are too meager now. Give me a song, a song for a sadness too vast for my heart, for a rage too wild for my throat.

-Joanna Macy

The pursuit of happiness is a cultural obsession. The constant need to be happy is to avoid the true of your ever-changing feelings. While standing before the mirror, witness your familiar appearance. What do you physically do to avoid your sadness? Underneath the thick skin of protective/defenses, where are your unexpressed sadness, loneliness, sorrow, remorse and despair hiding? When humming love cradle this part of you and ask its forgiveness.

Invoke your *Primal Name*. Encode this magical name with all the vulnerable sensibilities you have within you. Create an extended vocalization on each vowel in this chosen name. Emulate the tremor and sporadic qualities of sobbing through the consonants. Open up any backlog of vulnerable feelings that have been blocked from expression. While chanting this magical name, create an original Yoga posture that acts as the container for any feelings that resist being released. Imagine this posture becoming light and permeable as a balloon filled with helium.

Surrender to the inevitable. Step outside the posture and witness the resistance it hold, float away into the heavenly sky.

In this expressive art piece, your mirror is the movie screen being witnessed by all of humankind. Your task is to portray the Soul of Vulnerability that releases all that ails.

As a *Sacred Actor,* imagine humankind sitting before you. Many of these people have anesthetized themselves from feeling their vulnerable emotions. The part you play in the drama is the conscious expression of your vulnerable feelings as a synergistic, healing power. With all eyes upon you, turn around very slowly and bare the naked truth of your being. Create a simple hum of feeling that opens your heart to the broken hearts of all people, for the hungry creatures in the wild, for the mistreatment of the planet, and for the mystery and impermanence of life that is beyond all understanding.

Open the hum into a soul song whose sounds begin to dislodge the amnesia and paralysis of forgetting what is true in the heart. Let this soul song foster deepened understanding for our collective humanness – the fragility of life that contains the miracle of birth and death as one and the same. As your soul song comes to an end, see people everywhere moving from muteness to outcry. As this collective pain and despair is sounded out across the world, witness people opening up their vulnerability to care, not just for themselves, but also for the trials and tribulations of all of humanity. See children growing up feeling truly happy because their vulnerable feelings are respected as healthy. Imagine sitting in a business meeting and seeing someone announcing that they are going to cry and cry! Imagine the people around this person offering space for these feelings to run their course.

Vulnerability sleeps in the stones, dreams in the plants, stirs in the animals awakens in humanity and connects us to the heart of all life.

-Unknown

In closing this chapter, I am reminded of a lovely story of a Rabbi telling his students that he was going to lay the teaching on their heart. One child raised her hand and asked, "But Rabbi, why don't you put the teaching in our hearts?" Rabbi answered, "Oh no child, only God can do that. Here we put the teaching on our heart so that when it breaks, the teaching will fall in!"

It was still dark, so the music was close to silence, but the old narrow streets began to widen with the sound of God and I knew that it would not be long before the light followed.

-William Thompson

The bird of paradise alights only on a vulnerable, open hand.

-Unknown

But when the blast of war blows in our ears, then imitate the action of the tiger! Stiffen the sinews, summon up the blood, then lend the eye a terrible aspect! Now set the teeth, and stretch the nostrils wide, hold hard the breath, and bend up every spirit to his full height!

-Shakespeare

Volcanic Power
Pure Anger

Then in your play become one of the hated and despised animals.
Be one of the frightening ones. Battle with your enemy. Destroy him. Eat him!

–Laura Huxley

You Are Not The Target

In what area of your soul have you stored the profound pleasure of being big and bold in your physical expression? When was the last time you raised your fists to the sky and roared like a lion, just for the hell of it? Like a forest fire raging through the wilderness, explosive fire burns out the underbrush so that the seedlings of vegetation can receive nourishing sunlight and fiery heat. Exercising fierce energy in creative ways is absolutely essential in sustaining life long vigor and potent strength of purpose.

The sixth primal energizer coaches you to embody the Soul of Anger as the greatest strength you possess. By exercising anger as primal power, the intensity of this energy can be expressed in life-affirming ways.

When you allow a tornado here, a hurricane there, or a small volcanic eruption there, your emotions will not run rampant over your personal environment.

-Barbara Marchiniak

What makes anger so toxic is the 'length' of time this intense energy is held in the body. With few physical outlets, this primal power fumes in the mind of thought, which churns out conflicting dramas that can make soap operas look pale. Storing anger in the mind of thought stimulates the chemical adrenaline to work overtime. We can actually overdose on this chemical by developing a variety of painful illnesses, including heart disease. Jealous rages, drugs, alcohol, cigarettes, creating cataclysmic dramas, dwelling on deadly disasters and wallowing in bloody war and horror movies are all popular outlets to feed adrenaline addiction. As this destructive ferocity builds to even larger proportions, abuse, rape, terrorism, international crime and the horrifying effects of war reflect the building of toxic weapons that kill and wound millions of innocent people a year.

Embodying the strengthening potency of anger while identifying yourself with an elemental force of nature or an untamed creature safely transforms maladaptive anger into fit expressions of dynamic aliveness. When exercising the breath, sound and movement of thunder and lightning, there is renewed strength to move through tough obstacles without blaming or shaming anyone. By channeling anger into volcanic energy, there is confident courage to explode your unique talents into the world.

Land of the Dragon

When I was in college, I was involved in a children's theater play called *Land of the Dragon,* which was adapted from an old Chinese legend. I was understudying the part of a wicked, ruthless empress who dominated the entire kingdom with her volatile rage. At the last minute, the leading lady got sick and I had to step into the role. With no rehearsals, this seemed like an unbelievably overwhelming task. Shaking and trembling with fear, I slipped the magnificent black robe over my shoulders. A friend helped me paste on long red spiky fingernails that curled up at the tips. A half mask with eyebrows soaring to the sky was placed over my eyes. The last touch was putting on dark, purple lipstick that curved down at the corners of my mouth.

You can talk to other people in virtual reality, and that's great. You can also turn into an octopus– allot more fun!

-Jaron Lanier

When I peeked into a full-length mirror, I gasped in amazement at the transformation that had taken place. My nice girl self had completely disappeared into Lady Vicious Harp in all her terrifying aspects! Before I realized what was happening, someone pushed me on stage.

As I stood frozen in fear, a child in the audience screamed, "It's the witch! It's the witch!" In that timeless moment, the spark of creative fire blazed awake in my soul. With a high-pitched screech, I stuck out my blood red fingernails and clawed the air with ferocious intensity. As my servant in waiting came forward, I delivered my line with such fury; he stumbled backwards and fell over the couch! Without any hesitation, I wailed, "You stupid idiot!" As I gestured to the guards to carry him away, my red cummerbund snapped from my waist. My robe flew open and there I stood in my black Merry widow bra and panties. The audience of teachers and children went into pure hysteria. Their screams of laughter raised my fury to its highest peak.

Speaking of Mother Earth Her volcanic passions, her hurricane storms of temper, her trembings and shakings, her thrashings and lashings indicate that something other than serenity is going on.

-Paula Gunn Allen

Screaming back at them like a battle-axe out of hell, I picked up a sword to cut off their heads. As I struck the sword in the air, the paper mache' part of the blade flew off and spun across the stage. Without blinking my eye, I plunged the stick into the floor, screaming with utter frustration. At that moment, another kid shouted, " Kill the witch!" That was the last straw. I flew off the stage and went up to the kid and pounded my chest in fury! Now the audience went totally nuts with laughter and clapping. At the end, I got a standing ovation for the understudy who saves the play.

The profound value of playing out strong emotion and flamboyantly expurgating it in the name of art is a cathartic and enormously healing experience.

Large, eruptive expurgation of feelings, frustrations, anger, rage, dissatisfactions, create euphoria when used to set creative artistry alive in your work.

-Peter O'Toole

Bigger than Life

The absolute joy I experienced in that mad, uproarious evening is simply beyond my capacity to write about. When I took off the black robe, mask and red nails, I caught a bigger-than-life presence gazing back at me from the mirror. Sparks of red-hot dragon fire glowed from my eyes. It was such a revelation to unleash loud bombastic tantrums as pure unadulterated play.

Upon returning to my suburban world, all this big and bold expression went into hiding. If I even raised my voice, I was bad for doing so. While watching a TV program that depicted the brutality of animal experiments, I spontaneously danced out a ferocious lion roaring out against the atrocities inflicted on the animal kingdom. When the dance ended, a super-human power filled me with invincible strength. Whatever this energy was, I wanted more! While watering the lawn on the following day, I became a sword fighter swinging the hose as my magical sword. When I came home, a thunderstorm was brewing. Roaring with thunderous energy, I cleaned my room with lighting swiftness.

The Soul of Anger is the original intelligence of thunderous life force. When this elemental power is befriended, untold strength is achieved to create constructive change in the world.

The tragically clumsy way in which humanity handles its own aggression generates massive destructiveness. On our planet, one person kills another every twenty seconds.

-Piero Ferrucci
What We May Be

Activations

Look back into your life. What is your relationship with anger? Was anger ever valued as an intelligent power designed to give you the needed strength to meet your needs? Probably not. What beliefs have you absorbed that have shaped your perception of this intense emotion? When you were hurt or treated badly were you free to communicate your angry feelings? How do you normally discharge anger? Do you deny it, retreat or shout it out? When sensations of anger arise, do you blame others or blame yourself? How easy is it for you to say, *No!* pure and simple? Recall a moment in your life when you felt intense anger. While remembering this event, notice how your body reacts. Things to look for are locked jaw, clenched fist, stiffened back, jutting chin, smoldering eyes or gritting teeth. Let go of the event and simply be with the feelings that arise.

Blame and Shame

Over 80% of verbally aggressive relationships are physically violent. Programmed to value mental acumen over our primal instincts, dominant/subservient, top-down hierarchies get established early in life. A division of race, color, creed and religion occurs that is the source of 'holy wars' throughout the world. With this polarized outlook in place, we can get in the habit of blaming others for our mishaps or find ourselves taking the blame with subservient passivity.

If we continually use anger to feed our fire, eventually we burn out. Yet, if anger is the only way we know fire, when we suppress our anger, we suppress our fire.

-Diane Mariechild
The Inner Dance

Our mental mind is a brilliant computer, but it's not equipped to handle the job only our feeling heart can do. Living with repressed emotional energy that has no healthy outlet can have painful consequences. This was validated after a mass killing in Texas. The state government uncovered one significant factor in men who committed these crimes. As children, playful urges of emotional expression were punished as bad behavior.

Recall a person out of your past who hurt you when you were little. Imagine this person is in front of you. Start all your statements with: "You!" For instance, "You hurt me! You abused and abandoned me! You caused me so much pain!" Supply your own statements and shout them out. In the midst of this outpouring, listen to your tone and pay attention to your body language. Now transform 'you' statements into 'I' statements. For instance, "Feeling so much pain, I closed my heart to you. I was hurt and I hid my anger from you. I was filled with anger when you abandoned me." Notice the specific changes that occur in your vocal tone musculature when you go back and forth between making 'You' statements and 'I' statements. With heightened awareness of these two states, more opportunity is gained to communicate honest feelings with others.

The practice of exercising anger unleashes enormous personal power and tenacious strength to accomplish great tasks.

Deformed language wheels a million clubs. One must know innocence. Then language sparkles and shines.

-Richard Grossman
The Animals

Urban Mantra

With no healthy outlets to release the buildup of strong emotion, scapegoats are found that offer endless opportunities to rant and rave with justification. The sharp tongue of verbal abuse fires up pain, misunderstanding, and uncontrollable rage.

While leading groups at Esalen Institute, I decided to do some research on the physiology of the famous phrase, "Fuck You!" In front of a large mirror, I invited twenty people to recall an angry episode with someone and shout out that famous statement. I noticed, without exception, everyone contorted their voice and contracted their muscles–as if they were saying 'fuck you' to themselves! I also noticed that the body shape they assumed during the expression of the phrase was an amplification of the protective/defensive patterns of their social role.

Rage repressed is far less lethal when it is expressed in ritualized forms that honor this potent energy.

-George Bach
Aggression Lab

The whole point of amplifying the expression of negative words is to free you from being victimized by any word.

A belief exists that tightening the musculature is the most affective means of protecting ourselves from emotional abuse. Any chronic tightening of muscles dams energy and limits our creative options. Test this out now. Stand in front of a mirror and shout, "Fuck you!" a few times. At the height of this expression, freeze your body and observe your posture – how your muscles tighten, contract inward and twist your body parts in specific places.

Responding with feeling rather than reacting out of habit is one more way to strengthen personal power. Chant this popular mantra in dozens of zany, outrageous ways. Play with multitudes of improvised melodies while joyously roaring, snarling, squawking, snorting, bellowing and laughing through this urban manta. Sing it like an opera singer or rock star. I've wept with laughter while watching grown men skipping to cool jazz while wailing out, "Fuck You!'

Anger is often repressed or withheld, misdirected or projected onto others. The pushy, obnoxious kid in school or the father who threatens his children use bullying to express their shame or fear.

-Valerie Kack-Brice
The Emotion Handbook

The many creative uses for this simple phrase are almost unfathomable. Have fun creating a musical comedy song around the phrases: "I got fucked! Ahhhh fuck! I'm really fucked this time! What the Fuck? Oh, fuck me! This fucking thing is driving me nuts! Who gives a fuck! I'm all fucked up! Fuck it." Imagine a future episode when someone you really care about shouts at you with a barrage of abusive words. Listen more to the 'sound' of the interaction rather than personalizing the encounter.

When hearing abusive language as pure sound, more power is gained to change your tune in any way you please. In so doing the entire tone of the conflict will immediately change.

Thunder Grunt

An eighty-five year old client who works with abused children starts her day by having a grunting tantrum. She enters into this altered state by imagining she is exploding all the injustice in the world with primal power. Lying to rest her civilized ways of propriety, she writhes her body in unique shapes while breathing with volcanic fury. She ends this emotional fitness workout by stomping the ground and pounding her fists to the sky with pleasure. Needless to say, this vigorous, vocal cathartic releases tension and prepares her to hold the space for the children's unendurable pain.

All emotions, including anger are moving us towrad deepened union with the Source.

-Dan Johnson

Opening yourself up to express explosive power tiggers the deepest reverberations of sensation to flow through your body.

To start, visualize a thunderstorm brewing in the sky. Bring your hands into lightly clenched fists and pulse them in and out while grunting in rhythm with the action. Build and subside this rhythm until it explodes your arms outward like lightening streaking across the sky. For the next round, drum the ground with your feet while trembling your leg muscles free of tension. Loosening your legs in this way prevents jarring your spine.

As the energy builds, transform into a gorilla on the warpath! Jut out your jaw, narrow your eyes into slits, dilate your nostrils and turn your teeth into fangs. With wild, out of control gestures massacre all the jealous, envious, festering, hating, violent, destructive, vengeful, devious, manipulative, poisonous, fanatic, unscrupulous, callous, sly, ruthless thoughts you ever had! After this vibratory tirade, pause and feel the effects. Dwell in the sensations pulsing through your body. Breathe in the awe and wonder of new life flowing through you.

Reproducing the grunts of certain animals reaches down deep into our own primitive roots, and they excite the animal that lives in all of us.

-Eric Mooris
Irreverent Actiong

How Frustrating

Being caught in the middle of a frustrating dilemma is like being pulled in two directions at once. A new idea wants out and another one is fighting to keep it in. The more these push/pull deliriums can be physically amplified, the more new resolutions burst through any frustrating conflict. Is there some frustrating dilemma you're dealing with? Rather than think about how to resolve this conflict, physicalize the frustration. Imagine being tied up with rubbery strands of sticky gum that is holding in layers of annoyance, displeasure, exasperation, irritation and agitation.

Working with barbells releases tension while firming your muscles. Using the word 'frustration,' draw out the vowels while imagining a high-voltage electrical current running through your sounds. With all that juice in your veins, use all your muscular strength to pull off layers of exasperating frustration. Grunt with bravado while pumping the barbells out and in as if you are playing the accordion. Pause and feel the affects. For the next round, bring more swaying motions into your spine while enhancing your strength with vocal thunder power.

Exercising the primal power of anger as a daily fitness frees us from dumping thoughts on people we love.

-Wowza

Emergency Measures

When the energy of anger flares up after being caught in the mind of thought, the real question is what are you going to do with all that power? There is no question that many great musicians and creative artists had the ability to transform anger into artistic expression. It's been documented that Michelangelo channeled his anger into his works of art. It is said he hammered with such fury, the people around him were sure the whole marble stone would explode into bits. Beethoven made this comment, "You will ask me where I get my ideas. They are inspired by intense feelings, something uncontrollable anger that is translated into tones that surge and roar, until at last they stand before me as notes."

Great satisfaction can come from physically and vocally discharging rage in creative ways. Once the energy is spent, healthier options in solving the problem magically appears.

Listen to the thundering power ringing in your ears. Channel its flow into all your cells and feel the strength of the Creator.

-Jerome Tanner

One strong emergency measure is imagining your body as a 'dirty sponge' filled with toxins. Sniff in three quick breaths up into your head area. Release your breath by rounding your torso and loudly shout POW! into your belly. Hold your breath out while using writhing motions that squeeze out the toxins in your organs. When you can't hold your breath a second longer, 'pop' open and feel all of this compressed energy exploding in every direction. Then, take all the time in the world to gorge yourself on oxygen and more oxygen. This vigorous action tones your abdomen and charges your organs with vital energy.

Maddening events are often created to have a reason to unleash repressed anger. Amplifying anger as a fitness workout quickly restores balance. When dealing with unrequited anger, grab an old telephone directory and rip out all the pages. Roar like a lion while throwing the pieces of paper into the air like confetti. In the midst of this activity, play an aggressive game of tennis with your hips while yelling in rhythm with each thrust. Beat on a large conga drum that can transform rage into enormous satisfaction and downright pleasure.

POW WOW!

A family POW WOW when times get tough is a good way to maintain sanity. We can talk about an assumed conflict from here to doomsday, but physically releasing the tension in creative ways is a wondrous way to begin. I like to start by first going around to each member of the family and sharing what I appreciate about them; things I have noticed in their behavior and qualities that I value. For instance, my son often leaves the house saying, "I love you Mom." I let him know how much I appreciate hearing that. Step two is inviting each member to a pillow fight. The more noise the better. When the energy is spent, have everybody share one positive solution to a problem. You may have noticed I have left out expressing gripes, which by the way can take all night!

Put the wild hunger where it belongs, within the act of creation.

-Janie Canan

If you and your partner have a tendency to engage in full-blown, angry fighting, it's often difficult to bridge the gap so intimacy can be regained. When you're calm and relaxed, agree to mock up a typical fight with a chosen scenario. As sacred actors, become two wild samurai swinging swords while kicking and screaming *eahhhhhhhh! EEEHHH AAAEE!!* Let out all the emotional buildup with artful vigor. After your energy has been spent, bow to your partner for the magnificent power you both have to 'play' out any aggravating conflict with enjoyment!

Enacting our personal problems enables us to become cooperative participants rather than unconscious victims of illusionary dramas.

When tempers start to climb, pull out your imaginary six-guns from your holster and shout "Stick em' up! I'm taking over this relationship!" When you find yourself getting stuck in a tired old mother role attempting to speak reason to a five-year-old, take delight in transforming into a lion roaring, "Clean your room or I'll gobble you up for dinner!" More times than not, the room will be cleaned in a jiffy.

Carrying the mystical spear and dangling the bears power-laden claws from his arms, the shaman sings with roaring sounds that heal the sick.

-Nicholas Saunders
Animal Spirits

Last year I co-lead a seminar at the Oracle Corporation. Our message was, the more innovative we are in the body, the more inventive we will be in the mind. At the end of the seminar, I created a 'Pow Wow Brainstorming' session in which participants were guided to walk in a circle while vigorously sounding out different vowels with full voice. Once their energy was flowing, the manager of the department read out different questions that would evoke new ways to work smarter and more productive than before. While brainstorming on their feet, responses to the questions shot out so fast it was difficult for the person at the flip chart to get them all down. 'Strategic improvisation' is thinking on our feet.

Standing with fluid aliveness while brainstorming ideas, the brain receives 20% more vital energy. As a result, more innovative information flows from creative right brain.

But, finding true nature is not for the timid. It requires courage and a sense of adventure, a fearless heart, and optimistic strength.

-Hameed Ali

Song Talk

A decisive, assertive, potent voice commands attention, telling others we are in full possession of our inner authority. Taught to obey and never question the supremacy of outer authority, we find it increasingly difficult to speak our truth without needing agreement. Since anger has been so repressed, our throat muscles have clamped down on our voices, which make it very hard to express big and bold energy. Anger bound up in the mind of thought often has an attacking tone, a hardened toughness that masks the fear of intimacy. Many others attempt to shout out their words in a tense, muscularly armored body, which can cut through the hearts of other people like a sharp-edged knife.

One of my clients, Jean, was a brilliant artist who had learned that speaking with a bold tone was exhibiting bad manners. As a result, she projected a weak, apologetic, docile voice. Her quiet style of behavior seemed to attract men with loud voices that never failed to intimidate her. As she explored opening her voice with primal power, loud was heard as simply loud. It was not good or bad. By owning her vocal strength, her attraction to hard-hearted men diminished.

Think of anger as fuel, energy that can be harnessed behind creative new porjects and ways of being.

-Jeanne Segal

The voice of primal power is brimming with blood, guts and exalted passion. A big, resonant voice expressing the fullness of an experience is not hurtful to others. They can feel the tones pouring through an open heart that is not making them wrong.

I recall working with a group of mothers who lost their sons in the war. Most of them were raised to keep their pain bottled up inside. This well-worn strategy was making them sick. At the end of this event, I asked them to pour all their pain into the chant, ***"No more war!"*** As the energy built into a cone of power, we envisioned soldiers everywhere laying down their arms in mass relief for ending the insanity of war. If no young men are willing to participate in the perversity of war, then war, as we know it can no longer exist.

The great tragedy of life is not that men perish, but tthat they cease to love.

-W. Somerset Maugham

You may have to go to some remote place, ride in your car, or whatever it takes to create a safe place while releasing the phrases that follow. Ride the tiger into battle while belting them out with all the vigor you possess. As you open your throat with decisive, thunderous power, honor your capacity to assert the undaunted strength of your being.

Power, Power, Power!
I have the Power to move mountains and slay dragons!
I feast on fierce potency with total pleasure!
Red, hot fire is my indomitable strength!
Thunder power explodes my passion!

Walk Primal

The original dragons are said to have the head and horns of a ram, the foreleg of a lion, the body and tail of a snake, and the hind legs of an eagle. With their forked tongues, sharp teeth, glaring eyes and flaring nostrils, they breathed out sacred fire. Dragons of ancient times were also associated with water. With their enormous size they possessed agile swiftness to glide over the face of the earth with fluid power.

The celestial dragons represent the cosmic generative power. and lightning was its procreative intercourse with the feminine Earth.

-Ralph Metzner

When needing extra strength to go that extra mile, assume the power of a dragon breathing fire! Start by aligning with the gravitational power of the Earth.

Just as you shift gears in a car, take appropriate time to shift into different speeds. As momentum grows, shoot out the energy of your breath as an unstoppable firry flame that catapults you towards your goal with intense strength of conviction. Really feel this forward moving energy that can help you break through any physical, emotional or mental limitations that attempt to restrict your personal power.

To refine this process, curb the tendency to take big long strides that restricts the muscles of your pelvis. In other words, real strength is not about allowing your feet and legs to run ahead of the rest of your body. Instead, maintain a shorter stride while radiating an equal balance of strength to flow from belly, heart and head. Walking with equal distribution of energy builds a natural momentum of power that guides your forward with amazing confidence. As you shift gears into heightened speed, bend your forearms while lightly clenching your fists.

Feel your feet spring you into action. With wild grunts of roaring tenacity, pump your bent arms forward and backward in rhythm with your steps.

Slow down your walk and notice if you can still breathe with ease. As your breath returns to normal, create spontaneous, rhythmical 'power chants' by using a few syllables that are resounded over and over again. Feel your breath being drawn down into the deepest part of your lungs. This vision drops your energy deep inside your pelvis. Explore expanding the pressure and volume of air to support your tones. As the rhythms of your chant build with potent strength, grow a dragon tail that curves between your legs! Use these made up primordial chants whenever you approach a task that demands bigger than life energy for its accomplishment. Periodically shift into the *Whispers of Wow* bringing you into balance with the source of your being.

Walking with the speed of a tornato, I turned the corner and ran stright into love.

-Bettsy Drake
Opening to Inner Light

Embodying the Soul

We are coming out of a four thousand year history of domination and punishment that tell us how to act and behave by the rules and structures of patriarchal authority. This subservient/dominant structure is being reflected in our own minds. Without awareness of the game, we cannot change it. This ceremony before the mirror is about becoming free of dominant behaviors that resist expression of the essence of your being more thoroughly than any authoritarian institution. Lift the veils from your eyes and see your predicable tendencies with depth of clarity. What you label good or bad parts of your personality, reflects the dualistic drama that is keeping you in a state of perpetual conflict.

Expressive art is a holy ritual in which everything that is not holy is made sacred.

-Jeffory Tanne

As you gaze in the mirror, notice if there is an internal battle going on between the light and dark aspects of your public persona. Do you work hard to be positive, or is your rebellious side running the show? Do you ever get caught playing out the drama of victim and persecutor with someone you love?

The gap between who we really are and the role that is habitually played out is tightly wrapped in tension. The process of embodying the essence of our very own soul is an artful means of bridging this gap and experience wholeness.

As a *Sacred Actor*, you have been chosen to play the role of patriarchal supremacy intent on conquering and dominating the feelings of the human spirit. When identified with the *Sacred Actor,* the many disguises of God can be played out with total loving acceptance for the enormous raw energy that each role holds in its grasp. In this startling revelation, nothing in the world needs to be changed only dramatized with conscious awareness. In the new matrix there is only the 'play of opposites' reflecting the interconnected dance of life.

Once we learn the habit of accepting both sides of our nature, a self-supportive system develops, inviting greater challenge, expansion and growth.

-Antero Allir

In preparation for playing your part, invoke your *Primal Name* and encode it with the thunder power of primal anger. Before you start, call to mind potent sources of natural energy. For instance, a golden sun, fierce waves crashing on the rocks or exploding lava. As the Soul of Anger, let volcanoes erupt, tides rise and tornados spin as you chant this magical name. Intend these potent, combustive sounds to forever root you in personal power.

With the spotlight brightly highlighting your features, step into the shoes of the

Performance art need not exist only on the stage. Taking creative risks in the center of a family gathering is an exciting form of theatre!

-Ben Kingsley

badass, dominating, controlling power monger of the world! As you puff up your chest and flex all the muscles, let loose with a constant barrage of critical assessments and oppressing judgments that never cease. Do everything in your power to bring all of humankind under your control or be dammed to hell! With a hard edge growl, blast off with, "Shut up! Listen to me! I am the ruler of the world – the winner of the game! You take orders from no one but ME!!!" If you've really allowed yourself the room to play this role, don't be shocked by the extraordinary energy gushing through your body.

Feel the spotlight begin to spiral rainbow lights around your body. These lights are to support you in making the shift into enacting the great life-sustaining powers that have been lost in social conditioning. As you stand in the supporting field of gravity, feel potent roots of strength streaming from your feet into the Earth. Sense your roots diving deep into living soil, pushing into bones and fossils of all the ancients ones who lived before you. Still breathing deep, feel your roots intermingle with the fiery core of the Earth. Feel this fire as pure, transforming energy.

Consciously draw this fiery power back up from the Earth. Draw it through all the cells of your body and into the atmosphere around you. As you look out into the hearts of everyone before you, proclaim with massive red-hot potency, "I am the Soul of Anger! I am the originating power and strength that catapults all of life through the birth canal! This same thunderous power flows through me and you. Let us use our power to create a world based on love and peace."

I am beyond male and female. I embody the adventure of life. I bring courage to blast through insignificence. My name thunders across the skies.

-Alix Green

At the height of this intense outpouring, roar with the atomic intensity that births trillions of stars to shine in the sky! In this instant, the lost self-esteem that has keep a world of souls victimized in illusionary dramas, are being liberated in freedom. As a sacred embodiment of nature's elements, see everyone coming together to build strong, powerful communities that thrive in healthy self-worth. Suddenly being freed of guilt, shame and internalized blame, a celebration ensues in which young and old suddenly thumps their fists on their chest with unadulterated pleasure!

Hilarity

Authentic Laughter

At the height of laughter, the universe is flung into a kaleidoscope of new possibilities.

–Jean Houston,
The Possible Human

Authentic laughter is not only healthy, it continually uncovers life as it is - rational and irrational, complicated and simple, great and miserable, primitive and cultured - all rolled up into one. With a humorous outlook, there are no holier than thou images to protect or defend. Assumed imperfections are perceived as the growing part of being human. As the psychologist and mystic, Alan Watts, once wrote, "The whole art of life is in knowing how to transform negative thinking patterns into laughter."

The seventh primal energizer heals the disease of deadly seriousness by laughing in hundreds of different ways. Amplifying any feeling or mood with the percussive rhythms of laughter heals what ails.. The essential key is that you don't have to force yourself to be happy to laugh; you're happy because you laugh.

Research is confirming that laughter, happiness and a joyful heart are a great medicinal, therapeutic means to healing and increasing wellness. Popular writer, Norman Cousins, healed his cancer by laughing at old slapstick comedies for hours on end. The percussive impulses of laughter have a profound effect on the immune system by reducing the production of hormones associated with stress. Researchers have found that people with heart disease were 40% less likely to see the humor in life's everyday absurdities than people the same age with healthy hearts.

The real enlightenment is nothing more then a frequently occurring laugh at the Game of Life, beginning with the game called, "Your Life."

-Smothermon,MD

Deep belly laughs executed for a few minutes a day keeps the cardiovascular system stimulated and circulation flowing in the organs. The only problem is that because daily life is so stressful, it's hard to generate enough Ha! Ha! Ha's to gain sufficient benefit. Embodying the physiology of laughter with breath, sound and movement is a fit thing to do. It doesn't matter how you feel, miserable or bored, laughing with the quality of any feeling offers a high-impact internal aerobic workout for the diaphragm, abdominal organs and back muscles. It is estimated that hearty laughter can burn calories equivalent to several minutes on the rowing machine or exercise bike. This heightened increase in oxygen stimulates the production of endorphins, the chemical of joy that can shift us out of any doldrums in a jiffy.

Misgivings

As players, then, the gods are revealed to be delightful, joyful, graceful beings whose actions are completely spontaneous, unconditional, and expressive of their transcendent completeness and freedom.

-David R. Kinsley
The Sword and the Flute

After the breakup of my marriage, I thought my unhappy mood would never lift. I knew how healing laughter was, but even the thought of laughing was not a happy thought. One day, when self-pity reigned supreme, the 'misery phrase' chanted by millions: "Oueee veaaaa, how I suffer!" came pouring out of my mouth. Suddenly, the magic happened; I spontaneously laughed with misery! As good as it felt, I still believed that something had to be funny in order to laugh. To keep things moving, I exaggerated the laughter impulses through the syllables, *"OUEE!-EE!-EE!-EE!-VEA-A!-A!-A!- how I suffer!"*

In the middle of this strange behavior, I tripped over a rock and banged my knee. Instantly, I laughed with groaning, moaning pain. To my surprise, the pain quickly diminished. As I continued to jog, I laughed with a variety of different emotional energies. In the midst of this laughter tirade, I felt as if the sky, the trees and wildflowers were all laughing with me. When I arrived at my destination, a flood of tears filled my eyes. At first I wasn't sure if I was laughing or crying; for they both felt and sounded the same. I honored both of these masterful energies as the very energy I needed to heal my broken heart.

The weight of seriousness enervates the nervous system. Laughing reclaims a playful, joyous language of feeling uncovers a youthfulness of spirit that exists in all ages.

Old Age Renewed

Let all that you are merge with the energy of laughter. Let the motion of laughter dance and sing within you and discover your lost youth.

-Unknown

When teaching a class on the *Secrets of Ageless Vitality* to a group of seniors, I got their attention by enacting the inhibited posture I had as a child. While walking around the room with rounded shoulders and my head held forward, I let gravity amplify this posture to the extreme. When I stopped walking, I stood in the stooped, sagging posture of the elderly. I added a raspy sounding voice, which radically added years to my age.

Slowly, with a light-hearted laugh, I spontaneously unraveled this stooped posture into youthful balance. Awestruck by this shapeshifting feat, I invited them to walk around the room and pretend that they were over a hundred years old. They looked at me as if I were crazy. I kept shouting, "Come on, you can do it!" Finally they started hobbling around and becoming more decrepit by the minute. Looking at their friends bent down to the floor, they naturally started laughing their heads off.

Three-year old children laugh up to 500 times a day. If we laughed half that much, we would have the heart, lungs and nervous system of a six-year-old!

Sometimes I wake up Grumpy; other times I let him sleep.

-Bumper Sticker

The next step was demonstrating the bobbling bobble that brought their posture back into the support of gravity. With heightened fluidity I coached them to speak to each other with a higher, lighter tone of voice. Making the shift into a more youthful tone instantly shifted them out of their crotchety style of acting. We ended the session by *Wowing* each other in mutual admiration for our ability to grow young with ageless vitality. As we gathered together in our circle to share our experiences, many people agreed they spend too much precious energy fretting about old age instead of *Wowing* each other how great it is to be alive.

World Laughter Day

In many places throughout the world, laughter rituals are created to increase health, vitality and productivity. At present there are more than 5000 laughter clubs worldwide. Bombay, India celebrates World Laughter Day. When employees started work by laughing for 15 minutes, it was discovered that productivity doubled! When interspersing fun into work by offering permission to consciously laugh throughout the day, people feel better, think more optimistically, view problems more positively and get along better with others. I really laughed when reading that India also celebrates Machine Day. Rituals were created in which they decorated the machines with flowers and chanted affirmative sayings that supported long life. One day, while desperately struggling to get my computer to work, I reached out and tickled the computer all over! Instantly the computer started running.

You've got to realize when all goes well you have no comedy. It's when somebody steps on the bride's train, or belches during the ceremony that you've got comedy!

-Phyllis Diller

Activations

I dedicate the Activations to the laugh master, Charlie Chaplin. This Holy Fool possessed the supreme ability to rise above the worst experiences with his dignity intact. He accomplished this magical feat by blurring the lines between tragedy and comedy. They were simply intrinsic parts of a whole that played together in the dance of life. I'll never forget the moment when Chaplin was so hungry; he cooked the sole of his shoe for dinner and enjoyed every bit of it! The spirit of Chaplin invites us all to enter a magical realm in which God laughs through us. Come join the play.

Each of us is marvelously funny and absurd, but the fear of being laughed at is what holds most of us back from being our true selves. Learning to laugh for no reason at all, a fun house of liberating inspiration is unleashed.

Exploring the physiology of laughter can animate your aliveness with kaleidoscopic brilliance. With enough laughter ringing in your ears, anything is possible! When depressing states of mind get you down. never fear, the Soul of laughter is near. The trick is to leap into percussive breathing into a humorous state of mind. Enacting any mood you are in with the pulsing vitality of laughter creates distance from conditioned tendencies, and that distance makes all the difference in the world. What makes you laugh? Recall a humorous situation in which you laughed until you cried. Recall movies, cartoons, comedians and anything that pops into your mind that brought a hearty laugh through your lips and a merry twinkle to your eyes. Recall the

Playfulness is as sacred as any prayer. Laughter, singing and dancing will relax you. And the truth is only possible in a relaxed state of being.

-Oscho

nuances of laughter you've heard in conversation with others. Can you recreate your style of laughing now? Do you even know what it is? Laugh at a joke that amuses you and notice the predominant tone and where it is being generated in your body. Are your sounds predominantly high or low? Which vowel is expressed more than others?

I wish that every human life might be pure transparent freedom.

-Simone de Beauvoir
The Blood of Others

Don't get discouraged if you have difficulty recreating your laugh with conscious awareness. By sharpening your listening skills, you'll be able to recreate it and add many brilliant variations.

Hum Laughter

A delightful way to stretch your laughter muscles is by making little clicking breath sounds in your throat. Humming with laughter is great to do when you're down and out, with little energy to spare. I discovered this form of breath laughter one Sunday morning while singing in the church choir. A little boy accidentally knocked off an old lady's hat. She gave him the most devilish look I'd ever seen. Feeling the urge to laugh, I laughed in my throat! Playing with impulsive hum/laughter offers that extra added energy when going through laborious activities. So giggle, chortle, chuckle, grin and guffaw in all those odd moments of the day when you are just plain bored.

My greatest joy is when my soul laughs together with God.

-Meister Eckhart

Here is another humming way to get your funny bone in gear. Visualize yourself having a picnic with a teddy bear. Serenade your furry friend with your laughter harmonica. With your forefinger on your lips, rub it briskly across them, as if you're playing a harmonica. Using your finger to rub your lips, be light and aggressive, delicate and shockingly chaotic. Once you get going, create different vowel shapes that animate your expressiveness. Encourage every irreverent, impertinent and unashamedly childish impulse to have its way. Listen to the many magical intonations that appear. Irrational distortions of tone free up the doldrums with a happy-go-lucky-state to meet the demands of the moment.

Laughter is an instant vacation.

-Milton Berle

A great way to stretch your laughter muscles, is spending time in a public playground and witness young children laughing through their activities. Reflecting this exuberant vitality anytime you choose is to become young at heart.

Laughter Playout

Over 400 muscles in the torso are moved during five minutes of laughter. In fact, laughter has the same effects on the heart and blood vessels as aerobic exercise. Exercising with emotional dynamics of laughter turns fitness into a fun, joyous activity. Don't be surprised when you stop laughing to discover that your entire ribcage is trembling as if you've just finished a powerful weightlifting program. Put on peppy music and start bobbling in place.

Bobbling while laughing has increasingly more healthy benefits that sitting or standing in place with no aliveness streaming from the body. An image that takes the effort out of this process is imagining a tiny bouncing ball in your belly that's bouncing you. Start lightly laughing with the rhythms of your bobbling bounce. Imagine the bottoms of your feet are being tickled while loosening any tightness in your hinges and joints. As laughter bubbles up your spine and into your head, feel your 'clown' chakra opening! Laughter breaks can be perceived as 'internal aerobics' for all the systems of your body. Laughter is produced on the exhale breath. As you lightly bobble, shape your mouth into the different vowels with percussive articulation. You know what that sounds like: "Ho! Ho! HoHoHo! Hee! Hee! Ugh! Uh! Uhuh! Ho! Ho!Ha! Hahhs!" Lets bring more movement possibilities into your fitness playout. Double over with laughter and give your brain a 'laughitive' workout. As you dangle your head forward, chuckle, "Ha! Ha! Ha!" Once your head loosens up, encourage your shoulders to let go and dangle. Hang for a moment longer and enjoy rich flow of blood that rushes to your head. Take time coming up, so that you won't get dizzy.

Laughter is like changing a diaper. It may not permanently solve a problem, but it makes things acceptable for a while.

-Red Williams

If you feel a little self conscious, laugh as if you're tipsy! The more you laugh, bobble and bounce, the more the magical elixir of laughter is released.

For an extra bonus, take any physical exercise you know and laugh through it with impulsive rhythmic feeling. Or better yet, make up an original fitness pattern, in which you coordinate the rhythms of laughter. Once it's yours, let it go and create another movement pattern. Add different emotional qualities into this laughter playout and notice how your energy and creativity skyrockets! And more to the point, conscious laughter coordinated with physical activity keeps you in tune with your energy and your energy stays in tune with you.

Shaman healers learned to imitate bird songs and even imitate the sound of their wings. Through this embodiment, they could fly between the worlds.

-Nevill Drury
Music for Inner Space

Song Talk

Speaking with made up words filled with the percussive vibrations of laughter is the language of small children, poets, mystics and God. The Soul of Laughter speaks through us with short, strong contractions that raise and lower in pitch. Step across the threshold into an altered state by laughing through any 'quick essential language' you like. With endless combinations to explore, laugh up and down the scale with different emotions. Playing with incongruous combinations of laughing tonality unleashes pure joy to flow through your voice.

Laughing through enervating judgments creates a 'pattern disrupt' in the nervous system that turns 'clone-like' speech patterns into 'clown-like' relevance for new and different ways to express yourself.

Rap has gotten a bad rap. Rap evolved organically in the streets to express the dehumanization of life. Rap enables your left brain to talk with the instinctual side of your brain. One reason for this is that the brain processes speech in rhythm and rhyme differently from regular speech. Let your body rock and roll with this poetic rap: "Rhythm! Rhythm! Do you feel it? Put your mind in your feet and your body in the beat." Laugh/rapping through the phrase: "Ladies and jellybeans, pull up your sheets and lend me your rears!" Make up your own zany phrases and laugh/rap through them with gusto. Laughing with through the different emotions is a quick way to expand the range and resonance of your singing voice. Stretching out some of the vowels in the midst of laughter opens the purity and resonance of your tone.

Jump in and swim instead of thinking so hard about the process of swimming that you never get wet. There is no right or wrong;. there is only the giving or the non-giving of energy.

-Wesley Balk
The Complete Singer-Actor

Birdsong is pure laughter. Hum/laughing like a chirping bird is highly effective in opening the high range of your voice. A bird's singing sounds have enormous carrying power. A nightingale's song can fill a space measuring one square mile. If a bird were as big as a human being, its song would be heard up to one hundred miles away! If you're feeling a little nuts, warble like the Cuckoo! Interspersing lighter, higher tones in your speech clears out the raspy tones that come with age.

Making funny sound-sand faces with pleasure is a high form of art. It brings us more joy than anything.

-Jim Carry

Bring the comics to life for anyone who will listen. Get up and get your body language in the act. Watch kid's programs and imitate the cartoon characters voices. Weave these vocal tones into your conversation. If you're having difficulty communicating to a family member, create an unusual voice and say what needs to be said through a puppet. Tune up the 'startle reflex.' Enact scary stories to your family and watch them laugh, especially when you intersperse frightening tones. When you're riding in the car, have fun laugh/singing rhymes like *Old Mc Donald had a Farm.* Be the animals laughing! Or better yet, make up spontaneous laughter songs. When you hear a rhythm that attracts you, repeat and refine it into an original song. Exploring the art of laughter in a deadly serious world keeps us sane.

Radical fits of laughter for no reason at all, is not practical or reasonable, but it works. As a homeostatic response for reducing tension, shaking off anxiety, and healing the habit of monotonous living, *Ha, Ha, Ha!!!* work every time.

As we walk through life, the ring of laughter rises us to the free, exalted expression of our divine nature.

-Madan Kataria

Walk Primal

Every healthy, happy child mixes walking and skipping together, and intersperses this daily activity with sparkling laughter. Why on earth would we ever abandon such a fit activity? The intellect will tell you otherwise, but the rhythmical coordination of skipping and laughing is a healing, holy experience. To skip/laugh with all the different emotional energies is recapturing a child's joy of just being alive. Freeing the whimsical fun-loving spirit in childlike way releases mental burdens in a wink.

Skipping while laughing burns twice as many calories as walking and has less impact on your joints than running. Your inner critic will probably say, "People will think you're crazy doing a silly thing like that!" If you thank your intellect for sharing, and do it anyway, you will be amazed how great you can feel in the shortest period of time.

Laughter is the most direct route to Go – filling our heads with Light as we go.

-Henry Miller

Always start with the truth. Embarrassment often arises when even contemplating such a thing as skipping around the living room, kitchen and bedroom in full daylight. Even more resistance can come up when skipping while laughing. So skip with embarrassment! Visualize skipping in front of the whole world while laughing with extreme embarrassment. Now that's something to laugh at!

The point is, when skipping with the truth of your feelings, your skipping becomes artful and rings with truth. Imagining the ground is a trampoline filled with helium is a great way to get your skipping energy moving. Bobbling and laughing with gravity's buoyant support tickles the funny bone along with loosening the hinges and joints. With freedom to improvise, you can skip in place, in circles, quickly or slowly, daintily or rowdily, forward or backward with endless variations. Each one of these improvisations is a one-time experience. While you're at it, laugh your head off while galloping, jogging, hopping, jumping, sliding, turning and dancing. Combine all these qualities of movement and laugh to your hearts content. Shifting into the *Whispers of Wow* balances your energy and helps you become mindfully aware of the many changes that are occurring.

Humor Theater

Let's face it; everyday there is something or other we do to screw things up. What hellish dramas we create out of nothing at all. Oh how miserable we become when burning the toast, or when mispronouncing a word. Taking ourselves too seriously and viewing our problems as an unsolvable reality is a common malady in these trying times. What makes this truth palatable rather than depressing is the amusement that comes when we don't identify ourselves as an inferior human being. The point is any life that is well lived is full of foibles and mistakes. Mistakes are part of the learning process.

Learn to laugh at the absurdities of life as the child you once were who was ready and willing to laugh at anything at all

-Shad Helmstetter

When we take problems too seriously, rigidity rules the day. A grave attitude leads straight to the grave.

Laughter is when the unexpected occurs. A toddler puts on her father's big shoes -- and we laugh. The president forgets his lines in a speech -- and we laugh. When two contrary elements are juxtaposed, the sudden surprise catches us off guard. The more unexpected, the funnier it is. So, attune to the comedy of everyday life. Locked in seriousness means there is nothing in life to laugh about. If you have this tendency, laugh in deadly serious ways!

What is different is in the amplification of mistakes, which develops a humorous state of mind. Catch yourself when repeating the same lines thousands of times over with the same inflections and meaning. Now play the same scene again as an actor playing your part. Catch yourself going through the same lifeless motions day in and day out and this time laughing about it! The humor pops out when self-parodying our own behavior with enormous pleasure and delight.

Curtain up: There's the play of breakfast, the scene of going to work, the epilogue of supper and the epic of a Sunday outing - all grand possibilities for humorous improvisation.

Imagine how much laughter would fill the world if our unique talents were overflowing with spontaneous expression.

-Kitty Baker

Imagine a hidden movie camera filming you go through your daily scenes. Becoming the star of your movie will help you develop more courage to dramatize repetitive, daily soap operas from a humorous perspective. When needing to get someplace fast and your car won't start, laugh through your frustration! If limiting thoughts depress you, laugh them away with uproarious pleasure. It's downright magical how quickly emotional buildup is released. Embracing irreverence in reverence by mocking, satirizing and lampooning any state of mind that limits your natural genius is empowering.

When you feel stuck, it's good to ask questions. What is this scene about? What is the overriding emotional tone that your supporting actors are projecting? With this awareness, any new piece of business brings a breath of fresh air into an addiction called 'sameness.' For instance, I have a variety of red clown noses around the house. When dealing with a conflict that is going nowhere, slip on the red nose and amplify the conflict with a fresh new voice. One unexpected change in behavior can shift any deadlock into humorous interchange.

If you seek out the humor in your everyday life, it will be there. Collect a variety of character masks with unusual facial expressions that stretch your creative imagination.

When you're in need of a change of heart, put on a heroic mask. Strut your stuff for five minutes and notice how different you feel. Have a party and pass out masks to your guests and notice how amazing facets of their identity come forth that you never knew existed. Come to dinner with your face painted like a cat and watch how the moment comes alive with good-hearted fun.

Contagion of Laughter

God's kingdom is filled with childlike adults who know how to laugh in joyous communion with others. Laughter is contagious; it bonds us together by establishing a healthy emotional climate. In fact, we possess a built-in auditory laugh detector — a neural circuit in the brain that responds exclusively to laughter. Some people have never learned to laugh. The logical, reasonable path has run their life. The social masks they wear are so tight that it's difficult to crack a smile.

People tell me they feel so much more available to life once they learn how to clown around. It's about touching your soul and finally giving it room to laugh.

-Arina Issacson

Laughter is the shortest distance between two people. A burst of laughter is the most precious of all human experiences. When in the company of a heavy-hearted soul, generating more effervescent laughter is very infectious. Sometimes I share how the simple skill of humming with the vibrations of laughter lightens up my mood. As I demonstrate this skill more clearly, my companion will often catch the good vibes and automatically lighten up. Similarly, never laugh at another person's worries. Laughing with others is an ice-breaker while laughing at others is an ice-maker. Sarcasm, put downs, ethnic jokes, and anti jokes (anti-men, women, religious groups, nationalities, ethnicity, etc) can be hurtful as opposed to being uplifting.

Laugher brings people together because this emotive energy knows no boundaries and does not discriminate between caste, creed or color. It can break down gender and socioeconomic barriers in one second.

Where the comic spirit has departed, the company becomes constraint, reserve eats up the spirit and people fall into a penurious melancholy in their scruple to be exact, same and reasonable.

-George Santayana

Another way of transforming a gloomy interaction is to share some of your most embarrassing moments with full enjoyment. When conveying a comical perspective about an uncomfortable situation, people let down their built-in barriers. One of my favorite renditions is embodying 'miss fluidity,' the essence of grace, which trips over the stool on the way to the podium! It is the unexpected twist that is the source of all humor. With hilarious buffoonery, you're helping others to embrace the faux pas that make human life interesting. The ability to laugh together with friends boosts harmonious cooperation by dissolving value judgements.

When in conversation with friends, it's fun to mirror people's unique style of laughter. Merging your own style with someone else's style is a great way of expanding your laughter repertoire. Reflecting high-pitched laughter helps to release nervous, tense energy. Reflecting gravel-like laughter can stimulate gut-level potency to express your passion for life. Percussive tones radiating from the belly stimulates uproarious involvement with the moment. One more way to stimulate laughter with someone you feel close to, is to reach out and tickle them with living regard for all that they are. Tickling gets a quick response, as long as it comes from the heart and is not over done.

Developing an intimate relationship with laughter is making contact with an evanescent spirit that honors both incongruity and redundancy, eccentricity and conformity, seriousness and playfulness as the ingredients for a happy, successful life.

It is said that the Pricklies laughed for three days and things were never the same again. Now they celebrate the Festival of Laughter. Pricklies dress up in costumes. They hold a circus. They act like clowns. They do all kinds of foolish and fun things.

-Swami Beyondananda

Embodying the Soul

At the mirror, notice the typical mood the social role projects. How much humor and enjoyment do you allow to be seen? Don't be disappointed if there is little humor projected in your outlook. Many of us, as children, have been made fun of by the derisive sting of laughter filled with ridicule, loathing and belittlement. Being hurt by caustic humor, the mental mind builds an impressive fortress run by a protective/defense system that forgets how to laugh.

As we all know, the mental mind is notorious for prodding us to be better, smarter, and more together than we appear. Falling below our personal standards, is it any wonder that self-righteous pride, conceit, ambition, hypocrisy, vanity, cynicism and a ceaseless attempt to prove how worthy we are can rule our lives.

Changing the ego is too damn hard. Besides, this familiar anchor provides us with a security blanket in an unknown world. It is only when remaining identified with the ego as our real self that humor is stunted. When seeing yourself as a natural comedian, silly mistakes are perceived as new material that enriches your comedic style. With mischievous antics, amplify the emotional attitudes of the social role as your most glorious creation. Amplify that pretentious attitude and laugh! If you are sober or sweetly natured in attitude, exaggerate it all. With a humorous outlook, most conflicting aspects of the personality can be exposed with no guilt-absolving suffering. Frustrating situations can be dramatized with enjoyment. Pause and expand the inner light of your peripheral vision. Take a look at the sparkling joy shining from your eyes.

We each have a little clown inside us, waiting to pop out and express itself in fun ways.

-Mark Stolzenberg
Clown

Humorous performance art in front of the mirror can bring the light of humor back into the darkest hour.

Visualization and emotional energy joining together can create a life and a new world growing in expanding joy. You are requested in this expressive arts performance to play the Soul of laughter. To prepare for your role, play your mask on your face and invoke your *Primal Name*. Your task is to encode it with the emotive dynamics of laughter. Lift your spirits and lighten your heart while laughing with different emotions. Laugh as different characters that arise in your imagination. Laugh as sunlight spreading the warmth of joy throughout the world. Create an original Yoga posture that reflects pure hilarity. Living inside the shape of this inner mysterium, pulse all the boarders with laughter! Every time your recreate this posture, intend that unusual combinations of ideas are generating lavish inspired joy to fill your life.

The universe is a theater of mirrors in which consciousness laughs in all manner of ways.

-B. Myestra Slade

A profound opportunity is offered to create a magical time for children who have

Identifying with the actor in you, there is surprising freedom to play the fool, break into tears, shriek with laughter or fall dead!

-John Gielgud

been stricken with terminal illness. Open your field of vision and see these children sitting down before you. They want more than anything to give this serious plight a rest and laugh again. Remember, your ego of your social role can do very little in these moments, but there is an inner power within you that can tune you into the pure magic of the moment. Open your heart as wide as it gets and begin my communicating with the *Wow Language*. See their eyes grow wide with wonder as you commune with this pre-verbal language. Without any known words on your part, the whole group bursts a floodgate of chaotic feelings that have been stored in their soul. Within minutes, the energy shifts and they start to laugh. You laugh with them. Soon, every child is laughing with an open heart. Let this scene fade.

If you've been exploring these different playouts, give these questions some thought. Are you less hard on yourself than you used to be? Are you less afraid of critical assessments from others? Are you having more fun with things you used to take seriously? Is your negative self-talk lightening up? Are you feeling more tolerant of your friends and family's quirky behavior? Or better yet, are you able to bring more humor into trying relationships? It's time to laugh as much as you breathe and love as long as you live.

Developing resilience in handling the stresses of life with a humorous spirit, you can survive anything, and thrive on nothing more than simply being human.

Life is moving and alive, changing, laughing, playing, flowing ever into the new. This is the nature of what I bring.

-Ken Carey

Celebration

Natural Ecstasy

In the bright clouds tonight a luminous heart trembles. The moon goddess sings her song beckoning eternally to the deep flowing waters of my soul. Her song opens a yearning in me so vast, I fear my heart will burst. Softly, wordlessly, she sings, calling me deeper into this nameless rapture of a thousand dreams.

-David Schiffman
Songs of Big Sur

As the moon is reflected in the ocean at night, so the vast ecstasy of the universe, from the largest star to the smallest atom, exists in every primordial, protoplasmic molecule in your body. This erotic sensuality or this ecstatic power is forever eroticizing nerve fibers, warming the flesh, arousing the arteries and pumping blood into the heart with undivided passion. Conscious embodiment of natural ecstasy ignites the fire in your eyes, the flowing motion of your spine, the joy in your walk and the resonant warmth in your voice. Moving through day breathing and humming with the Soul of Ecstasy as your divine companion, is becoming a lover of life beyond all reason.

This last primal energizer weaves all emotional energies together in a celebration of radiant wholeness. Coming into union with the rapturous force of your ecstatic soul is living life in celebration for the life you have been given.

Embracing all emotions; from peace to chaos as the language of your soul is what self-love is all about. It is honoring the multidimensional nature of your expression in all its glory. Conscious embodiment of this rapturous passion there is unlimited freedom to moan with pain, to roar with potent fury, to tremble with excitement, to wail with gasping sobs, to burst with laughter, to throb with joy, to swell with bliss and to whisper with peaceful calm. With freedom of expression, radiant health, harmony, success and abundance abound.

Tapping into the bliss of ecstatic passion, every movement you make, your soul sings with unbounded love.

-Arvind

God as a Woman

Several years ago, I was asked to do a performance ritual depicting *God as a Woman* at the All Saints Episcopal Church. Their mission was to heal past wounds and bring people of all religions together in harmonious interchange. Leaders from many different religions shared how to transform the painful results that occurred when identifying

Mother, flung down in vengeance before your time. You will return on limbs flaming. Rolling back the stone.

-Celeste Newbrough
Pagan Psalms

For thousands of years, pleasure has been disdained and demoralized. It's time to proclaim the true wisdom of a life informed by pleasure.

-Stella Resnick Ph.D.
Pleasure Zone

the flesh, nature, woman, and sexuality, with the forces of evil. I started my performance by saying, "There is nothing outside of God. I see both the masculine and feminine energies of God in everything.

With a series of masks, I enacted many of the Goddess archetypes who embodied the ecstatic energies of nature to effect changes in consciousness. I interjected stories in my performance that many of these women were the original midwives and herbalists that sustained the health and vitality of the community. Their most powerful magic was delighting in the wisdom of the body and the beauty of soul. Breathing, sounding and moving with ecstatic energy was the regenerative source of their healing power.

As the evening transpired, different religious leaders shared about the reign of patriarchy, which instigated the Inquisition that is reported to have burned millions of women at the stake. In order to gain control of this ecstatic power, women healers were labeled witches who were 'cavorters with the devil.' No matter what brutal force was used to control and suppress, the potency of ecstatic energy does not evaporate into smoke. As the climate of guilt, shame, fear, suspicion, and terror grew throughout the land, thousands of people would spontaneously fling themselves into wild, out-of-control dance frenzies that swept Europe like raging epidemics.

Luminous, multicolored transparencies emerge into my awareness, streaming out from this teeming profusion of radiant energy.

-Deborah Koo-Chapin
At the Pool of Wonder.

The church condemned these eruptions as the work of the devil. Ecstatic power is not the culprit; suppressing ecstatic energy by separating the heart from the mind creates conflict on all levels. Until now, societal morality has trained us not to see this obvious truth. As long as the body, emotions and spirit are perceived as separate, the God force will remain in the image of a transcendent man, removed from the Earth, from the seasons of nature and the cycles of birth and death.

When our ecstatic/spiritual nature reawakens, institutions of domination will be forced to become more humanized. When each religion is honored for their unique expression of God and joins in respectful harmony with all other religions, 'holy wars' will no longer be a valid choice in handling conflict.

Developing a co-creative partnership with a meta-spirituality is the first step in dissolving polarized forces that no longer fight in war but dance together in love.

Sensual Discovery

I recall a client named Randa, who came to me because she wanted to cure her epileptic seizures. She had spent many years going through one verbal therapy after another and had taken a variety of drugs, but the dreaded disease still plagued her. During our session together, I learned she was sexually abused as a child and her religious upbringing taught her that she was born in original sin. Still living with this early trauma and believing she was rooted in sin, mistrust in her body and her sexuality grew strong.

I asked Ronda to view her seizures as a dance drama of ecstatic expression that was exploding with healing information. I encouraged her to physically enact the specific breath, sound and movements she undergoes during a seizure. With a shocked look on her face, she expressed not having a clue what happens when taken over by this severe experience. She also expressed shame in revealing such gross, ugly movements. As we talked further, Ronda conveyed that her religious upbringing judged dance, song, laughter, delight, joy and celebration as amusements and nothing to be taken seriously. My parting words were, "In spite of everything you were taught, a wind dance is exploding out of you beyond your control. Let us learn from this dance. Become a fly on the wall and witness this experience. When your seizure subsides, see what you can to recreate the breath, sound and movements of this dance in slow motion."

Passion, like a plant, has a seed from which it springs, has roots from which its stem emerges, has a stem, leaves, flowers which crown its development. It is the 'roots of passion' a passion in which love blossoms.'

-Constantin Stanislavski, Creating a Role

Two weeks later, Ronda came back and demonstrated the most erotic movements, sensual breathing patterns and passionate sounds I have ever witnessed. I asked her to go through the dance again while I mirrored her expression back to her. Ronda appeared awestruck when watching this hellacious experience transforming into a passionate outpouring of sensuous expression.

I whispered, "Ronda, ask this uncontrollable power if it has a message for you." Soon the words came, "Your sexuality is a sacred gift of God. If you continuously judge and inhibit your passion, it will continue to erupt out of your control." Ronda caressed her shoulders and said, "Oh, I feel such relief. I'm not bad for being sexually abused as a child. I have a right to express my sensual self and enjoy the pleasure of my body!"

The world is only for celebration. Manifestation is just a Cosmic Drama to be enjoyed.

-Sri H. W. L. Poonja

I suggested that when she feels the first impulse of a seizure coming on, rather than tighten her body against it, to expand her breath, sound and movement to support its release. In this way, more intuitive information will be conveyed for how to heal and transform this condition.

I saw Rhonda a year later. She confided to me that she had gone a year without any serious mishap. Whenever she felt the slightest tremor, she writhed out the pain by breathing with ecstatic energy. With huge amounts of oxygen flowing through her system, the terrifying pressure that would build to the extreme would relax its hold. With her heightened self-esteem, Rhonda, confided that she was enjoying the company of a very special man for the first time in her life.

Without access to ecstatic experience, addiction to substances is reaching epidemic proportions throughout the world. It's time to get high naturally on the breath, sound and movements of ecstatic energy.

Activations

Take a voyage that carries you through your life experiences. Recall different memories from your past that have opened up states of ecstatic passion. Choose one of these experiences to focus your attention on. What do you actually see, hear, smell, taste, or touch in this moment? Immerse yourself in

the sensuous, richly textured colors and sounds connected to this ecstatic event. It may be something simple, like feeling the pleasure of moist grass beneath your feet, or breathing in the intoxicating smell of a rose, or experiencing the wind blowing through your hair, or a puppy licking your face, or seeing the moonlight reflected on the water while you were kissed with rapture under the stars.

The expression of ecstatic energy involves the wholeness of our being. It is total involvement in what we do, whether we are eating, working, meditating or loving.

The balmy wind, one brilliant day, called to my soul with an aroma of jasmine.

-Antonio Machado

If you have difficulty remembering such an experience, make one up that would give you great pleasure. For instance, visualize yourself devouring the most delicious orange while humming with ecstatic energy. Savor and relish the sensory sensations; the fragments of color, taste, sound and touch that will warm the temperature of your blood. With your entire senses alert, dig your fingers into the orange and peel off its thick-skin covering, and *Hum Mmm* with feeling! As you handle the lush flesh of the orange and watch the juice pouring out on your fingers, *Hum Mmmm.* Awaken your taste buds while placing the slice of orange on your tongue. Feel its juicy rich textures melt in your mouth. *Hum Mmm!* You can give no greater gift to yourself than the quality of your attention. With the full presence of your being, slowly swallow the rich, juicy flesh of the orange. Now let go of the experience and dwell in the lingering feelings that have been stirred.

Millions and millions of times deeper, millions and millions of times higher, it is a total orgasm with the Whole, with the universe. It is melting into the source of Being

-Tilopa
Song of Mahamudra

Ecstatic Breathing

Ecstatic breathing is making love to God. Becoming one with the Soul of Ecstasy is breathing with the depths and heights of a fathomless mystery that lies below all labels and concepts. With all the emotional energies at your disposal, now is the time to celebrate your union with this bigger than life force. A fluidity of being is paramount in the expression of passion. Bring the root of your pelvis – the tailbone and the PG muscle – vitally alive. This is accomplished by imagining the entire floor of your pelvis as a high-powered elevator that catapults the inflow and outflow of ecstatic breath up the spinal column and out through your open mouth.

With a fluid spine and a fully adaptable mouth, the varied expressions of passion can be artfully articulated. Picture a baby bird being fed by its mother. Witness how this creature opens its mouth and throat in anticipation of gobbling up a worm! As you whisper-breathe with the different vowels, sense your mouth opening clear down to the floor of your pelvis.

To see the world in a grain of sand, a heaven in a wild flower, to hold infinity in the palm of your hand and eternity in an hour,

-William Blake

The expression of ecstatic passion needs the entire spectrum of emotional energy to bring it authentically to life. Breathing with total freedom of expression a lust for life is revitalized.

With uninhibited facial expression perceive your spine as a luminous rubber band that can arch and round, bend and curve in any direction with effortless ease. While audibly inhaling, arch your back, lift your chest and tilt your head upward. Suspend your breath at the peak of the inhalation. When breathing out, round your back, soften your chest and tilt your head downward. Keep refining these spinal movements while building and subsiding the rhythmical currents of your whispering breath. Slowing and speeding up your breath coordinated with an elastic spine is the magical key that taps you into a rapturous state deeper than all roses.

Participating in a beautifully co-ordinated flow of motion, is to come in harmony with the universal rhythm of life.

-Gertrude Enelow
Body Dynamics

Breathing with thrilling impulses and rapturous crescendos of feeling revives lost passion and moistens everything that has become dry.

Speeding up and slowing down your breath – grown and moan deep in your throat. Building and subsiding the rhythms of your breath – pant with aggressive, pounding tones – faster and faster! Open to the expression of peace, rage, fragility, fear and laughter – all blending together into expressions of uninhibited love! When your energy is spent, dwell in the spacious void where all thoughts, all sense of time, location and identity merge into the divine mystery and magic of the eternal now.

My body, which in a long spell of enforced immobility has stored up an accumulation of vital energy, I am now obliged, like a spinning top wound and let go, to spin in every direction.

-Proust

Whirling into Bliss

The eternal dance of the universe is a swirling sea of spiraling energy that reflects life's eternal motion – the spinning formations of the solar system and the whirling of atoms. More specifically, it represents the Earth revolving on its axis while orbiting the sun. The ancient spiral dances were designed to stimulate ecstasy in order to sustain a woman's fertility and a man's virility.

Put on music that inspires your passion to flow. Clear a space so you can move with uncensored abandon. If you have physical handicaps and find it difficult to move, don't worry; you can achieve great benefit from imagining yourself whirling around the space. The secret is sensuously breathing while undulating your spine. All this oxygenation will energize you as if you are actually participating in this whirling dance.

To start, intend to become fluidity in creative motion. Take a gliding walk through the space you have chosen. Explore taking a few steps forward, sideward and backward. Once you can shift into different directions, turn in a circle for a few seconds and return to your gliding walk. Add more turns while exploring which direction feels the easiest. Visualize a current of life force spiraling up the arches of your feet. Intend this spiraling electromagnetic field to turn your breathing body with effortless ease. While fluidly turning in place, shake loose your hinges and joints to release the buildup of tension.

Feel the ground come alive under your feet. With supportive energy coming up from the ground, spontaneously whirl again. With each turn, discover the space in which your body

When she danced the Blue Danube, her simple waltzing forward and back, like the oncoming and receding waves on the shore, had such an ecstacy of rhythms that audiences became frenzied with the contagion of it, and rose from their seats, cheering, applauding, laughing and crying. We felt as if we had recived the blessing of God.

-Magherita Duncan watching her sister-inlaw Isadora Duncan, dancer

feels light, lifted and supported in the field of gravity. Become a conduit for the universes most powerful energies. Light up your *Diamond Mind* by opening your peripheral vision. Seeing the space you occupy prevents you from bumping into anything in the room. Imagine your arms filled with helium as you expand them in air like the wings of a bird soaring into flight. To avoid getting nauseous, keep your eyes on the horizon rather than trying to spot a target. With practice, you'll be able to look in any direction without getting dizzy.

Miraculous changes are set in motion when spinning with the primal powers of nature's elements. Whatever you wish to accomplish, visualize it unfolding beautifully before you.

Tremble as leaves shaking in the wind. Quiver as the ocean waves traveling through your veins. Shimmy as seaweed undulating in the currents of your spine. Float your head like a cloud hovering in the sky. Whisper as the life force igniting the wisdom of the ages. Pulse your insides as sparkling moonbeams shimmering on a lake. Undulate your arms and gyrate your pelvis with intense animal magnetism. As passion builds, open your voice as thunderous streaks of lightning across the sky. If you falter in your turns, clap your hands very loudly and forcefully. This surprising tactic grounds your energy and jolts you into an alert state of mind.

Become a silkworm spinning a cocoon that is birthing your future self. In the coolness of your inner sanctuary, trillions of molecules are metabolizing into a new radiant form. What shape is your body taking? As a magical dancer and ecstatic alchemist, perceive a living embryo of creative possibility increasing in size and pressing outward. Feel this new life pushing forward with greater and greater tenacity. With a sudden explosion, the walls of your chrysalis crack open. Breaking free from everything that binds you, release the butterfly inside.

When ending your dance, slow down your breath while slowing down your rotations. And above all else, keep your eyes on the horizon. Sense the pulsing vibrations and shimmering particles of light whirling in the atmosphere around you.

Song Talk

Creating melodic beauty in the voice involves a synergistic relationship of the parts with the whole.

-H. Wesley Balk The Radiant Performer

Truth is erotic. The ecstatic voice reflects the uninhibited freedom of expression your soul rejoicing in simply being alive. As Fred Alan Wolf, who wrote *The Spiritual Universe,* wrote, "Humanity needs to listen, until such a time as the Voice of the Soul is heard throughout the universe as the only voice of compassion and reason that has ever existed. When this occurs, all of humanity will be truly free and the Voice of the Soul will sing until the end of time."

Repression of vocal power often reflects a wounded sexuality. To extrapolate on this point, it has been discovered that the larynx resembles the female vagina. Tissue samples taken from the cervix and the larynx cannot be distinguished, one from another. Denial of vocal expression sustains self-conscious, protective/defensive behavior. The fear of opening the mouth may explain why many people feel 'naked' when speaking before a group or when sharing feelings with one another. It may even account for the fact that stage fright is the number one fear, even over death itself.

Ecstacy resounds in my throat and dances in my footsteps and I wonder who is who.

-Eveline Banks

The media is obsessed in projecting women with sexy attitudes speaking with an affected tone of voice with no real passionate life force behind the act. This means, the self-image becomes more real than the feelings underneath the projection. True sensuality is not putting on a sexy attitude to get attention. It is fully enjoying the body in which you dwell.

The author is unknown but this saying touched my heart: "The song of words sang through the trees and swirled through the chasms of space. In reflection of this song, man formed the vowels, and, therein found the name of God."

Undress yourself for the naked truth of your being to shine. Become a vessel for the Soul of Ecstasy to sing through you. May the holy sounds of infinite creative possibility guide your way. In the deepest, wordless place in your heart, sink into the spacious silence of an indescribable joy waiting to be born. With the wind as your breath, sigh out long flowing *ahhhhhhhsss* that rises and falls, slides and soars with increased abandon.

Take another vowel and let it have its way with you. When each vowel is clarified, sing with a universal language that transmutes all inhibitory sonic barriers into a cathartic release. If any self-consciousness still exists, sing ugly! Embrace all discordant sound – moaning and groaning, violent, frenzied, wailing torrents of notes that gush up from the forgotten realm of your primordial soul. Resounding between the sacred and the profane, from deep timbre into melodic resonance, astonish yourself with your voice!

Listen to the ecstatic voice of the world, with which it makes love to you.

-Tagore

Below are phrases to read aloud. Turn the printed word into erotic flesh and blood. Excite your ecstatic soul by making love to the sounds within the words. Immerse yourself in the living currents of tone that run through the words. Ride the nucleus of creative possibility as you savor and relish the exotic tastes of these phrases.

There lives within you a sense of the possible, a yearning to move forward to embrace life in all its fullness. Say YES TO LIFE!

-Danaan Parry
Warriors of the Heart

I am the Soul of Ecstasy loving life beyond all reason.
Deeper than all roses, I am the flame of passion burning bright.
All acts of love and pleasure are my rituals.
Lying naked, I moon bathe on a black velvet sky.
Ecstasy kisses me with limitless love.
Every aware moment is making love to God.

Increasing the depth of your relationships into archetypal proportions broadens your interdependent connection with a holistic identity.

-Beth Jarman

Mirror Interplay

Most of the Activations in this manual have been solitary pursuits. Without personal embodiment of your soul essence, it is difficult to be truly intimate with another. Inviting a friend to playfully reflect your spontaneous physical gestures, vocal tone and feeling states is a great way to introduce the work. Energetically reflecting each other's body language is a profound spiritual practice. Throughout this pre-verbal mirror play, you are saying, "I see you, I accept you, I am you."

Reflecting facial expression and vocal tone is what supports a baby's self-awareness. When caretakers respond with the monotone quality of their grownup image, babies become emotionally agitated. Without proper mirroring of their expressive language, boundaries of protection get established. Feeling separate from others and the rest of the world makes it difficult to merge in union with others when growing into adults.

The art of mirroring is not about slavishly following every movement with exactitude, it's more like playfully tracing or sketching the essence of your partner's expression. Taking the lead to express the dynamics of energy builds rapid rapport. After playfully expressing spontaneous feelings, encourage your partner to take the lead. Be surprised how quickly your partner can express sounds and movements you've never heard or seen before. When you take the lead once again, in all likelihood, you probably some of your partner's movement qualities enrich your own expression.

The phrase, "mirror me," is the magical switch, the shock of illumination that engenders genuine emotional involvement and authentic feeling with another person.

Sound and hearing, vocalizing and speaking, involve a rich dimensional conversation with the world around us.

-Andrea Olsen
Body and Earth

Speaking with your whole body is becoming a cohesive force of inspired beauty and power. Create a simple phrase enhanced with fluid gestures. Play with, repeat and transform any emotive expressions as they spontaneously arise. Now signal your partner to make up a phrase and express it in whatever way feels good. Blend these two phrases into an interactive dialogue. This means there is no one leading or following. You are both interlaying with the dynamics of energy that is being created.

Wisdom lives inside emotional expression. To end this mirroring process, hold hands and gaze into each other's third eye. Open yourself to see the hidden essence behind all mask-like concealments. Being together in this creative state, you can never take anyone for granted because they are forever growing and changing right before your eyes. Blending and merging passionate power in action reveals that we are all 'master teachers' for each other.

Primal Wrestling Massage

Many of us have a great desire for innocent, playful bodily contact, yet worry about looking foolish, losing control or getting hurt. Within the narrow confines of sex, lovemaking can get routine and boring. *Primal wrestling massage* is not displaying crude aggressive tactics and brutal hammer locks to subdue your opponent. Do you remember

192

moments in your childhood of roly-poly play with a playmate, laughing and tumbling with delight? Joining with the healing power of touch provides the fullest openness that is as pure as the driven snow.

It is the primal call not to separate but to blend, to contribute, to cocreate, and to serve.

-David Spangler

This writhing serpent-like 'contact improvisation' uses your whole body to massage another's body. Elbows, knees, hips and head can all act as instruments of massage.

With the aerobic diversity of breath and sound as the prime mover of inspiration, a playful preverbal dialogue occurs that directs you out of your head and into your feeling sensations. With the guiding power of breath and sound, you are less likely to be hurt because your tones are communicating how much pressure is appropriate.

A good warm up is lying down on the floor with knees up, and rolling on different size balls. This simple self-massage enhances fluidity and creates more subtle flexibility in your body. Once you're limbered up, sit back-to back with your partner. Bring your knees up and probe each other's back with an inquiring, open state of mind. Another variation is getting on all fours and letting your partner slowly roll over your back. While supporting your partner's back, maintain a fluid, wiggling spine. You'll be amazed how much weight you can handle when your back remains subtle. Wiggling the spine as a creature would is playing by heart in the primordial moment. Once you both have had a turn, move with spontaneous pleasure into new realms of being.

Blended attention is the state where we are expanded throughout the activity, but we are not asleep or spaced out.

-Wendy Palmer
The Intuitive Body

A tiny patch of flesh houses over three million cells, a hundred sweat glands, twelve feet of nerves and hundreds of nerve endings. Massaging another with your whole body provides an extraordinary depth of feeling that nothing else can provide. Shapeshifting into the rhythms and forces of nature deepens contact with your original innocence. As Alan Watts is quoted saying, "Life is at root playing." This playful contact celebrates original innocence as an enlightened state of being. The need to play and enjoy the sophistication of the adult role can dance together.

It is time to meet the challenges of relationship through integrative harmony with the child player and the serious adult.

Instead of talking a problem to death, play out the conflict by getting on your hands and knees and become two rams grunting with unadulterated feeling. Bring your foreheads together while widening your eyes. Being in this close proximity, your faces will take on a surreal quality. Imagine, as you do this, your 'third eye' is opening to see the truth of the situation. Have fun and move together as two serpent creatures, slowly hissing and slivering over each other's body in slow motion. Become two dolphins playfully rolling together while sounding out a unique sonar language.

Neither a woman, nor a man, we are joined, we are one. Yes, at last we are free.

-Sally Potter

Primal Lovemaking

I was six when I saw that everything was God.

-J.D Salinger

Perceiving sex as a ritual sacrament of divine worship is a new concept in the western world.' With a legacy of repression, expressing erotic pleasure with our naked bodies is often fraught with inhibition. Primalizing' lovemaking recapitulates the ancient dance of the universe that takes us back to the original urge that transforms scales into feathers, seawater into blood and caterpillars into butterflies. In this eternal moment, sex and spirit are perceived as inherently intertwined and inseparable. Sexual energy is the primal power that links everything in the universe in its embrace.

The pattern that connects all living creatures is erotic play. Metamorphosing into a creature or an element of nature while making love releases inhibited, self-conscious concerns.

Someday, after we have mastered the winds, the waves, the tides and gravity, we shall harness for God the energies of love. Then for the second time in the history of the world, man will have discovered fire.

-Teillard de Chardin

In preparation for the sacred dance of love, focus on creating a sensuous atmosphere with burning candles, fresh flowers and delicious aromas to intoxicate the senses. Turning the bathtub into an exotic pool filled with floating flowers clears the mind and relaxes the body. Emerging from the bath dressed in flowing garments that feel good to the touch prepares you to touch and be touched.

Before any lovemaking experience, reawaken the Soul of Ecstasy by opening the floodgate to your feeling nature. Become orgasmic with your emotions. Ecstatically breathe while weaving all the emotional energies spontaneously together. Real anger and tears and pain may appear. Embrace all your feelings with equal value. Emotional catharsis releases tension and heightens real passion to flow.

Sacred sexuality is merging soul with soul. While loving, become love, while caressing, become the caress, while kissing, be the kiss

When coming together, gazing into each other's eyes establishes trust and intimacy. Share simple intention: "By my breath, by my words, by my prayer, I honor you. I honor the expression of our love as sacred." Massaging each other's body with warm essential oils is an exquisite way to heighten arousal. With ecstatic breathing, playfully titillate, torment, tantalize, incite, inflame, tease, bewitch and dazzle each other's body. Become one 'organ of delight!' I quote Anne Hillman, "The guttural eruptions from my mouth, seemed to spew from my belly, NGGNAAAGH!THE! The sensation was beyond exhilarating."

The interplay of a breath, sound language of infinite meanings is pure intimacy in action. Being erotically charged, open, and present with your love is the essence of primal love making. It is trusting in the sensations of fearless responsiveness, and in any moment hovering the the valley of peaceful repose.The rapture of unbridled feeling gains in strength with moments of peaceful interchange. This means the more pleasure you can sustain, the more ecstatic passion you will enjoy.

But even in our hugs, kisses, and even in our genital sexuality, we might suddenly gbe the fields, the wheat, the grapes, the grain, the bee, the and the stars.

-Glen Mazis
Earthbodies

Floating on timeless waves of pleasure adrift on a sea of bliss sexual union is shared shameless and guilt free. As St. John of the Cross so beautiful said, "My face I reclined on the beloved. All ceased and I abandoned myself, leaving my cares forgotten among the lilies."

Like the power of gravity, attraction between two people springs from the same unifying force that holds the world together in its embrace.

I quote Barbara Marx Hubbard, in her book, *The Revelation,* "The sexual drive to reproduce the species would be transformed into the suprasexual drive to evolve the species. We would desire to join, not only our genes but also our genius, to evolve ourselves and our world. Sexuality and supra-sexuality would merge in one great orgasmic effort to evolve!" The concept of supra-sexuality is fully awakening to the unified field, the supreme catalyst for harmonious expression global transformation. Glen Mazis, in his book, *Earthbodies* builds on this illuminating idea. He writes, "We become a multiplicity of beings that have entered this inercoursing current – from frog, to turtle, to oozing jelly, to all the waters of the world.....It is the fluidity of identity, of selves, of bodies becoming one rhythm that goes beyond the human."

The embodiment of an ecstatic consciousness allows you to be more resourceful as you confront the collapse of your old world and ride the wave into the new world that is not yet fully born.

-Unknown

Embodying the Soul

In an atmosphere of ritual celebration, light candles around the mirror. Witness the auric light that shimmers around your body. As you gaze into your eyes, see yourself as the soul sees you. To perceive yourself in the presence of your soul, you are an equal among equals. With natural ecstasy as your primal power, your hopes, dreams and desires can be more fully magnetized into actuality.

Blessed are the beings who grow as flowers. Their roots arise from the flowing water, their faces turn toward the light.

-Odes of Solomon

All life is evolving from the One Word of creation. As Mathew Fox wrote in his book *Original Blessing,* "There is one divine word carrying the one creative energy flowing through all things, all time, all space. We are all apart of that flow." In this last ritual, place your mask on your face and encode your *Primal Name* with ecstatic power. Inspire all the emotional energies to merge together into one flowing continuum while pronouncing this magical name. Whisper it, shout it and magnetize it with the force that binds atoms to atoms, molecules to molecules. Now you possess a trigger-ready tool that can support you in moving through any activity of the day with all the passion necessary to accomplish your tasks.

With heightened electrical energy flooding your nervous system, create an original Yoga posture in which to concentrate this passionate energy in form. Intend in the creation of this form, all mental distraction cease. Relax in this posture and breathe with ease.

With expressive art before the mirror, direct experience is gained to sing the song only you can sing, to express the wisdom buried in your bones, and flesh out what is truly original within your soul.

Our planet, our country, our families, and our souls cry for unity. Your final performance is demonstrating, for all the world to see, an ecstatic state of consciousness. Step forward unto the cosmic stage and witness your sub-personalities that represent all of humankind sitting before you. The opening of your peripheral vision turns on the multidimensional radiance of your *Diamond Mind.* With the expansion of increasing space, perceive all human life and the elements of nature become an extension of your unlimited identity. The ecology of your body merges into the ecology of the planet. The largeness of the macrocosm and the smallness of microcosm that you are, mirror each other. They are one and the same. In the presence of the *One in All,* breathe as the first cell of existence, which grew, diversified, multiplied and evolved into all the biota of the earth. Audibly breathe as the algae and original green plants that produce oxygen. Open your throat and breathe as the coral, snails, fish, amphibian, reptile, early mammal and monkey that define your primal nature.

This new race is in act of being born from us, and in the near future, will walk on the earth with greater beauty and grace.

-Richard Bucke
Cosmic Consciousness

Honoring the vulnerable heart of nature's fragility, sing a soul song for a million species of plants and animals living in the rain forests that are quickly becoming extinct. As this song reaches the atmosphere, become the trees, the rivers, sky and creatures singing out their tumultuous feelings for the Earth that is perishing. Feel this song arousing humankind's heart of compassion. This is the song that has been ringing through the ages. We are born here on account of this song.

The first and future consciousness is one and the same. What is true on one plane is true on all planes. The greater and more inclusive your consciousness, the greater your inner power will become. All 'godness' lies dormant in everything, only waiting to be awakened. With this knowledge, the consensus reality that has separated truth from illusion is being shattered at last. The world is approximately 24,000 miles in circumference. Being of one mind and heart living in the unified field of this awe-inspiring creation, is coming into intimate relationship with all this is. As the giver and the gift are one, witness ecstatic passion thrilling the hearts of all beings with renewed passion.

See people everywhere joining together to speak with one voice and sing the song that can reunite us all in unconditional love.

As massive waves of love are magnetizing life-enhancing activities in people everywhere, effortless miracles abound to uncover all the sustainable resources possible to foster a world of magical coexistence for all. Carolyn Mary Kleefeld author of The Alchemy of Possibility writes, "We are cosmic dancers holding hands in space, our songs ascending in eternal symphony. Our suspension is supported by our interconnection with the invisible primal forces that be."

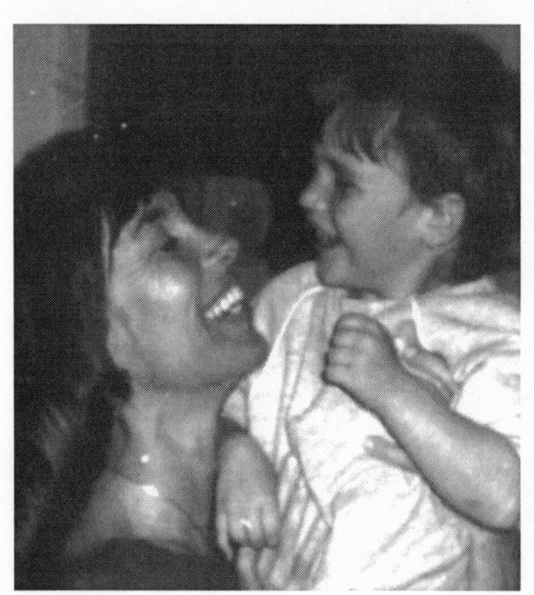

Original Child

New reports are growing that children born in the new millennium are more evolved than previous generations. I personally feel it is our expanding consciousness that is finally recognizing what has been glowing from children's faces forever – the natural genius and boundless energy of their authentic essence. As the anthropologist, Ashley Montague, is quoted saying, "Every baby born is the forerunner of humanity - possessing all the traits that lead to a healthy and fulfilled human being, and thus to a healthy and fulfilled humanity."

Behold the miracle of life. A baby is the original blessing of the universe. Babies born into the world require an ecstatic passage into life. Being born in amniotic fluid, a water birth is a natural birthing practice. There are no sudden changes leaving the womb and the entry into a new world is imprinted as a nurturing, loving space. A baby born in normal circumstances is unable to move around or even lift its head. The same baby, under water, can move effortlessly with a fluidity of being. In this way, the fluid nature of all life is honored.

This original being will not be programmed to be dully obedient and unauthentic. Born brilliant, every child is an 'artist of being,' an extraordinary work of art in progress. As the great artist Picasso noted before his death, "It took me years to paint like Raphael, but a lifetime to paint like a child."

The new education will support and develop the 'play instinct' as an intrinsic means of teaching all serious human endeavors. Being driven by millions of years of genetic encoding, giving up worship of the isolated intellect for the intelligence of the entire universe is a smart thing to do. Joseph Chilton Pearce builds on this idea by saying, "A playful consciousness is the only way the highest intelligence of humankind can unfold." This means that all subject matter will be enacted with physical/emotional involvement.

I saw the sun-eyed children of a marvelous dawn, the massive barrier-breakers of the world, bodies made beautiful by the Spirits light, carrying the magic word, the mystic fire, carrying the Dionysian cup of joy.

- Sri Aurobindo

Theater practices illuminating communication skills that reflect healthy adaptation with others, will receive the highest priority. Turning work into the living art of play, our definition of fun transforms into change, novelty and surprise.

As children learn to use their logical left-brain while being in fluid motion, numbers will be drawn out with the whole body and words will be creatively sounded with spontaneous innovation. Along with historic characters, universal archetypes will also be enacted as extensions of their multidimensional nature.

Instigating the expressive arts into sports and fitness training programs will create a world of 'primal athletes' who will emulate the astonishing mobility of their animal ancestors. They come not to compete, but to demonstrate the universality of the life force in embodied action.

Before conditioning has been instilled, young children possess an inherent compassion for their fellow creatures, both human and non-human. There is a natural kinship with the environment in which they are intrinsically apart. This deep-rooted connection needs to be supported and encouraged. As children become aware that they are fully interconnected with the world, global community consciousness will be regenerated. As Rachel Carson expressed in her book, *The Sense of Wonder,* "If a child is to keep alive his inborn sense of wonder for the Earth and all living creatures, he or she needs the companionship of at least one adult who can share it, rediscovering with this child, the joy, excitement and mystery of the world we live in."

A world-soul resides in each of us, capable of speaking to us as if broadcast from a single television atenna, no matter where we are in space or when we exist in time.

-Fred Wolf

Original innocence needs to be nurtured in every adult's heart. The freshness of spring is forever born through the power of love. This gift lives in the mystery of here and now. The holy child, ancient and wise is coming forth to guide us into a new Eden. A Wow Consciousness is celebrating radical self-expression as sacred.

Blessed are the pure in spirit, for theirs is the kingdom of heaven. **This is the beginning of life – be pure in spirit."**

Passing On

Sensuous during life, do not deny me in death! Wash me with scent of apple blossom, anoint me with essence of lilac. Fill my veins with honeysuckle nectar, sprinkle me with perfume of purple violets. Rest me in moss velvet earth. Cover me with soil exuding flavor of maple and oak leaves. Command a white birch to stand guard!

-Lois Wickenhauser

Until now, dying in a technological society is a demeaning procedure. In our attempt to conquer death, massive life-support systems go to work to numb people with drugs and seclude them in sterilized spaces with little natural light. This great crossing into a new domain of consciousness needs to be honored and treated with dignity. Within the primordial depths of nature, all life is being recycled back into the welcoming arms of the Great Mother. Constant change into new domains of existence keeps the whole evolutionary show operating. Just as every cell in our body is being replaced many times, transformation requires old structures to compost into the dust of the Earth and be reformed into a new order of being.

Brighter than a thousand suns, don't wait to die in order to enter the luminous light. Live the preciousness of your life basking in the pure illumination of your soul. Science has discovered the pineal gland contains an ecstatic aphrodisiac. When the heart stops beating, it is released. Ecstatic bliss has been so greatly inhibited in our culture, that this euphoric chemical remains dormant throughout our lifetime. It is time to spend more time activating this force while we're alive. Let us imagine 'passing on' as the birth of new ecstatic states of being. Many people who went through near-death experiences all say the same thing. After the initial trauma of leaving the body, they were overtaken by ecstatic feelings of bliss. The presence of brilliant white light was perceived as a pure loving force waiting to help them make the crossing into a new life. It has also been reported that sounds of indescribable beauty, pervade the entire atmosphere. One woman said, "I heard thousands of angels humming with infinite harmonies filled with profound beauty of tone. In that moment, the whole would appeared to be pure, living music."

Yet now when all seems lost, miraculously a new dawn has come. The sun shines bright again, earth rises again from the sea, clad with green pastures and forests - beauty to behold.

-The Ragnorok
Ancient Norse Prophecy

When returning from a near-death experience, people report that they are in greater attunement with their soul's wise counsel. As the great genius, Goethe, once said, "I am firmly convinced that the Spirit is indestructible. It is like the sun, which to our eyes seems to disappear beyond the horizon, while in actual fact it goes on shining continuously." And Leonardo da Vinci expressed, "Behold now the hope or desire of going back to one's own country or returning to primal chaos, like that of the moth to the light, of the man who with perpetual longing always looks forward with joy to each new spring and each new summer." Midwifing someone transitioning to a new domain of consciousness is a profound spiritual practice. Being a bridge between the worlds is embracing the realization that life and death comprise a dual unity, inseparable and complementary in nature. Humming with love to someone transitioning is a beautiful way to support them through the portal into a new domain of being.

Doro te devote. **May our expanding ecstatic nature set off rippling tides of bliss flowing through the matrix of the world, bringing humankind ever closer to reclaiming paradise on earth.**

A New Dawn

When I finally had to let go of this manuscript by accepting it as a 'work of art in progress,' I looked for some meaningful piece of completion. An inner urge directed me to go to my library and stand for a few minutes in a meditative state of awareness. I asked my inner guidance to pick appropriate information that could help me in this task. I closed my eyes and picked up a book of poetry I hadn't opened in over forty years. As I open the book, a frayed and yellow piece of paper fell on the floor. As I opened it up, I gasped with disbelief. In my hands was the dramatic presentation I had delivered at the Miss America Pageant in 1957. It was a letter written by a Yugoslavia soldier to his unborn child just before he died of a bullet wound. Soldiers found the letter and passed it around from hand to hand. This letter became a source of inspiration and hope to the whole platoon. With the growing awareness of the cosmos as One Body, I offer this letter to the first and future child of creation who is coming forth to celebrate the play of creative expression as our soul's glory.

Letter to an Unborn Child

My Child. Sleeping now in the dark and gathering strength for the struggle of birth, I send you boundless love. At present you have no form or shape, yet when your time comes, there will be something in you that will give you power to struggle free, to breathe in air and open your eyes to the light. Such is your heritage. Such is your destiny as a child born of woman, to fight for life and hold on without knowing why.

May the passionate flame that tempers the bright steel of your youth never die, but burn always with wonder and awe. The spirit of challenge and adventure will be given you as a child. May you keep it always.

Keep your soul hungry for new knowledge by firing the power of your imagination. Receive and accept everything that comes to you, only learn to select and act on what your instinct tells you is true. In this world where men grow so tired, keep your capacity for faith, but discern what you know is true in your heart. Remain open to all your feelings, the laughter, the fear and the tears - for they will not lead you astray. Above all, keep your love of life. Know life must be loved or it is lost.

Keep your delight in friendship by staying attuned to the soul of everyone who crosses your path. Keep your wonder at great and noble things like sunlight and thunder, the rain and the stars, the wind and the sea, the growth of trees, the return of harvest and the greatness of a life well lived. With high courage, may you seek and cherish the gold beyond the rainbow, the green pastures beyond the desert, the dawn beyond the sea, the light beyond the dark. When your work is done and your long days ended, may you still be like a watchman's light – a fire at the end of a lonely road, loved and cherished for your gracious glow and the warmth you have shown to others.

Now I must die, and you must be born to stand upon the humbleness of my life. Forgive me for leaving you an untidy, uncomfortable world. But so it must be. In thought, as a last benediction, I kiss your forehead. Dear child, good night. May you awaken to a bright morning and a clear dawn.

Made in the USA